✳

Ethics

Discovering Right and Wrong

SIXTH EDITION

LOUIS P. POJMAN
Late of the United States Military Academy, West Point

JAMES FIESER
University of Tennessee, Martin

WADSWORTH
CENGAGE Learning™

Australia • Brazil • Japan • Korea • Mexico • Singapore • Spain • United Kingdom • United States

WADSWORTH
CENGAGE Learning™

Ethics: Discovering Right and Wrong, **Sixth Edition**
Louis P. Pojman and James Fieser

Acquisitions Editor:
Worth Hawes

Assistant Editor:
Patrick Stockstill

Editorial Assistant:
Kamilah Lee

Technology Project Manager:
Julie Aguilar

Marketing Manager:
Christina Shea

Marketing Assistant:
Mary Anne Payumo

Marketing Communications
Manager: Darlene Amidon-Brent

Project Manager, Editorial
Production: Matt Ballantyne

Creative Director: Rob Hugel

Art Director: Maria Epes

Print Buyer: Judy Inouye

Permissions Editor: Mardell
Glinski-Schultz

Production Service:
Ruth Cottrell

Copy Editor: Betty Duncan

Cover Designer: RHDG/Tim
Heraldo

Compositor: International
Typesetting and Composition

For product information and technology assistance, contact us at
Cengage Learning Customer & Sales Support, 1-800-354-9706.
For permission to use material from this text or product, submit all requests online at **cengage.com/permissions.** Further permissions questions can be e-mailed to **permissionrequest@cengage.com.**

Library of Congress Control Number: 2007942487

ISBN-13: 978-0-495-50235-7

ISBN-10: 0-495-50235-9

Wadsworth
10 Davis Drive
Belmont, CA 94002-3098
USA

Cengage Learning is a leading provider of customized learning solutions with office locations around the globe, including Singapore, the United Kingdom, Australia, Mexico, Brazil, and Japan. Locate your local office at **international.cengage.com/region.**

Cengage Learning products are represented in Canada by Nelson Education, Ltd.

For your course and learning solutions, visit **academic.cengage.com.**

Purchase any of our products at your local college store or at our preferred online store **www.ichapters.com.**

Printed in the United States of America
1 2 3 4 5 6 7 12 11 10 09 08

The painting on the cover, The Death of Socrates *by Jacques Louis David, shows Socrates carrying out his own execution by taking the poison hemlock as described in Plato's dialogue* Crito *in 399 B.C. Socrates had been unjustly condemned to death by an Athenian court for corrupting the youth and not honoring the Athenian deities. Offered a way to escape by his friends, he reasons that it would be immoral to accept their offer. Being the first person in recorded history to put philosophy to work in the area of morals, Socrates is called the "Father of Ethics." The* Metropolitan Museum of Art, Catharine Lorillard Wolfe Collection, Wolfe Fund, 1931. Copyright © 1980 The Metropolitan Museum of Art. Corbis Images.

*

I am indebted to my wife, Trudy, for living a morally inspiring life. I can identify with Brutus when he said regarding his Portia, "O ye gods, Render me worthy of this noble wife!" (Shakespeare's Julius Caesar*) Without her love and devotion, my life would be less joyous and this book would not have been written. To her this book is dedicated.*

Louis P. Pojman, Clare Hall, Cambridge University
September 20, 2004

About the Authors

Louis P. Pojman (1935–2005) was Professor of Philosophy, Emeritus, at the United States Military Academy and a Life Member of Clare Hall, Cambridge University. He received an M.A. and a Ph.D. from Union Theological Seminary/ Columbia University and a D. Phil. from Oxford University. He has written in the areas of philosophy of religion, epistemology, ethics, and political philosophy and is the author or editor of more than 30 books and 100 articles. Among these are *Ethics: Discovering Right and Wrong* (6/e 2009), *Environmental Ethics* (5/e 2008), *Who Are We?* (2005), and *Global Political Philosophy* (2003).

James Fieser is Professor of Philosophy at the University of Tennessee at Martin. He received his BA. from Berea College and his M.A. and Ph.D. in philosophy from Purdue University. He is the author, co-author, or editor of ten textbooks, including *Moral Philosophy through the Ages* (2001), *A Historical Introduction to Philosophy* (2003), and *Socrates to Sartre and Beyond* (8/e 2008). He has edited and annotated the ten-volume *Early Responses to Hume* (2/e 2005) and the five-volume *Scottish Common Sense Philosophy* (2000). He is founder and general editor of the *Internet Encyclopedia of Philosophy* website (www.iep.utm.edu).

Contents

PREFACE   xi

1   What Is Ethics?   1
Ethics and Its Subdivisions   2
Morality as Compared with Other Normative Subjects   3
Traits of Moral Principles   7
Domains of Ethical Assessment   8
Conclusion   11
For Further Reflection   12
For Further Reading   13

2   Ethical Relativism   14
Subjective Ethical Relativism   16
Conventional Ethical Relativism   18
Criticisms of Conventional Ethical Relativism   21
Conclusion   27
For Further Reflection   28
For Further Reading   29

3   Moral Objectivism   30
Aquinas's Objectivism and Absolutism   32
Moderate Objectivism   38
Ethical Situationalism   43
Conclusion   44

For Further Reflection   45

For Further Reading   45

4   Value and the Quest for the Good   46

Intrinsic and Instrumental Value   47

The Value of Pleasure   50

Are Values Objective or Subjective?   53

The Relation of Value to Morality   54

The Good Life   57

Conclusion   61

For Further Reflection   62

For Further Reading   62

**5   Social Contract Theory and the Motive
to Be Moral   64**

Why Does Society Need Moral Rules?   66

Why Should I Be Moral?   70

Morality, Self-Interest, and Game Theory   72

The Motive to Always Be Moral   75

Conclusion   78

For Further Reflection   79

For Further Reading   80

6   Egoism, Self-Interest, and Altruism   81

Psychological Egoism   82

Ethical Egoism   87

Arguments against Ethical Egoism   91

Evolution and Altruism   95

Conclusion   97

For Further Reflection   98

For Further Reading   99

7   Utilitarianism   100

Classic Utilitarianism   102

Act- and Rule-Utilitarianism   105

Criticism of Utilitarianism   109

Criticism of the Ends Justifying Immoral Means   114

Conclusion   118

For Further Reflection   119
For Further Reading   119

8 Kant and Deontological Theories   121
Kant's Influences   122
The Categorical Imperative   126
Counterexamples to the Principle of the Law of Nature   131
Other Formulations of the Categorical Imperative   134
The Problem of Exceptionless Rules   138
The Problem of Posterity   141
Conclusion: A Reconciliation Project   142
For Further Reflection   144
For Further Reading   145

9 Virtue Theory   146
The Nature of Virtue Ethics   147
Criticisms of Action-Based Ethics   151
Connections between Virtue-Based and
Action-Based Ethics   157
Feminism and the Ethics of Care   165
Conclusion   167
For Further Reflection   169
For Further Reading   169

10 Religion and Ethics   170
Does Morality Depend on Religion?   171
Is Religion Irrelevant or Even Contrary to Morality?   176
Does Religion Enhance the Moral Life?   180
Conclusion   185
For Further Reflection   186
For Further Reading   187

11 The Fact–Value Problem   188
Hume and Moore: The Problem Classically Stated   189
Ayer and Emotivism   192
Hare and Prescriptivism   196
Naturalism and the Fact–Value Problem   203
Conclusion   206

For Further Reflection 207

For Further Reading 208

12 Moral Realism and the Challenge of Skepticism 209

Mackie's Moral Skepticism 211

Harman's Moral Nihilism 215

A Defense of Moral Realism 219

Conclusion 222

For Further Reflection 223

For Further Reading 223

APPENDIX 224
GLOSSARY 228
INDEX 233

Website

Additional student and instructor supplemental materials are available free online at academic.cengage.com/philosophy/Pojman/Ethics6e. For both students and instructors, the companion website includes Tutorial Quizzing, Essay Questions, and Weblinks for various topics introduced throughout the text. On the instructors' version of the companion website, there are PowerPoint slides for lessons.

In addition, we have included content from the fifth edition of this book, in their complete and unedited form, which were condensed or modified in this edition. These include:

- the complete "A Concluding Reflection: Minimal Morality, Virtue Ethics, and the Development of Character"
- the complete "An Analysis of the Modified Divine Command Theory" from Appendix 1
- the complete "Questions for Reflection"
- the complete discussion of Lord of the Flies and Ayn Rand

Preface

In 1977 Australian philosopher John L. Mackie published his famous book *Ethics: Inventing Right and Wrong* in which he takes the skeptical position that there are no objective moral values. Rather, Mackie says, the values we hold are *inventions* of society: "We have to decide what moral views to adopt, what moral stands to take."

The title of this book, *Ethics: Discovering Right and Wrong*, is both an acknowledgment of the importance of Mackie's critique and an answer to it. Morality is not a mere invention as Mackie claims but, more optimistically, a *discovery*. We may compare morality to the development of the wheel. Both are creations based on discoverable features. The wheel was invented to facilitate the transportation of objects with minimal friction. The construction of a wheel adheres to the laws of physics to bring about efficient motion. Not just anything could function as a good wheel. A rectangular or triangular wheel would be inefficient, as would one made out of sand or bird feathers or heavy stones. Analogously, morality has been constructed to serve human needs and desires—for example, the need to survive and the desires to prosper and be happy. The ideal morality should serve as the blueprint for individual happiness and social harmony. Human beings have used their best minds over millennia to discover those principles that best serve to promote individual and social well-being. Just as the construction of the wheel depends on the laws of physics, so the construction of morality has depended on human nature, on discoverable features of our being. It is in this spirit of moral discovery that *Ethics: Discovering Right and Wrong* surveys the main theories of moral philosophy today.

The philosophical community experienced a great loss in 2005 with the death of Louis Pojman, the original author of this book, who succumbed to his battle with cancer. His voluminous writings—over 30 books and 100 articles—have been uniformly praised for their high level of scholarship and insights, and countless philosophy students and teachers have benefited from them (see www.louispojman.com for biographical and bibliographical details).

Ethics: Discovering Right and Wrong was first published in 1990 and quickly established itself as an authoritative yet reader-friendly introduction to ethics. In an earlier preface, Louis expresses his enthusiasm for his subject and his commitment to his reader:

> I have written this book in the spirit of a quest for truth and understanding, hoping to excite you about the value of ethics. It is a subject that I love, for it is about how we are to live, about the best kind of life. I hope that you will come to share my enthusiasm for the subject and develop your own ideas in the process.

Over the years, new editions of this book have appeared in response to the continually evolving needs of college instructors and students. Sections were added and most everything else was at some point updated and refined. This newly revised sixth edition attempts to reflect the spirit of change that governed previous editions. As with most textbook revisions, the inclusion of new material in this edition required the deletion of a comparable amount of previously existing material. In making these tough decisions, I have tried to retain the full substance of each chapter's narrative while rewording some existing discussions more concisely to free up space. As to the newly added material, many of the changes were suggested by previous book users, both faculty and students, for which I am very grateful. The more global changes include these:

- New illustrations, particularly in the chapter openings
- More heading divisions and subdivisions for better navigation throughout the chapters
- Additional explanation provided to elucidate the more difficult discussions
- Updated bibliographies
- Revised closing questions for further discussion

Below are the more prominent changes in each chapter, which may help reorient instructors who are accustomed to the previous edition of this book.

- Chapter 1: "What Is Ethics?" This incorporates material previously appearing in "A Word to the Student"; the discussion of "Why Do We Need Morality?" has been moved to the new Chapter 5.
- Chapter 2: "Ethical Relativism" The discussion of subjective ethical relativism has been moved to the beginning of the chapter to avoid splitting the discussion of conventional ethical relativism.
- Chapter 3: "Moral Objectivism" There are no major changes.
- Chapter 4: "Value and the Quest for the Good" There are no major changes.
- Chapter 5: "Social Contract Theory and the Motive to Be Moral" This is a new chapter created from combining related material from two separate chapters in the fifth edition: the section "Why Do We Need Morality?" in Chapter 1 ("What Is Ethics?") and Chapter 9 ("Why Should I Be Moral?").

The discussion of *Lord of the Flies* has been shortened, and a new discussion of game theory has been included.

- Chapter 6: "Egoism, Self-Interest, and Altruism" A new introduction on Nestlé's infant formula has been included; the discussion of psychological egoism has been moved to the beginning to avoid splitting the discussion of ethical egoism; the discussion of Rand has been condensed; the discussion of egoism and the problem of posterity has been expanded with material on the subject from the utilitarianism chapter; separate sections containing criticisms and responses have been combined into a single section where each response directly follows its related criticism.

- Chapter 7: "Utilitarianism" A new discussion of Epicurus's influence has been included; the discussion of egoism and the problem of posterity has been moved to Chapter 6; separate sections containing criticisms and responses have been combined; the order of criticisms has been rearranged to group them into different types.

- Chapter 8: "Kant and Deontological Theories" A new discussion of Pufendorf's rule intuitionism has been included; the discussion of Ross has been moved toward the end of the chapter; the discussion of religion and morality has been moved to Chapter 10.

- Chapter 9: "Virtue Theory" A new discussion regarding attacks on virtue theory by utilitarians and Kant is included, and the subsequent decline of virtue theory is discussed; the terms *virtue-based* and *rule-based* are used consistently throughout the chapter replacing the occasional synonyms *aretaic ethics* and *deontic ethics*; the fifth edition's final brief chapter, "A Concluding Reflection" (that is, the discussion of Norton) has been condensed and inserted into this chapter.

- Chapter 10: "Religion and Ethics" The discussion of Kant on religion has been expanded; a new section is included on Hume's antireligious ethics; the term *autonomy thesis* has been renamed *independence thesis* to differentiate it from the argument from autonomy that appears later in this chapter; more antireligious points are listed in the section on whether religion enhances moral life.

- Chapter 11: "The Fact–Value Problem" A new opening introduction has been included; new expositions of Hume, Moore, and Ayer replace the previous ones.

- Chapter 12: "Moral Realism and the Challenge of Skepticism" The chapter opens with a new example regarding Amnesty International; new definitions and examples of moral realism have been included in the introduction; new criticisms of Mackie have been included; the discussions of noncognitivism have been consolidated and moved to the chapter's end.

- "Glossary" The glossary has been revised with twice as many entries (glossary terms are shown boldface in text).

ACKNOWLEDGMENTS

The preface to the fifth edition of this book lists the following acknowledgments, which I present here verbatim:

> Michael Beaty, Sterling Harwood, Stephen Kershnar, Bill Lawhead, Michael Levin, Robert Louden, Laura Purdy, Roger Rigterink, Bruce Russell, Walter Schaller, Bob Westmoreland, and Mark Discher were very helpful in offering trenchant criticisms on several chapters of this book. The students in my ethical theory classes at the University of Mississippi and the U.S. Military Academy at West Point for the past twenty years have served as a challenging sounding board for many of my arguments. Ronald F. Duska, Rosemont College; Stephen Griffith, Lycoming College; Arthur Kuflik, University of Vermont; James Lindemann Nelson, Michigan State University; Peter List, Oregon State University; Ann A. Pang-White, University of Scranton; Fred Schueler, University of New Mexico; Nancy A. Stanlick, University of Central Florida; R. Duane Thompson, Indiana Wesleyan University; Peter Vallentyne, Virginia Commonwealth University; and David A. White, Marquette University reviewed the manuscript for an earlier edition and provided guidance in revising this latest edition.

I also wish to thank Worth Hawes, Patrick Stockstill, and the rest of the talented editorial staff at Wadsworth for their thoroughness and good nature throughout the production of this new edition. Thanks also to my students, fellow colleagues, and the following reviewers of this book for their helpful suggestions on improvements: Jason Glenn, Baton Rouge Community College; Vicki Lynn Harper, St. Olaf College; Elizabeth Hodge, Gavilan College; Steve Magarian, California State University–Fresno; Robert Whiteley, Suffolk County Community College; Alice Wood, Bethune-Cookman College; and James Woolever, Foothill College. I offer a special word of thanks to Louis's wife, Trudy Pojman, for her input on the changes that I have made to this edition.

James Fieser
April 26, 2007 (Hume's birthday)

1

✳

What Is Ethics?

In all the world and in all of life there is nothing more important to
determine than what is right. Whatever the matter which lies before us
calling for consideration, whatever the question asked us or the problem
to be solved, there is some settlement of it which will meet the situation
and is to be sought.... Wherever there is a decision to be made or any
deliberation is in point, there is a right determination of the matter in
hand which is to be found and adhered to, and other possible
commitments which would be wrong and are to be avoided.
C. I. LEWIS, *THE GROUND AND NATURE OF RIGHT*

We are discussing no small matter, but how we ought to live.
SOCRATES, IN PLATO'S *REPUBLIC*

Some years ago, the nation was stunned by a report from New York City. A
young woman, Kitty Genovese, was brutally stabbed in her own neighborhood
late at night during three separate attacks while thirty-eight respectable, law-abiding
citizens watched or listened. During the thirty-five minute struggle, her assailant
beat her, stabbed her, left her, and then returned to attack her two more times
until she died. No one lifted a phone to call the police; no one shouted at the criminal, let alone went to Genovese's aid. Finally, a seventy-year-old woman called the
police. It took them just two minutes to arrive, but by that time Genovese was
already dead.

Only one other woman came out to testify before the ambulance showed up
an hour later. Then residents from the whole neighborhood poured out of their
apartments. When asked why they hadn't done anything, they gave answers ranging from "I don't know" and "I was tired" to "Frankly, we were afraid."[1]

This tragic event raises many questions about our moral responsibility to others. What should these respectable citizens have done? Are such acts of omission morally blameworthy? Is the Genovese murder an atypical situation, or does it represent a disturbing trend? This story also raises important questions about the general notion of morality. What is the nature of morality, and why do we need it? What is the good, and how will we know it? Is it in our interest to be moral? What is the relationship between morality and religion? What is the relationship between morality and law? What is the relationship between morality and etiquette? These are some of the questions that we explore in this book. We want to understand the foundation and structure of morality. We want to know how we should live.

ETHICS AND ITS SUBDIVISIONS

Ethics is that branch of philosophy that deals with how we ought to live, with the idea of the Good, and with concepts such as "right" and "wrong." But what is *philosophy*? It is an enterprise that begins with wonder at the marvels and mysteries of the world; that pursues a rational investigation of those marvels and mysteries, seeking wisdom and truth; and that results in a life lived in passionate moral and intellectual integrity. Taking as its motto Socrates' famous statement that "the unexamined life is not worth living," philosophy leaves no aspect of life untouched by its inquiry. It aims at a clear, critical, comprehensive conception of reality.

The main characteristic of philosophy is rational argument. Philosophers clarify concepts and analyze and test propositions and beliefs, but their major task is to analyze and construct arguments. Philosophical reasoning is closely allied with scientific reasoning, in that both build hypotheses and look for evidence to test those hypotheses with the hope of coming closer to the truth. However, scientific experiments take place in laboratories and have testing procedures through which to record objective or empirically verifiable results. The laboratory of the philosopher is the domain of ideas. It takes place in the mind where imaginative thought experiments take place. It takes place in the study room where ideas are written down and examined. It also takes place wherever conversation or debate about the perennial questions arises, where thesis and counterexample and counterthesis are considered.

The study of ethics within philosophy contains its own subdivisions, and dividing up the territory of ethics is a tricky matter. A word must be said first about the specific terms *moral* and *ethical* and the associated notions of *morals/ethics* and *morality/ethicality*. Often these terms are used interchangeably—as will frequently be the case in this book. Both terms derive their meaning from the idea of "custom"—that is, normal behavior. Specifically, "moral" comes from the Latin word *mores* and "ethical" from the Greek *ethos*.

The key divisions within the study of ethics are (1) descriptive morality, (2) moral philosophy (ethical theory), and (3) applied ethics. First, **descriptive morality** refers to actual beliefs, customs, principles, and practices of people and cultures. Sociologists in particular pay special attention to the concrete moral practices of social groups around the world, and they view them as cultural "facts," much like facts about what people in those countries eat or how they dress. Second, **moral philosophy**—also called **ethical theory**—refers to the systematic effort to understand moral concepts and justify moral principles and theories. It analyzes key ethical concepts such as "right," "wrong," and "permissible." It explores possible sources of moral obligation such as God, human reason, or the desire to be happy. It seeks to establish principles of right behavior that may serve as action guides for individuals and groups. Third, **applied ethics** deals with controversial moral problems such as abortion, premarital sex, capital punishment, euthanasia, and civil disobedience.

The larger study of ethics, then, draws on all three of these subdivisions, connecting them in important ways. For example, moral philosophy is very much interrelated with applied ethics: Theory without application is sterile and useless, but action without a theoretical perspective is blind. There will be an enormous difference in the quality of debates about abortion, for example, when those discussions are informed by ethical theory as compared to when they are not. More light and less heat will be the likely outcome. With the onset of multiculturalism and the deep differences in worldviews around the globe today, the need to use reason, rather than violence, to settle our disputes and resolve conflicts of interest has become obvious. Ethical awareness is the necessary condition for human survival and flourishing.

If we are to endure as a free, civilized people, we must take ethics more seriously than we have before. Ethical theory may rid us of simplistic extremism and emotionalism—where shouting matches replace arguments. Ethical theory clarifies relevant concepts, constructs and evaluates arguments, and guides us on how to live our lives. It is important that the educated person be able to discuss ethical situations with precision and subtlety.

The study of ethics is not only of instrumental value but also valuable in its own right. It is satisfying to have knowledge of important matters for its own sake, and it is important to understand the nature and scope of moral theory for its own sake. We are rational beings who cannot help but want to understand the nature of the good life and all that it implies. The study of ethics is sometimes a bit off-putting because so many differing theories often appear to contradict each other and thus produce confusion rather than guidance. But an appreciation of the complexity of ethics is valuable in offsetting our natural tendency toward inflexibility and tribalism where we stubbornly adhere to the values of our specific peer groups.

MORALITY AS COMPARED WITH OTHER NORMATIVE SUBJECTS

Moral principles concern standards of behavior; roughly speaking, they involve not what is but what ought to be. How should I live my life? What is the right thing to do in this situation? Is premarital sex morally permissible? Ought a woman ever to have an abortion? Morality has a distinct action-guiding, or *normative,* aspect, which it shares with other practices such as religion, law, and etiquette. Let's see how morality differs from each of these.

Religion

Consider first the relation between morality and religion. Moral behavior, as defined by a given religion, is usually believed to be essential to that religion's practice. But neither the practices nor principles of morality should be identified with religion. The practice of morality need not be motivated by religious considerations, and moral principles need not be grounded in revelation or divine authority—as religious teachings invariably are. The most important characteristic of ethics is its grounding in reason and human experience.

To use a spatial metaphor, secular ethics is horizontal, lacking a vertical or higher dimension; as such it does not receive its authority from "on high." But religious ethics, being grounded in revelation or divine authority, has that vertical dimension although religious ethics generally uses reason to supplement or complement revelation. These two differing orientations often generate different moral principles and standards of evaluation, but they need not do so. Some versions of religious ethics, which posit God's revelation of the moral law in nature or conscience, hold that reason can discover what is right or wrong even apart from divine revelation.

Law

Consider next the relationship between morality and law. The two are quite closely related, and some people even equate the two practices. Many laws are instituted in order to promote well-being, resolve conflicts of interest, and promote social harmony, just as morality does. However, ethics may judge that some laws are immoral without denying that they are valid. For example, laws may permit slavery, spousal abuse, racial discrimination, or sexual discrimination, but these are immoral practices. A Catholic or antiabortion advocate may believe that the laws permitting abortion are immoral.

In a PBS television series, *Ethics in America,* a trial lawyer was asked what he would do if he discovered that his client had committed a murder some years earlier for which another man had been wrongly convicted and would soon be executed.[2] The lawyer said that he had a legal obligation to keep this information confidential and that, if he divulged it, he would be disbarred. It is arguable that he has a moral obligation that overrides his legal obligation and demands that he act to save the innocent man from execution.

Furthermore, some aspects of morality are not covered by law. For example, although it is generally agreed that lying is usually immoral, there is no general law against it—except under such special conditions as committing perjury or falsifying income tax returns. Sometimes college newspapers publish advertisements by vendors who offer "research assistance," despite knowing in advance that these vendors will aid and abet plagiarism. Publishing such ads is legal, but its moral correctness is doubtful.

Similarly, the thirty-eight people who watched the attacks on Kitty Genovese and did nothing to intervene broke no New York law, but they were very likely morally responsible for their inaction. In our legal tradition, there is no general duty to rescue a person in need. In 1908 the Dean of Harvard Law School proposed that a person should be required to "save another from impending death or great bodily harm, when he might do so with little or no inconvenience to himself." The proposal was defeated, as its opponents argued: Would a rich person to whom $20 meant very little be legally obliged to save the life of a hungry child in a foreign land? Currently, only Vermont and Minnesota have "Good Samaritan" laws, requiring that one come to the aid of a person in grave physical harm but only to the extent that the aid "can be rendered without danger or peril to himself or without interference with important duties owed to others."

There is another major difference between law and morality. In 1351 King Edward of England instituted a law against treason that made it a crime merely to think homicidal thoughts about the king. But, alas, the law could not be enforced, for no tribunal can search the heart and discover the intentions of the mind. It is true that *intention,* such as malice aforethought, plays a role in determining the legal character of an act once the act has been committed. But, preemptive punishment for people who are presumed to have bad intentions is illegal. If malicious intentions by themselves were illegal, wouldn't we all deserve imprisonment? Even if one could detect others' intentions, when should the punishment be administered? As soon as the offender has the intention? How do we know that the offender won't change his or her mind? Furthermore, isn't there a continuum between imagining some harm to X, wishing a harm to X, desiring a harm to X, and intending a harm to X?

Although it is impractical to have laws against bad intentions, these intentions are still bad, still morally wrong. Suppose I buy a gun with the intention of killing Uncle Charlie to inherit his wealth, but I never get a chance to fire it (for example, suppose Uncle Charlie moves to Australia). Although I have not committed a crime, I have committed a moral wrong.

Etiquette

Consider next the relation between morality and etiquette. Etiquette concerns form and style rather than the essence of social existence; it determines what is polite behavior rather than what is *right* behavior in a deeper sense. It represents society's decision as to how we are to dress, greet one another, eat, celebrate festivals, dispose of the dead, express gratitude and appreciation, and, in general, carry out social transactions. Whether people greet each other with a handshake, a bow, a hug, or a kiss on the cheek depends on their social system. Russians wear their wedding rings on the third finger of their right hands whereas Americans wear them on their left hands. The English hold their forks in their left hands whereas people in other countries are more likely to hold them in their right hands. People in India typically eat without a fork at all, using the fingers of their right hands to deliver food from their plate to their mouth. Whether we uncover our heads in holy places (as males do in Christian churches) or cover them (as females do in Catholic churches and males do in synagogues), none of these rituals has any moral superiority. Polite manners grace our social existence, but they are not what social existence is about. They help social transactions to flow smoothly but are not the substance of those transactions.

At the same time, it can be immoral to disregard or defy etiquette. Whether to shake hands when greeting a person for the first time or put one's hands together in front as one bows, as people in India do, is a matter of cultural decision. But, once the custom is adopted, the practice takes on the importance of a moral rule, subsumed under the wider principle of showing respect to people.

Similarly, there is no moral necessity to wear clothes, but we have adopted the custom partly to keep warm in colder climates and partly to be modest. Accordingly, there may be nothing wrong with nudists who decide to live together in nudist colonies. However, for people to go nude outside of nudist colonies—say, in classrooms, stores, and along the road—may well be so offensive that it is morally insensitive. Recently, there was a scandal on the beaches of south India where American tourists swam in bikinis, shocking the more modest Indians. There was nothing immoral in itself about wearing bikinis, but given the cultural context, the Americans willfully violated etiquette and were guilty of moral impropriety.

Although Americans pride themselves on tolerance, pluralism, and awareness of other cultures, custom and etiquette can be—even among people from similar backgrounds—a bone of contention. A Unitarian minister tells of an experience early in his marriage. He and his wife were hosting their first Thanksgiving meal. He had been used to small celebrations with his immediate family whereas his wife had been used to grand celebrations. He writes, "I had been asked to carve, something I had never done before, but I was willing. I put on an apron, entered the kitchen, and attacked the bird with as much artistry as I could muster. And what reward did I get? [My wife] burst into tears. In *her* family the turkey is brought to the table, laid before the [father], grace is said, and *then* he carves! 'So I fail patriarchy,' I hollered later. 'What do you expect?' "[3]

Law, etiquette, and religion are all important institutions, but each has limitations. A limitation of religious commands is that they rest on authority, and we may lack certainty or agreement about the authority's credentials or how the authority would rule in ambiguous or new cases. Because religion is founded not on reason but on revelation, you cannot use reason to convince someone from another religion that your view is the right one. A limitation of law is that you can't have a law against every social problem, nor can you enforce every desirable rule. A limitation of etiquette is that it doesn't get to the heart of what is vitally important for personal and social existence. Whether or not one eats with one's fingers pales in significance with the importance of being honest, trustworthy, or just. Etiquette is a cultural invention, but morality is more like a discovery.

In summary, morality differs from law and etiquette by going deeper into the essence of our social existence. It differs from religion by seeking reasons, rather than authority, to justify its principles. The central purpose of moral philosophy is to secure valid principles of conduct and values that can guide human actions and produce good character. As such, it is the most important activity we know, for it concerns how we are to live.

TRAITS OF MORAL PRINCIPLES

A central feature of morality is the moral principle. We have already noted that moral principles are practical action guides, but we must say more about the traits of such principles. Although there is no universal agreement on the traits a moral principle must have, there is a wide consensus about five features: (1) prescriptivity, (2) universalizability, (3) overridingness, (4) publicity, and (5) practicability. Several of these will be examined in chapters throughout this book, but let's briefly consider them here.

First is **prescriptivity,** which is the practical, or action-guiding, nature of morality. Moral principles are generally put forth as commands or imperatives, such as "Do not kill," "Do no unnecessary harm," and "Love your neighbor." They are intended for use: to advise people and influence action. Prescriptivity shares this trait with all normative discourse and is used to appraise behavior, assign praise and blame, and produce feelings of satisfaction or guilt.

Second is **universalizability.** Moral principles must apply to all people who are in a relevantly similar situation. If one judges that act X is right for a certain person P, then it is right for anyone relevantly similar to P. This trait is exemplified in the Golden Rule, "Do to others what you would want them to do to you (if you were in their shoes)." We also see it in the formal principle of justice: It cannot be right for A to treat B in a manner in which it would be wrong for B to treat A, merely on the ground that they are two different individuals.[4]

Universalizability applies to all evaluative judgments. If I say that X is a good Y, then I am logically committed to judge that anything relevantly similar to X is a good Y. This trait is an extension of the principle of consistency: One ought to be consistent about one's value judgments, including one's moral judgments. Take any act that you are contemplating doing and ask, "Could I will that everyone act according to this principle?"

Third is **overridingness.** Moral principles have predominant authority and override other kinds of principles. They are not the only principles, but they also take precedence over other considerations including aesthetic, prudential, and legal ones. The artist Paul Gauguin may have been aesthetically justified in abandoning his family to devote his life to painting beautiful Pacific Island pictures, but morally he probably was not justified. It may be prudent to lie to save my reputation, but it probably is morally wrong to do so—in which case, I should tell the truth. When the law becomes egregiously immoral, it may be my moral duty to exercise civil disobedience. There is a general moral duty to obey the law because the law serves an overall moral purpose, and this overall purpose may give us moral reasons to obey laws that may not be moral or ideal. There may come a time, however, when the injustice of a bad law is intolerable and hence calls for illegal but moral defiance. A good example would be laws in the South prior to the Civil War requiring citizens to return runaway slaves to their owners.

Religion is a special case: Many philosophers argue that a religious person may be morally justified in following a perceived command from God that overrides a normal moral rule. John's pacifist religious beliefs may cause him to renege on an obligation to fight for his country. On face value, religious morality qualifies as morality and thus has legitimacy.

Fourth is **publicity.** Moral principles must be made public in order to guide our actions. Publicity is necessary because we use principles to prescribe behavior, give advice, and assign praise and blame. It would be self-defeating to keep them a secret.

Fifth is **practicability.** A moral principle must have practicability, which means that it must be workable and its rules must not lay a heavy burden on us when we follow them. The philosopher John Rawls speaks of the "strains of commitment" that overly idealistic principles may cause in average moral agents.[5] It might be desirable for morality to require more selfless behavior from us, but the result of such principles could be moral despair, deep or undue moral guilt, and ineffective action. Accordingly, most ethical systems take human limitations into consideration.

Although moral philosophers disagree somewhat about these five traits, the above discussion offers at least an idea of the general features of moral principles.

DOMAINS OF ETHICAL ASSESSMENT

At this point, it might seem that ethics concerns itself entirely with rules of conduct that are based solely on evaluating acts. However, it is more complicated than that. Most ethical analysis falls into one or more of the following domains: (1) action, (2) consequences, (3) character, and (4) motive. Again, all these domains will be examined in detail in later chapters, but an overview here will be helpful.

Let's examine these domains using an altered version of the Kitty Genovese story. Suppose a man attacks a woman in front of her apartment and is about to kill her. A responsible neighbor hears the struggle, calls the police, and shouts from the window "Hey you, get out of here!" Startled by the neighbor's reprimand, the attacker lets go of the woman and runs down the street where he is caught by the police.

Action

One way of ethically assessing this situation is to examine the *actions* of both the attacker and the good neighbor: The attacker's actions were wrong whereas the neighbor's actions were right. The term *right* has two meanings. Sometimes, it means "obligatory" (as in "the right act"), but it also can mean "permissible" (as in "a right act" or "It's all right to do that"). Usually, philosophers define *right* as permissible, including in that category what is obligatory:

1. A *right act* is an act that is permissible for you to do. It may be either (a) obligatory or (b) optional.
   a. An **obligatory act** is one that morality requires you to do; it is not permissible for you to refrain from doing it.
   b. An **optional act** is one that is neither obligatory nor wrong to do. It is not your duty to do it, nor is it your duty not to do it. Neither doing it nor not doing it would be wrong.
2. A *wrong act* is one you have an obligation, or a duty, to refrain from doing: It is an act you ought not to do; it is not permissible to do it.

In our example, the attacker's assault on the woman was clearly a wrong action (prohibited); by contrast, the neighbor's act of calling the police was clearly a right action—and an obligatory one at that.

But, some acts do not seem either obligatory or wrong. Whether you take a course in art history or English literature or whether you write a letter with a pencil or pen seems morally neutral. Either is permissible. Whether you listen to rock music or classical music is not usually considered morally significant. Listening to both is allowed, and neither is obligatory. Whether you marry or remain single is an important decision about how to live your life. The decision you reach, however, is usually considered morally neutral or optional. Under most circumstances, to marry (or not to marry) is considered neither obligatory nor wrong but permissible.

Within the range of permissible acts is the notion of **supererogatory acts,** or highly altruistic acts. These acts are neither required nor obligatory, but they exceed what morality requires, going "beyond the call of duty." For example, suppose the responsible neighbor ran outside to actually confront the attacker rather than simply shout at him from the window. Thus, the neighbor would assume an extra risk that would not be morally required. Similarly, while you may be obligated to give a donation to help people in dire need, you would not be obligated to sell your car, let alone become impoverished yourself, to help them. The complete scheme of acts, then, is this:

1. Right act (permissible)
   a. Obligatory act
   b. Optional act
      (1) Neutral act
      (2) Supererogatory act
2. Wrong act (not permissible)

One important kind of ethical theory that emphasizes the nature of the act is called *deontological* (from the Greek word *deon,* meaning "duty"). These theories hold that something is inherently right or good about such acts as truth telling and promise keeping and inherently wrong or bad about such acts as lying and promise breaking. Classical deontological ethical principles include the Ten

Commandments and the Golden Rule. Perhaps the leading proponent of deontological ethics in recent centuries is Immanuel Kant (1724–1804), who defended a principle of moral duty that he calls the categorical imperative: "Act only on that maxim whereby you can at the same time will that it would become a universal law." Examples for Kant are "Never break your promise" and "Never commit suicide." What all of these deontological theories and principles have in common is the view that we have an inherent duty to perform right actions and avoid bad actions.

Consequences

Another way of ethically assessing situations is to examine the *consequences* of an action: If the consequences are on balance positive, then the action is right; if negative, then wrong. In our example, take the consequences of the attacker's actions. At minimum he physically harms the woman and psychologically traumatizes both her and her neighbors; if he succeeds in killing her, then he emotionally devastates her family and friends, perhaps for life. And what does he gain from this? Just a temporary experience of sadistic pleasure. On balance, his action has overwhelmingly negative consequences and thus is wrong. Examine next the consequences of the responsible neighbor who calls the police and shouts down from the window "Hey you, get out of here!" This scares off the attacker, thus limiting the harm of his assault. What does the neighbor lose by doing this? Just a temporary experience of fear, which the neighbor might have experienced anyway. On balance, then, the neighbor's action has overwhelmingly positive consequences, which makes it the right thing to do.

Ethical theories that focus primarily on consequences in determining moral rightness and wrongness are called **teleological ethics** (from the Greek *telos,* meaning "goal directed"). The most famous of these theories is *utilitarianism,* set forth by Jeremy Bentham (1748–1832) and John Stuart Mill (1806–1873), which requires us to do what is likeliest to have the best consequences. In Mill's words, "Actions are right in proportion as they tend to promote happiness; wrong as they tend to produce the reverse of happiness."

Character

Whereas some ethical theories emphasize the nature of actions in themselves and some emphasize principles involving the consequences of actions, other theories emphasize *character,* or virtue. In our example, the attacker has an especially bad character trait—namely, malevolence—which taints his entire outlook on life and predisposes him to act in harmful ways. The attacker is a bad person principally for having this bad character trait of malevolence. The responsible neighbor, on the other hand, has a good character trait, which directs his outlook on life—namely, benevolence, which is the tendency to treat people with kindness and assist those in need. Accordingly, the neighbor is a good person largely for possessing this good trait.

Moral philosophers call such good character traits **virtues** and bad traits **vices.** Entire theories of morality have been developed from these notions and are called **virtue theories.** The classic proponent of virtue theory was Aristotle (384–322 BCE), who maintained that the development of virtuous character traits is needed to ensure that we habitually act rightly. Although it may be helpful to have action-guiding rules, it is vital to empower our character with the tendency to do good. Many people know that cheating, gossiping, or overindulging in food or alcohol is wrong, but they are incapable of doing what is right. Virtuous people spontaneously do the right thing and may not even consciously follow moral rules when doing so.

Motive

Finally, we can ethically assess situations by examining the motive of the people involved. The attacker intended to brutalize and kill the woman; the neighbor intended to thwart the attacker and thereby help the woman. Virtually all ethical systems recognize the importance of motives. For a full assessment of any action, it is important to take the agent's intention into account. Two acts may appear identical on the surface, but one may be judged morally blameworthy and the other excusable. Consider John's pushing Mary off a ledge, causing her to break her leg. In situation (A), he is angry and intends to harm her, but in situation (B) he sees a knife flying in her direction and intends to save her life. In (A) he clearly did the wrong thing, whereas in (B) he did the right thing. A full moral description of any act will take motive into account as a relevant factor.

CONCLUSION

The study of ethics has enormous practical benefits. It can free us from prejudice and dogmatism. It sets forth comprehensive systems from which to orient our individual judgments. It carves up the moral landscape so that we can sort out the issues to think more clearly and confidently about moral problems. It helps us clarify in our minds just how our principles and values relate to one another, and, most of all, it gives us some guidance in how to live. Let's return to questions posed at the beginning of this chapter, some of which we should now be able to better answer.

What is the nature of morality, and why do we need it? Morality concerns discovering the rules that promote the human good, as elaborated in the five traits of moral principles: prescriptivity, universalizability, overridingness, publicity, and practicability. Without morality, we cannot promote that good.

What is the good, and how will I know it? The good in question is the human good, specified as happiness, reaching one's potential, and so forth. Whatever we decide on that fulfills human needs and helps us develop our deepest potential is the good that morality promotes.

Is it in my interest to be moral? Yes, in general and in the long run, for morality is exactly the set of rules most likely to help (nearly) all of us if nearly all of us follow them nearly all of the time. The good is good for you—at least most of the time. Furthermore, if we believe in the superior importance of morality, then we will bring children up so that they will be unhappy when they break the moral code. They will feel guilt. In this sense, the commitment to morality and its internalization nearly guarantee that if you break the moral rules you will suffer.

What is the relationship between morality and religion? Religion relies more on revelation, and morality relies more on reason, on rational reflection. But, religion can provide added incentive for the moral life, offering the individual a relationship with God, who sees and will judge all our actions.

What is the relationship between morality and law? Morality and law should be very close, and morality should be the basis of the law, but there can be both unjust laws and immoral acts that cannot be legally enforced. The law is shallower than morality and has a harder time judging human motives and intentions. You can be morally evil, intending to do evil things, but as long as you don't do them, you are legally innocent.

What is the relationship between morality and etiquette? Etiquette consists in the customs of a culture, but they are typically morally neutral in that the culture could flourish with a different code of etiquette. In our culture, we eat with knives and forks, but a culture that eats with chopsticks or fingers is no less moral.

NOTES

1. Martin Gansberg, "38 Who Saw Murder Didn't Call Police," *New York Times,* March 27, 1964.
2. *Ethics in America,* PBS, 1989, produced by Fred Friendly.
3. John Buehrens and Forrester Church, *Our Chosen Faith* (Beacon Press, 1989), p. 140.
4. Henry Sidgwick, *The Methods of Ethics,* 7th ed. (Macmillan, 1907), p. 380.
5. John Rawls, *A Theory of Justice* (Harvard University Press, 1971), pp. 176, 423.

FOR FURTHER REFLECTION

1. Consider the Kitty Genovese story and what you think a responsible neighbor should have done. Are there any situations in which the neighbors might be morally justified in doing nothing?

2. The study of philosophy involves three main divisions: descriptive morality, moral philosophy, and applied ethics. Explain how these three divisions interrelate with a moral issue such as abortion, euthanasia, or capital punishment.

3. Illustrate the difference between a moral principle, a religious principle, a legal rule, a principle of etiquette. Are these sometimes related?

4. Take a moral principle such as "Don't steal" and analyze it according to the four traits of moral principles.

5. French painter Paul Gauguin (1848–1903) gave up his job as a banker and abandoned his wife and children to pursue a career as an artist. He moved to Martinique and later to Tahiti, eventually becoming one of the most famous postimpressionist artists in the world. Did Gauguin do what was morally permissible? Discuss this from the perspective of the four domains of ethical assessment.

6. Siddhartha Gautama (560–480 BCE), appalled by the tremendous and pervasive suffering in the world, abandoned his wife and child to seek enlightenment. He eventually attained enlightenment and became known as the Buddha. Is there a moral difference between Gauguin and the Buddha?

FOR FURTHER READING

Fieser, James. *Moral Philosophy through the Ages.* New York: McGraw Hill, 2001.

Frankena, William. *Ethics.* Englewood Cliffs, N.J.: Prentice-Hall, 1988.

MacIntyre, Alasdair. *A Short History of Ethics,* 2nd ed. Macmillan, 1998.

MacKinnon, Barbara. *Ethics: Theory and Contemporary Issues.* Belmont, Calif.: Thomson/ Wadsworth, 2007.

Pojman, Louis, ed. *Ethical Theory: Classical and Contemporary Readings.* Belmont, Calif: Thomson/Wadsworth, 2007.

Rachels, James. *The Elements of Morality.* New York: Random House, 2006.

Singer, Peter, ed. *A Companion to Ethics.* Oxford, Engl.: Blackwell Reference, 1997.

Timmons, Mark. *Moral Theory.* Lanham, Md.: Rowman & Littlefield, 2002.

Williams, Bernard. *Morality: An Introduction to Ethics.* New York: Cambridge University Press, 1993.

2

✳

Ethical Relativism

Ethical relativism is the doctrine that the moral rightness and wrongness
of actions varies from society to society and that there are no absolute
universal moral standards binding on all men at all times. Accordingly, it
holds that whether or not it is right for an individual to act in a certain
way depends on or is relative to the society to which he belongs.

JOHN LADD, *ETHICAL RELATIVISM*

1. The individual realizes his personality through his culture; hence
respect for individual differences entails respect for cultural differences.
2. Respect for differences between cultures is validated by scientific fact
that no technique of qualitatively evaluating cultures has been discovered.
3. [Therefore] How can the proposed Declaration [of Universal Human
Rights] be applicable to all human beings and not be a statement
of rights conceived only in terms of values prevalent in countries in
western Europe and America?

THE AMERICAN ANTHROPOLOGICAL ASSOCIATION POSITION PAPER (1947)

In the nineteenth century, Christian missionaries sometimes used coercion to
change the customs of pagan tribal people in parts of Africa and the Pacific
Islands. Appalled by the customs of public nakedness, polygamy, working on the
Sabbath, and infanticide, they went about reforming the "poor pagans." They
clothed them, separated wives from their husbands to create monogamous house-
holds, made the Sabbath a day of rest, and ended infanticide. In the process, they
sometimes created social disruption, causing the women to despair and their children to be orphaned. The natives often did not understand the new religion but
accepted it because of the white man's power. The white people had guns and
medicine.

Since the nineteenth century, we've made progress in understanding cultural diversity and now realize that the social conflict caused by "do-gooders" was a bad thing. In the last century or so, anthropology has exposed our fondness for **ethnocentrism,** the prejudicial view that interprets all of reality through the eyes of one's own cultural beliefs and values. We have come to see enormous variety in social practices throughout the world. Here are a few examples.

For instance, Eskimos allow their elderly to die by starvation, whereas we believe that this is morally wrong. The Spartans of ancient Greece and the Dobu of New Guinea believe that stealing is morally right, but we believe that it is wrong. Many cultures, past and present, have practiced or still practice infanticide.

A tribe in East Africa once threw deformed infants to the hippopotamus, but our society condemns such acts. Sexual practices vary over time and from place to place. Some cultures permit homosexual behavior, whereas others condemn it. Some cultures, including Muslim societies, practice polygamy, whereas Christian cultures view it as immoral. Anthropologist Ruth Benedict describes a tribe in Melanesia that views cooperation and kindness as vices, and anthropologist Colin Turnbull has documented that a tribe in northern Uganda have no sense of duty toward their children or parents. There are societies that make it a duty for children to kill their aging parents, sometimes by strangling.

The ancient Greek historian Herodotus (485–430 BCE) told the story of how Darius, the king of Persia, once brought together some Callatians (Asian tribal people) and some Greeks. He asked the Callatians how they disposed of their deceased parents. They explained that they ate the bodies. The Greeks, who cremated their parents, were horrified at such barbarous behavior and begged Darius to cease from such irreverent discourse. Herodotus concluded that "Custom is the king over all."[1]

Today, we condemn ethnocentrism as a form of prejudice equivalent to racism and sexism. What is right in one culture may be wrong in another, what is good east of the river may be bad west of the same river, what is virtue in one nation may be seen as a vice in another, so it behooves us not to judge others but to be tolerant of diversity.

This rejection of ethnocentrism in the West has contributed to a general shift in public opinion about morality so that for a growing number of Westerners consciousness raising about the validity of other ways of life has led to a gradual erosion of belief in **moral objectivism,** the view that there are universal and objective moral principles valid for all people and social environments. For example, in polls taken in my philosophy classes over the past several years, students affirmed by a two-to-one ratio a version of moral relativism over moral objectivism, with barely 3 percent seeing something in between these two polar opposites. A few students claim to hold the doctrine of **ethical nihilism,** the doctrine that no valid moral principles exist, that morality is a complete fiction. Of course, I'm not suggesting that all these students have a clear understanding of what relativism entails, for many of those who say they are ethical relativists also state on the same questionnaire that "abortion, except to save a woman's life, is always wrong," that "capital punishment is always morally wrong," or that "suicide is never morally permissible." The apparent contradictions signal some confusion on the matter.

In this chapter, we examine the central notions of **ethical relativism** and look at the implications that seem to follow from it. There are two main forms of ethical relativism as defined here:

> **Subjective ethical relativism (subjectivism):** All moral principles are justified by virtue of their acceptance by an individual agent him- or herself.

> **Conventional ethical relativism (conventionalism):** All moral principles are justified by virtue of their cultural acceptance.

Both versions hold that there are no objective moral principles but that such principles are human inventions. Where they differ, though, is with the issue of whether they are inventions of individual agents themselves or of larger social groups. We begin with the first of these, which is the more radical of the two positions.

SUBJECTIVE ETHICAL RELATIVISM

Some people think that morality depends directly on the individual—not on one's culture and certainly not on an objective value. As my students sometimes maintain, "Morality is in the eye of the beholder." They treat morality like taste or aesthetic judgments, which are person relative. Ernest Hemingway wrote,

> So far, about morals, I know only that what is moral is what you feel good after and what is immoral is what you feel bad after and judged by these moral standards, which I do not defend, the bullfight is very moral to me because I feel very fine while it is going on and have a feeling of life and death and mortality and immortality, and after it is over I feel very sad but very fine.[2]

This form of moral subjectivism has the sorry consequence that it makes morality a very useless concept: On its premises, little or no interpersonal criticism or judgment is possible. Hemingway may feel good about killing bulls in a bullfight, whereas Saint Francis or Mother Teresa would no doubt feel the opposite. No argument about the matter is possible. Suppose you are repulsed by observing John torturing a child. You cannot condemn him if one of his principles is

"Torture little children for the fun of it." The only basis for judging him wrong might be that he was a *hypocrite* who condemned others for torturing. However, one of his or Hemingway's principles could be that hypocrisy is morally permissible (he "feels very fine" about it), so it would be impossible for him to do wrong. For Hemingway, hypocrisy and nonhypocrisy are both morally permissible (except, perhaps, when he doesn't feel very fine about it).

On the basis of subjectivism, Adolf Hitler and the serial murderer Ted Bundy could be considered as moral as Gandhi, as long as each lived by his own standards whatever those might be. Witness the following paraphrase of a tape-recorded conversation between Ted Bundy and one of his victims, in which Bundy justifies his murder:

> Then I learned that all moral judgments are "value judgments," that all value judgments are subjective, and that none can be proved to be either "right" or "wrong." I even read somewhere that the Chief Justice of the United States had written that the American Constitution expressed nothing more than collective value judgments. Believe it or not, I figured out for myself—what apparently the Chief Justice couldn't figure out for himself—that if the rationality of one value judgment was zero, multiplying it by millions would not make it one whit more rational. Nor is there any "reason" to obey the law for anyone, like myself, who has the boldness and daring—the strength of character—to throw off its shackles. . . . I discovered that to become truly free, truly unfettered, I had to become truly uninhibited. And I quickly discovered that the greatest obstacle to my freedom, the greatest block and limitation to it, consists in the insupportable "value judgment" that I was bound to respect the rights of others. I asked myself, who were these "others"? Other human beings, with human rights? Why is it more wrong to kill a human animal than any other animal, a pig or a sheep or a steer? Is your life more to you than a hog's life to a hog? Why should I be willing to sacrifice my pleasure more for the one than for the other? Surely, you would not, in this age of scientific enlightenment, declare that God or nature has marked some pleasures as "moral" or "good" and others as "immoral" or "bad"? In any case, let me assure you, my dear young lady, that there is absolutely no comparison between the pleasure I might take in eating ham and the pleasure I anticipate in raping and murdering you. That is the honest conclusion to which my education has led me—after the most conscientious examination of my spontaneous and uninhibited self.[3]

Notions of good and bad or right and wrong cease to have interpersonal evaluative meaning. We might be revulsed by Bundy's views, but that is just a matter of taste.

In the opening days of my philosophy classes, I often find students vehemently defending subjective relativism: "Who are you to judge?" they ask. I then give them their first test. In the next class period, I return all the tests, marked "F," even though my comments show that most of them are of a very high caliber. When the students express outrage at this (some have never before seen that letter on their papers and inquire about its meaning), I answer that I have accepted subjectivism for marking the exams. "But that's unjust!" they typically insist—and then they realize that they are no longer being merely subjectivist about ethics.

Absurd consequences follow from subjectivism. If it is correct, then morality reduces to aesthetic tastes about which there can be neither argument nor interpersonal judgment. Although many students say they espouse subjectivism, there is evidence that it conflicts with some of their other moral views. They typically condemn Hitler as an evil man for his genocidal policies. A contradiction seems to exist between subjectivism and the very concept of morality, which it is supposed to characterize, for morality has to do with *proper* resolution of interpersonal conflict and the improvement of the human predicament. Whatever else it does, morality has a minimal aim of preventing a Hobbesian **state of nature** in which life is "solitary, nasty, poor, brutish and short." But if so, then subjectivism is no help at all, for it rests neither on social agreement of principle (as the conventionalist maintains) nor on an objectively independent set of norms that binds all people for the common good. If there were only one person on earth, then there would be no occasion for morality because there wouldn't be any interpersonal conflicts to resolve or others whose suffering that he or she would have a duty to improve. Subjectivism implicitly assumes **moral solipsism,** a view that isolated individuals make up separate universes.

Subjectivism treats individuals as billiard balls on a societal pool table where they meet only in radical collisions, each aimed at his or her own goal and striving to do the others in before they do him or her in. This view of personality is contradicted by the facts that we develop in families and mutually dependent communities—in which we share a common language, common institutions, and similar rituals and habits—and that we often feel one another's joys and sorrows. As John Donne wrote, "No man is an island, entire of itself; every man is a piece of the continent."

Subjective ethical relativism is incoherent, and it thus seems that the only plausible view of ethical relativism must be one that grounds morality in the group or culture. Thus, we turn now to conventional ethical relativism.

CONVENTIONAL ETHICAL RELATIVISM

Again, conventional ethical relativism, also called conventionalism, is the view that all moral principles are justified by virtue of their cultural acceptance. There are no universally valid moral principles, but rather all such principles are valid relative to culture or individual choice. This view recognizes the social nature of morality, which is the theory's key asset. It does not seem subject to the same absurd consequences that plague subjectivism. Recognizing the importance of our social environment in generating customs and beliefs, many people suppose that ethical relativism is the correct theory. Furthermore, they are drawn to it for its liberal philosophical stance. It seems to be an enlightened response to the arrogance of ethnocentricity, and it seems to entail or strongly imply an attitude of tolerance toward other cultures.

The Diversity and Dependency Theses

John Ladd gives a typical characterization of the theory:

> Ethical relativism is the doctrine that the moral rightness and wrongness of actions varies from society to society and that there are no absolute universal moral standards binding on all men at all times. Accordingly, it holds that whether or not it is right for an individual to act in a certain way depends on or is relative to the society to which he belongs.[4]

If we analyze this passage, we find two distinct theses that are central to conventional ethical relativism:

> *Diversity thesis.* What is considered morally right and wrong varies from society to society, so there are no universal moral standards held by all societies.

> *Dependency thesis.* All moral principles derive their validity from cultural acceptance.

The diversity thesis is simply an anthropological thesis acknowledging that moral rules differ from society to society; it is sometimes referred to as *cultural relativism.* As we illustrated earlier in this chapter, there is enormous variety in what may count as a moral principle in a given society. The human condition is flexible in the extreme, allowing any number of folkways or moral codes. As Ruth Benedict has written,

> The cultural pattern of any civilization makes use of a certain segment of the great arc of potential human purposes and motivations, just as we have seen . . . that any culture makes use of certain selected material techniques or cultural traits. The great arc along which all the possible human behaviors are distributed is far too immense and too full of contradictions for any one culture to utilize even any considerable portion of it. Selection is the first requirement.[5]

It may or may not be the case that there is no single moral principle held in common by every society, but if there are any, they seem to be few, at best. Certainly, it would be very hard to derive one single "true" morality on the basis of observation of various societies' moral standards.

Turning to the second element of conventional ethical relativism—the *dependency thesis*—this asserts that individual acts are right or wrong depending on the nature of the society in which they occur. Morality does not exist in a vacuum; rather, what is considered morally right or wrong must be seen in a context that depends on the goals, wants, beliefs, history, and environment of the society in question. As William Graham Sumner says,

> We learn the [morals] as unconsciously as we learn to walk and hear and breathe, and [we] never know any reason why the [morals] are what they

are. The justification of them is that when we wake to consciousness of life we find them facts which already hold us in the bonds of tradition, custom, and habit.[6]

Trying to see things from an independent, noncultural point of view would be like taking out our eyes to examine their contours and qualities. We are simply culturally determined beings.

In a sense, we all live in radically different worlds. Each person has a different set of beliefs and experiences, a particular perspective that colors all of his or her perceptions. Do the farmer, the real estate dealer, and the artist looking at the same spatiotemporal field actually see the same thing? Not likely. Their different orientations, values, and expectations govern their perceptions, so different aspects of the field are highlighted and some features are missed. Even as our individual values arise from personal experience, so social values are grounded in the particular history of the community. Morality, then, is just the set of common rules, habits, and customs that have won social approval over time so that they seem part of the nature of things, like facts. There is nothing mysterious about these codes of behavior. They are the outcomes of our social history.

There is something conventional about *any* morality, so every morality really depends on a level of social acceptance. Not only do various societies adhere to different moral systems, but the very same society could (and often does) change its moral views over time and place. For example, in the southern United States, slavery is now viewed as immoral, whereas just over one hundred years ago, it was not. We have greatly altered our views on abortion, divorce, and sexuality as well.

Conventional Ethical Relativism and Tolerance

Defenders of conventional ethical relativism often advertise another benefit of their theory: It supports the value of tolerance. As the anthropologist Ruth Benedict says, in recognizing ethical relativity, "We shall arrive at a more realistic social faith, accepting as grounds of hope and as new bases for tolerance the coexisting and equally valid patterns of life which mankind has created for itself from the raw materials of existence.[7]

Consider this example. In parts of northern Africa, many girls undergo female circumcision, cutting out their external genitalia. It has been estimated that 80 million living women have had this surgery and that 4 to 5 million girls suffer it each year. The mutilating surgery often leads to death or sickness and prevents her as a woman from experiencing sexual orgasm. Some African women accept such mutilation as a just sacrifice for marital stability, but many women and ethicists have condemned it as a cruel practice that causes women unjustified pain and mutilation and robs them of pleasure and autonomy. Some anthropologists such as Nancy Scheper-Hughes accept relativism and argue that we Westerners have no basis for condemning genital mutilation.[8] Scheper-Hughes advocates tolerance for other cultural values. She writes, "I don't like the idea of clitoridectomy any better than any other woman I know. But I like even less the western 'voices of reason' [imposing their judgments]. " She argues that judging other cultures irrationally supposes that we know better than the people of that culture do what is right or wrong.

The most famous proponent of this position is anthropologist Melville Herskovits,[9] who argues even more explicitly than Benedict and Scheper-Hughes that ethical relativism entails intercultural tolerance:

(1) If morality is relative to its culture, then there is no independent basis for criticizing the morality of any other culture but one's own.

(2) If there is no independent way of criticizing any other culture, then we ought to be *tolerant* of the moralities of other cultures.

(3) Morality is relative to its culture.

(4) Therefore, we ought to be *tolerant* of the moralities of other cultures.

Tolerance is certainly a virtue, but is this a good argument for it? No. If morality simply is relative to each culture and if the culture in question has no principle of tolerance, its members have no obligation to be tolerant. Herskovits and Scheper-Hughes, as well, seem to be treating the *principle of tolerance* as the one exception. They are treating it as an absolute moral principle.

But, from a relativistic point of view, there is no more reason to be tolerant than to be intolerant, and neither stance is objectively morally better than the other. If Westerners condemn clitoridectomies on the basis of their cultural values, they are no more to be condemned than those people are who, because of their cultural values, perform clitoridectomies. One cannot consistently assert that all morality is relative and then treat the principle of tolerance as an absolute principle.

CRITICISMS OF CONVENTIONAL
ETHICAL RELATIVISM

So far we've examined the main ingredients of conventional ethical relativism and considered its strengths. We now turn to the problems with this view.

Conventional Ethical Relativism Undermines Important Values

One serious problem with conventional ethical relativism is that it undermines the basis of important values. If conventional ethical relativism is true, then we cannot legitimately criticize anyone who espouses what we might regard as a heinous principle. If, as seems to be the case, valid criticism supposes an objective or impartial standard, then relativists cannot morally criticize anyone outside their own culture. Adolf Hitler's genocidal actions, as long as they are culturally accepted, are as morally legitimate as Mother Teresa's works of mercy. If conventional relativism is accepted, then racism, genocide of unpopular minorities, oppression of the poor, slavery, and even the advocacy of war for its own sake are as moral as their opposites. And if a subculture decided that starting a nuclear war was somehow morally acceptable, we could not morally criticize these people. Any actual morality, whatever its content, is as valid as every other and more valid than ideal moralities—since no culture adheres to the latter.

Another important value that we commonly hold is that regarding moral reformers: people of conscience like Mohandas Gandhi and Martin Luther King who go against the tide of cultural standards. However, according to conventional ethical relativism, by going against dominant cultural standards, their actions are technically wrong. Consider the following examples. William Wilberforce was wrong in the eighteenth century to oppose slavery. The British were immoral in opposing *suttee* in India (the burning of widows, which is now illegal there). The early Christians were wrong in refusing to serve in the Roman army or bow down to Caesar because the majority in the Roman Empire believed that these two acts were moral duties.

Yet, we normally feel just the opposite, that the reformer is a courageous innovator who is right, has the truth, and stands against the mindless majority. Sometimes the individual must stand alone with the truth, risking social censure and persecution. In Ibsen's *Enemy of the People,* after Dr. Stockman loses the battle to declare his town's profitable but polluted tourist spa unsanitary, he says,

> The most dangerous enemy of the truth and freedom among us—is the compact majority. Yes, the damned, compact and liberal majority. The majority has *might*—unfortunately—but *right* it is not. Right—are I and a few others.

Yet, if relativism is correct, the opposite is necessarily the case: Truth is with the crowd and error with the individual.

A third important value that conventional ethical relativism undermines is our moral duties toward the law. Our normal view is that we have a duty to obey the law because law, in general, promotes the human good. According to most objective systems, this obligation is not absolute but relative to the particular law's relation to a wider moral order. Civil disobedience is warranted in some cases in which the law seems to seriously conflict with morality. However, if ethical relativism is true, then neither law nor civil disobedience has a firm foundation. On the one hand, from the side of the society at large, civil disobedience will be morally wrong as long as the majority culture agrees with the law in question. On the other hand, if you belong to the relevant subculture that doesn't recognize the particular law in question (because it is unjust from your point of view), then disobedience will be morally mandated. The Ku Klux Klan, which believes that Jews, Catholics, and African Americans are evil and undeserving of high regard is, given conventionalism, morally permitted or required to break the laws that protect these people. Why should I obey a law that my group doesn't recognize as valid?

Thus, unless we have an independent moral basis for law, it is hard to see why we have any general duty to obey it. And unless we recognize the priority of a universal moral law, we have no firm basis for justifying our acts of civil disobedience against "unjust laws." Both the validity of the law and morally motivated disobedience of unjust laws are voided in favor of a power struggle.

Conventional Ethical Relativism Leads to Subjectivism

An even more basic problem with the concept that morality depends on cultural acceptance for its validity is that the notion of a *culture* or *society* is notoriously difficult to define. This is especially so in a pluralistic society like our own where the notion seems to be vague, with unclear boundary lines. One person may belong to several societies (subcultures) with different value emphases and arrangements of principles. A person may belong to the nation as a single society with certain values of patriotism, honor, courage, and laws (including some that are controversial but have majority acceptance such as the current law on abortion). But, he or she may also belong to a church that opposes some of the laws of the state. He or she may also be an integral member of a socially mixed community where different principles hold sway and belong to clubs and a family where still other rules prevail. Relativism would seem to tell us that if a person belongs to societies with conflicting moralities, then that person must be judged both wrong and not wrong whatever he or she does. For example, if Mary is a U.S. citizen and a member of the Roman Catholic Church, then she is wrong (as a Catholic) if she has an abortion and not wrong (as a citizen of the United States) if she acts against the church's teaching on abortion. As a member of a racist university fraternity, KKK, John has no obligation to treat his fellow African American students as equals, but as a member of the university community (which accepts the principle of equal rights), he does have the obligation; but as a member of the surrounding community (which may reject the principle of equal rights), he again has no such obligation; but then again, as a member of the nation at large (which accepts the principle), he is obligated to treat his fellow students with respect. What is the morally right thing for John to do? The question no longer makes much sense in this moral confusion. It has lost its action-guiding function.

Perhaps the relativist would adhere to a principle that says in such cases the individual may choose which group to belong to as his or her primary group. If Mary has an abortion, she is choosing to belong to the general society relative to that principle. John must likewise choose among groups. The trouble with this option is that it seems to lead back to counterintuitive results. If Murder Mike of the company "Murder Incorporated" feels like killing a bank president and wants to feel good about it, he identifies with the "Murder Incorporated" society rather than the general public morality. Does this justify the killing? In fact, couldn't one justify anything simply by forming a small subculture that approved of it? Ted Bundy would be morally pure in raping and killing innocents simply by virtue of forming a little coterie. How large must the group be in order to be a legitimate subculture or society? Does it need ten or fifteen people? How about just three? Come to think of it, why can't my burglary partner and I found our own society with a morality of its own? Of course, if my partner dies, I could still claim that I was acting from an originally social set of norms. But, why can't I dispense with the interpersonal agreements altogether and invent my own morality because morality, in this view, is only an invention anyway? Conventionalist relativism seems to reduce to subjectivism. And subjectivism leads, as we have seen, to moral solipsism, to the demise of morality altogether.

The relativist may here object that this is an instance of the slippery slope fallacy—that is, the fallacy of objecting to a proposition on the erroneous grounds that, if accepted, it will lead to a chain of events that are absurd or unacceptable. In response to this objection, though, the burden rests with the relativist to give an alternative analysis of what constitutes a viable social basis for generating valid (or true) moral principles. Perhaps we might agree (for the sake of argument, at least) that the very nature of morality entails two people who are making an agreement. This move saves the conventionalist from moral solipsism, but it still permits almost any principle at all to count as moral. What's more, one can throw out those principles and substitute their contraries for them as the need arises. If two or three people decide to make cheating on exams morally acceptable for themselves, via forming a fraternity, Cheaters Anonymous, at their university, then cheating becomes moral. Why not? Why not rape as well?

However, I don't think that you can stop the move from conventionalism to subjectivism. The essential force of the validity of the chosen moral principle is that it depends on *choice*. The conventionalist holds that it is the group's choice, but why should I accept the group's "silly choice" when my own is better for me? If this is all that morality comes to, then why not reject it altogether—even though, to escape sanctions, one might want to adhere to its directives when others are looking? Why should anyone give such grand authority to a culture of society? I see no reason to recognize a culture's authority unless that culture recognizes the authority of something that *legitimizes* the culture. It seems that we need something higher than culture by which to assess a culture.

Moral Diversity Is Exaggerated

A third problem with conventional ethical relativism is that the level of moral diversity that we actually see around the world is not as extreme as relativists like Sumner and Benedict claim. One can also see great similarities among the moral codes of various cultures. Sociobiologist E. O. Wilson has identified over a score of common features:

> Every culture has a concept of murder, distinguishing this from execution, killing in war, and other "justifiable homicides." The notions of incest and other regulations upon sexual behavior, the prohibitions upon untruth under defined circumstances, of restitution and reciprocity, of mutual obligations between parents and children—these and many other moral concepts are altogether universal.[10]

Colin Turnbull's description of the sadistic, semidisplaced, disintegrating Ik tribe in northern Uganda supports the view that a people without principles of kindness, loyalty, and cooperation will degenerate into a Hobbesian state of nature.[11] But, he has also produced evidence that, underneath the surface of this dying society, there is a deeper moral code from a time when the tribe flourished, which occasionally surfaces and shows its nobler face.

From another perspective, the whole issue of moral diversity among cultures is irrelevant to the truth or falsehood of conventional ethical relativism. There is indeed enormous cultural diversity, and many societies have radically different moral codes. Cultural diversity seems to be a fact, but, even if it is, it does not by itself establish the truth of ethical relativism. Cultural diversity in itself is neutral with respect to theories. The objectivist could concede complete cultural relativism but still defend a form of universalism; for he or she could argue that some cultures simply lack correct moral principles.[12]

By the same reasoning, a denial of complete cultural relativism (that is, an admission of some universal principles) does not disprove ethical relativism. For even if we did find one or more universal principles, this would not prove that they had any objective status. We could still *imagine* a culture that was an exception to the rule and be unable to criticize it. Thus, the diversity thesis doesn't by itself imply ethical relativism, and its denial doesn't disprove ethical relativism.

Weak Dependency Does Not Imply Relativism

A final problem with conventional ethical relativism concerns the dependency thesis that all moral principles derive their validity from cultural acceptance. On close inspection, this principle is rather unclear and can be restated in two distinct ways, a weak and a strong version:

> *Weak dependency.* The application of moral principles depends on one's culture.

> *Strong dependency.* The moral principles themselves depend on one's culture.

The weak thesis says that the application of principles depends on the particular cultural predicament, whereas the strong thesis affirms that the principles themselves depend on that predicament. The nonrelativist can accept a certain relativity in the way that moral principles are *applied* in various cultures, depending on beliefs, history, and environment. Indeed, morality does not occur in a vacuum but is linked with these cultural factors. For example, a raw environment with scarce natural resources may justify the Eskimos' brand of euthanasia to the objectivist, who would consistently reject that practice if it occurred in another environment. One Sudanese tribe throws its deformed infants into the river because the tribe believes that such infants *belong* to the hippopotamus, the god of the river. We believe that these groups' belief in euthanasia and infanticide is false, but the point is that the same principles of respect for property and respect for human life operate in such contrary practices. The tribe differs with us only in belief, not in substantive moral principle. This is an illustration of how nonmoral beliefs (for example, deformed infants belong to the hippopotamus), when applied to common moral principles (for example, give to each his or her due), generate different actions in different cultures. In our own culture, the difference in the nonmoral belief about the status of a fetus generates opposite moral stands. The major difference between pro-choicers and pro-lifers is not whether we should kill persons but whether fetuses are really persons. It is a debate about the facts of the matter, not the principle of killing innocent persons.

Thus, the fact that moral principles are weakly dependent doesn't show that ethical relativism is valid. Despite this weak dependency on nonmoral factors, there could still be a set of general moral norms applicable to all cultures and even recognized in most, which a culture could disregard only at its own expense.

Accordingly, the ethical relativist must maintain the stronger thesis, which insists that the very validity of the principles is a product of the culture and that different cultures will invent different valid principles. This, though, is a more difficult position to establish because it requires ruling out all rival sources of substantive moral principles such as human reason, human evolution, innate notions of human happiness, and God. In fact, a detailed examination of these rival explanations will take us on through to the end of this book. In short, while it is reasonable to accept the weak dependency thesis—the application of moral principles depends on one's culture—the relativist needs the stronger thesis which is a challenge to prove.

The Indeterminacy of Language

Relativists still have at least one more arrow in their quiver—the argument from the **indeterminacy of translation.** This theory, set forth by Willard V. Quine (1908–2000),[13] holds that languages are often so fundamentally different from each other that we cannot accurately translate concepts from one to another. Language groups mean different things by words. Quine holds that it may be impossible to know whether a native speaker who points toward a rabbit and says "gavagai" is using the word to signify "rabbit," or "rabbit part," or something else. This thesis holds that language is the essence of a culture and fundamentally shapes its reality, cutting the culture off from other languages and cultures. This, then, seems to imply that each society's moral principles depend on its unique linguistically grounded culture.

But experience seems to falsify this thesis. Although each culture does have a particular language with different meanings—indeed, each person has his or her own particular set of meanings—we do learn foreign languages and learn to translate across linguistic frameworks. For example, people from a myriad of language groups come to the United States, learn English, and communicate perfectly well. Rather than causing a complete gap, the interplay between these other cultures and ours eventually enriches the English language with new concepts (for example, *forte, foible, taboo,* and *coup de grace*), even as English has enriched (or "corrupted," as the French might argue) other languages. Even if some indeterminacy of translation exists between language users, we should not infer from this that no translation or communication is possible. It seems reasonable to believe that general moral principles are precisely those things that can be communicated transculturally. The kind of common features that Kluckhohn and Wilson advance—duties of restitution and reciprocity, regulations on sexual behavior, obligations of parents to children, a no-unnecessary-harm principle, and a sense that the good people should flourish and the guilty people should suffer—these and other features constitute a common human experience, a common set of values within a common human predicament of struggling to survive and flourish in a world of scarce resources.[14]

Thus, it is possible to communicate cross-culturally and find that we agree on many of the important things in life. If this is so, then the indeterminacy-of-translation thesis, which relativism rests on, must itself be relativized to the point at which it is no objection to objective morality.

What the relativist needs is a strong thesis of dependency, that somehow all principles are essentially cultural inventions. But, why should we choose to view morality this way? Is there anything to recommend the strong thesis of dependency over the weak thesis of dependency? The relativist may argue that in fact we lack an obvious impartial standard to judge from. "Who's to say which culture is right and which is wrong?" But this seems dubious. We can reason and perform thought experiments to make a case for one system over another. We may not be able to *know* with certainty that our moral beliefs are closer to the truth than those of another culture or those of others within our own culture, but we may be *justified* in believing this about our moral beliefs. If we can be closer to the truth about factual or scientific matters, why can't we be closer to the truth on moral matters? Why can't a culture simply be confused or wrong about its moral perceptions? Why can't we say that a culture like the Ik, which enjoys watching its own children fall into fires, is less moral in that regard than a culture that cherishes children and grants them protection and equal rights? To take such a stand is not ethnocentrism, for we are seeking to derive principles through critical reason, not simply uncritical acceptance of one's own mores.

CONCLUSION

Ethical relativism—the thesis that moral principles derive their validity from dependence on society or individual choice—seems plausible at first glance, but on close scrutiny it presents some severe problems. Subjective ethical relativism seems to boil down to anarchistic individualism, an essential denial of the interpersonal feature of the moral point of view. Conventional ethical relativism, which does contain an interpersonal perspective, fails to deal adequately with the problem of the reformer, the question of defining a culture, and the whole enterprise of moral criticism. Nevertheless, unless moral objectivism—the subject of the next chapter—can make a positive case for its position, relativism may survive these criticisms.

NOTES

1. *History of Herodotus,* trans. George Rawlinson (Appleton, 1859), Bk. 3, Ch. 38.
2. Ernest Hemingway, *Death in the Afternoon* (Scribner's, 1932), p. 4.
3. Harry V. Jaffa, *Homosexuality and the Natural Law* (Claremont Institute of the Study of Statesmanship and Political Philosophy, 1990), pp. 3–4.
4. John Ladd, *Ethical Relativism* (Wadsworth, 1973), p. 1.

5. Ruth Benedict, *Patterns of Culture* (New American Library, 1934), p. 257.

6. W. G. Sumner, *Folkways* (Ginn & Co., 1905), Sec. 80, p. 76.

7. Ruth Benedict, *Patterns of Culture* (New American Library, 1934), p. 257.

8. Nancy Scheper-Hughes, "Virgin Territory: The Male Discovery of the Clitoris," *Medical Anthropology Quarterly* 5, no. 1 (March 1991): 25–28.

9. Melville Herskovits, *Cultural Relativism* (Random House, 1972).

10. E. O. Wilson, *On Human Nature* (Bantam Books, 1979), pp. 22–23.

11. Colin Turnbull, *The Mountain People* (Simon & Schuster, 1972).

12. Clyde Kluckhohn, "Ethical Relativity: Sic et Non," *Journal of Philosophy* 52 (1955).

13. See W. V. Quine, *Word and Object* (MIT Press, 1960) and *Ontological Relativity* (Columbia University Press, 1969); Benjamin Whorf, *Language, Thought and Reality* (MIT Press, 1956).

14. Kluckhorn, "Ethical Relativity"; Wilson, *On Human Nature*.

FOR FURTHER REFLECTION

1. Examine the position paper of the American Anthropological Association, quoted at the opening of this chapter, which rhetorically concludes that there are no universal human rights. How sound is this argument implying that all morality, as well as human rights, is relative to culture? What does this mean regarding women's rights? Discuss the implications of this argument.

2. Go over John Ladd's definition of ethical relativism, quoted at the beginning of this chapter and discussed within it. Is it a good definition? Can you find a better definition of ethical relativism? Ask your friends what they think ethical relativism is and whether they accept it. You might put the question this way: "Are there any moral absolutes, or is morality completely relative?" Discuss your findings.

3. Examine the notion of subjective ethical relativism. It bases morality on *radical individualism,* the theory that each person is the inventor of morality: "Morality is in the eye of the beholder." Consider this assumption of individualism. Could there be a morality for only one person? Imagine that only one person existed in the world (leave God out of the account). Suppose you were that person. Would you have any moral duties? Certainly there would be *prudential* duties—some ways of living would help you attain your goals—but would there be moral duties?

4. Now imagine a second person has come into your world—a fully developed, mature person with wants, needs, hopes, and fears. How does this change the nature of the situation of the solitary individual?

5. Can you separate the anthropological claim that different cultures have different moral principles (the diversity thesis—called cultural relativism) from the judgment that *therefore* they are all equally good (ethical relativism)?

Are there independent criteria by which we can say that some cultures are "better" than others?

6. Ruth Benedict has written that our culture is "but one entry in a long series of possible adjustments" and that "the very eyes with which we see the problem are conditioned by the long traditional habits of our own society." What are the implications of these statements? Is she correct? How would an objectivist respond to these claims?

7. Consider the practice of clitoridectomies in parts of Africa, discussed in this chapter. How would an ethical relativist defend such a practice? How would a nonrelativist argue against the practice?

FOR FURTHER READING

Cook, John W. *Morality and Cultural Differences*. New York: Oxford University Press, 1999.

Harman, Gilbert, and Judith Jarvis Thomson. *Moral Relativism and Moral Objectivity*. Cambridge, Mass: Blackwell, 1996.

Kellenberger, James. *Moral Relativism, Moral Diversity and Human Relationships*. University Park: Pennsylvania State University Press, 2001.

Ladd, John. *Ethical Relativism*. Belmont, Calif.: Wadsworth, 1973.

Levy, Neil. *Moral Relativism: A Short Introduction*. Oxford, Engl.: Oneworld, 2002.

Moser, Paul K., and Thomas L. Carson, eds. *Moral Relativism: A Reader*. New York: Oxford University Press, 2001.

Wong, David. *Moral Relativity*. Berkeley: University of California Press, 1984.

3

※

Moral Objectivism

There is a great uniformity among the actions of men, in all nations and ages, and that human nature remains still the same, in its principles and operations. The same events follow from the same causes. Ambition, avarice, self-love, vanity, friendship, generosity, public spirit; these passions, mixed in various degrees, and distributed through society, have been, from the beginning of the world, and still are, the source of all the actions and enterprises which have ever been observed among mankind. . . . [History's] chief use is only to discover the constant and universal principles of human nature, by showing men in all varieties of circumstances and situations, and furnishing us with materials, from which we may form our observations, and become acquainted with the regular springs of human action and behavior.
DAVID HUME, *AN ENQUIRY CONCERNING HUMAN UNDERSTANDING*

Here is the story of Seba, a girl from Mali:

I was raised by my grandmother in Mali, and when I was still a little girl a woman my family knew came and asked her if she could take me to Paris to care for her children. She told my grandmother that she would put me in school, and that I would learn French. But when I came to Paris I was not sent to school. I had to work every day. In her house I did all the work; I cleaned the house, cooked the meals, cared for the children, and washed and fed the baby. Every day I started work before 7 a.m. and finished about 11 p.m.; I never had a day off. My mistress did nothing; she slept late and then watched television or went out.

One day I told her that I wanted to go to school. She replied that she had not brought me to France to go to school but to take care of her children. I was so tired and run down. I had problems with my teeth; sometimes my cheek would swell and the pain would be terrible. Sometimes I had stomachaches, but when I was ill I still had to work. Sometimes when I was in pain I would cry, but my mistress would shout at me.

... She would often beat me. She would slap me all the time. She beat me with a broom, with kitchen tools, or whipped me with electric cable. Sometimes I would bleed; I still have marks on my body.

Once in 1992, I was late going to get the children from school; my mistress and her husband were furious with me and beat me and then threw me out on the street. I didn't understand anything, and I wandered on the street. After some time her husband found me and took me back to the house. There they stripped me naked, tied my hands behind my back, and began to whip me with a wire attached to a broomstick. Both of them were beating me at the same time. I was bleeding a lot and screaming, but they continued to beat me. Then she rubbed chili pepper into my wounds and stuck it in my vagina. I lost consciousness.[1]

Surely, this case of modern slavery is an instance of injustice. Seba was treated with malicious cruelty. What happened to Seba should not happen to a dog, let alone a little girl. It is morally wrong, even if the people who enslaved Seba believed what they were doing was morally permissible. You can be sincere but mistaken. The people who enslaved Seba violated at least three basic moral principles: (1) respect the freedom of rational beings; (2) don't cause unnecessary suffering; and (3) always treat people as ends in themselves, never merely as means (that is, don't exploit people). We will examine such principles throughout the rest of this book.

One way of testing our behavior is by applying the Golden Rule: "Do unto others as you would have them do unto you." This is a good rule of thumb, for generally in everyday life we can decide what is right or wrong by putting ourselves in the shoes of people with whom we are interacting. I wouldn't want you to steal my property, so I shouldn't steal yours. As we will see in Chapter 8, this rule is not always correct, but it's a good rule of thumb. It's the beginning but not the last word in moral philosophy.

In Chapter 2, we examined moral relativism, the thesis that moral principles gain their validity only through approval by the culture or the individual, and concluded that it was plagued with severe problems. However, showing that relativism is loaded with liabilities is one thing; showing that moral principles have objective validity, independent of cultural acceptance, is quite another. A rival theory to moral relativism attempts to do just that—namely, the position of **moral objectivism:** There are objective universal moral principles, valid for all people and all social environments. In this chapter, we examine several versions of this theory and ultimately accept a view that may be called **moderate objectivism.**

First, it is important to distinguish between moral objectivism and the closely related view of **moral absolutism.** The absolutist believes that there are nonoverrideable moral principles that one ought never violate. Moral principles are exceptionless. For example, some absolutists hold that one ought never break a promise, no matter what. The objectivist shares with the absolutist the notion that moral principles have universal, objective validity. However, objectivists deny that moral norms are necessarily exceptionless. The objectivist could believe that no moral duty has absolute weight or strict priority; each moral principle must be weighed against other moral principles. For example, the duty to tell the truth might be overridden in a situation where speaking the truth would lead to serious harm. In this case, the duty to avoid harm would override the duty to tell the truth. Some versions of objectivism indeed do adopt the absolutist stance that moral principles are exceptionless and nonoverrideable. Other objectivist theories, though, reject absolutism and maintain instead that, in special situations, one moral duty might be overridden by a different and more compelling duty.

We begin our discussion with the views of one influential moral objectivist, Thomas Aquinas (1225–1274).

AQUINAS'S OBJECTIVISM AND ABSOLUTISM

Aquinas's moral philosophy has two components. First, he followed an objectivist approach called natural law theory. Second, he was a moral absolutist, and he developed this theme in a theory known as the doctrine of double effect. Let's look at each of these.

Natural Law Theory

Natural law theory is the view that there exists an eternal moral law that can be discovered through reason by looking at the nature of humanity and society. The idea of natural law first appears among the Stoics (first century BCE), who believed that human beings have within them a divine spark (from the Greek *logos spermatikos,* meaning "the rational seed or sperm") that enables them to discover the essential eternal laws necessary for individual happiness and social harmony. The whole universe is governed by laws that exhibit rationality. Nature in general and animals in particular obey these laws by necessity, but humans have a choice. Humans obey these laws because they can perceive the laws' inner reasonableness. This notion enabled the Stoics to be *cosmopolitans* ("people of the cosmos") who imposed a universal standard of righteousness (*jus naturale*) on all societies, evaluating various human-made or "positive laws" (from the Latin *jus gentium,* meaning "laws of the nations") by this higher bar of reason.

Aquinas combined the sense of cosmic natural law with Aristotle's view that human beings, like every other natural object, have a specific nature, purpose, and function. A knife's function is to cut sharply, a chair's function is to support the body in a certain position, and a house's function is to provide shelter from the elements. Humanity's essence or proper function is to live the life of reason. As Aristotle put it,

> Reason is the true self of every man, since it is the supreme and better part. It will be strange, then, if he should choose not his own life, but some other's. What is naturally proper to every creature is the highest and pleasantest for him. And so, to man, this will be the life of Reason, since Reason is, in the highest sense, a man's self.[2]

Humanity's function is to exhibit rationality in all its forms: contemplation, deliberation, and action. For Aquinas, reason's deliberative processes discover the natural laws. They are universal rules, or "ordinances of reason for the common good, spread by him who has the care of the community":

> To the natural law belong those things to which a man is inclined naturally; and among these it is proper to man to be inclined to act according to reason.... Hence this is the first precept of law, that good is to be done and promoted, and evil is to be avoided. All other precepts of the natural law are based upon this; so that all the things which the practical reason naturally apprehends as man's good belong to the precepts of the natural law under the form of things to be done or avoided.
>
> Since, however, good has the nature of an end, and evil, the nature of the contrary, hence it is that all those things to which man has a natural inclination are naturally apprehended by reason as good, and consequently as objects of pursuit, and their contraries as evil, and objects of avoidance. Therefore, the order of the precepts of the natural law is according to the order of natural inclinations.[3]

Aquinas and other Christians who espoused natural law appealed to the "Epistle to the Romans" in the New Testament, where Paul wrote

> When the Gentiles, who have not the [Jewish-revealed] law, do by nature what the law requires, they are a law to themselves, even though they do not have the law. They show that what the law requires is written on their hearts, while their conscience also bears witness and their conflicting thoughts accuse or perhaps excuse them. (Romans 2: 14–15)

The key ideas of the natural law tradition are the following:

1. Human beings have an essential rational nature established by God, who designed us to live and flourish in prescribed ways (from Aristotle and the Stoics).
2. Even without knowledge of God, reason, as the essence of our nature, can discover the laws necessary for human flourishing (from Aristotle; developed by Aquinas).

3.   The natural laws are universal and unchangeable, and one should use them to judge individual societies and their positive laws. Positive (or actual) laws of societies that are not in line with the natural law are not truly laws but counterfeits (from the Stoics).

Moral laws have objective validity. Reason can sort out which inclinations are part of our true nature and how we are to relate them to one another. Aquinas listed the desires for life and procreation as fundamental values without which other values could not even get established. Knowledge and friendship (or sociability) are two other intrinsic values. These values are not good because we desire them; rather, we desire them because they are good—they are absolutely necessary for human flourishing.

The Doctrine of Double Effect

Aquinas's position is not only objectivist but also absolutist. For Aquinas, humanity has an essentially rational nature, and reason can discover the right action in every situation by following an appropriate *exceptionless* principle. But, sometimes we encounter moral conflicts, "dilemmas" in which we cannot do good without also bringing about evil consequences. To this end, Aquinas devised the *doctrine of double effect* (DDE), which provides a tidy method for solving all moral disputes in which an act will have two effects, one good and the other bad. The doctrine says, roughly, that it is always wrong to do a bad act intentionally in order to bring about good consequences, but that it is sometimes permissible to do a good act despite knowing that it will bring about bad consequences. This doctrine consists in four conditions that must be satisfied before an act is morally permissible:

1.   *The nature-of-the-act condition.* The action must be either morally good or indifferent. Lying or intentionally killing an innocent person is never permissible.

2.   *The means–end condition.* The bad effect must not be the means by which one achieves the good effect.

3.   *The right-intention condition.* The intention must be the achieving of only the good effect, with the bad effect being only an unintended side effect. If the bad effect is a means of obtaining the good effect, then the act is immoral. The bad effect may be foreseen but must not be intended.

4.   *The proportionality condition.* The good effect must be at least equivalent in importance to the bad effect.

Let's illustrate this doctrine by applying it to a woman whose life is endangered by her pregnancy. Is it morally permissible for her to have an abortion to save her life? The DDE says that an abortion is not permissible.

Because abortion kills an innocent human being and intentionally killing innocent human beings is always wrong, it is always wrong to have an abortion—even to save the woman's life. Abortion also fails condition 2 (the means–end condition).

Killing the innocent to bring about a good effect is never justified, not even to save a whole city or the world. As the Stoics said, "Let justice be done, though the heavens fall." However, if the woman's uterus happens to be cancerous, then she may have a hysterectomy, which will result in the death of the fetus. This is because the act of removing a cancerous uterus is morally good (thus passing condition 1). The act of performing a hysterectomy also passes condition 3 because the death of the fetus is the unintended (although foreseen) effect of the hysterectomy. Condition 2 is passed because the death of the fetus isn't the means of saving the woman's life—the hysterectomy is. Condition 4 is passed because saving the woman's life is a great good, at least as good as saving the fetus. In this case, given the DDE, the woman is really lucky to have a cancerous uterus.

On the other hand, if the doctor could save the woman's life only by changing the composition of the amniotic fluid (say, with saline solution), which in turn would kill the fetus, then this would not be morally permissible according to the DDE. In this case, the same result occurs as in the hysterectomy, but killing the fetus is *intended* as the means of saving the woman's life. Similarly, crushing the fetus's head to remove the fetus vaginally and thus save the mother's life would be disallowed because this would violate conditions 2 and 3.

The Roman Catholic Church uses this doctrine to prohibit not only most abortions but also the use of contraceptives. Because the procreation of life is good and the frustration of life is bad and because the natural purpose of sexual intercourse is to produce new life, it is wrong to use devices that prevent intercourse from producing its natural result.

The doctrine is also used by just-war theorists in defending strategic bombings in contrast with terrorist bombings. In a strategic bombing, the intention is to destroy a military target such as a munitions factory. One foresees that in the process of destroying this legitimate target, noncombatants will be killed. On the basis of DDE, the bombing is justified because the civilians were not the intended target. In a terrorist bombing, on the other hand, noncombatants are the intended target. The Allied fire bombings of Hamburg and Dresden in World War II and the dropping of the atom bomb on Hiroshima and Nagasaki are condemned on the basis of the DDE because they clearly intended to kill civilians. Utilitarians, by contrast would permit such bombings because they were likely to produce overall benefit—namely, ending the war sooner, thus saving thousands of lives.

Consider another example. Suppose that Sally's father has planted a nuclear bomb that will detonate in a half hour. Sally is the only person who knows where he hid it, and she has promised him that she will not reveal the location to anyone. Although she regrets his act, as a devoted daughter she refuses to break her promise and give away the secret. However, if we do not discover where the bomb is and dismantle it within the next half hour, it will blow up a city and kill a million people. Suppose we can torture Sally to get this information from her. According to the DDE, is this permissible? No, for the end does not justify the means. Condition 2 is violated. We are using a bad act to bring about a good effect.

On the other hand, suppose someone has tampered with the wires of my television set in such a way that turning it on will send an electrical signal to the next town where it will detonate a bomb. Suppose I know that this will happen. Is it morally wrong, according to the DDE, to turn on my television to watch an edifying program? Yes it is because condition 4 is violated. The unintended evil outweighs the good.

Problems with the Doctrine of Double Effect

If we interpret the proportionality principle in this way, then a lot of other seemingly innocent or good actions would also violate it. Suppose that I am contemplating joining the true religion (I leave you to tell me which one that is) to save my eternal soul. However, I realize that, by doing so, I will create enormous resentment in my neighborhood over my act, resentment that will cause five neighbors to be damned. Or, suppose that my marrying the woman of my heart's desire generates such despair in five other fellows (who, we may imagine, would be reasonably happy as bachelors as long as no one married her) that they all commit suicide. We may suppose that the despair I cause these five fellows will make their free will nonoperational. I understand ahead of time that my act will have this result. Is my act morally justified? In both of these cases, the DDE seems to imply that my actions are not morally justified because, according to condition 4, the good effects would be much less than the bad effects.

The DDE has problems. First, some of the prescriptions seem patently counterintuitive. It seems absurd to prohibit someone from changing his or her religion or marrying the person of his or her choice because other people will feel depressed or do evil deeds. Normally, we want to say, "That's their problem." And, regarding the abortion example, we generally judge the mother's life to be more valuable than the fetus's life, so commonsense morality would permit all abortions that promise to save the mother's life. The response to this may be that our intuitions are not always correct. They can lead us astray. Some people have intuitions that it is bad luck to walk under a ladder or have a black cat cross one's path, but these are simply superstitions. The counterresponse is that intuitions about a person's right to life are not superstitions but a fundamental moral right.

Second, it's not always clear how closely an effect must be connected with the act to be counted as the intended act. Consider the trolley problem, first set forth by Philippa Foot. A trolley is speeding down a track, and Edward the driver notices that the brakes have failed. Five people who will be killed if something is not done are standing on the track a short distance ahead of the trolley. To the right is a sidetrack in a tunnel on which a single worker is working. Should Edward turn the wheel onto the sidetrack, killing the single worker? Utilitarians and many others would say that Edward should turn the trolley onto the sidetrack, for it is better to kill one person than allow five equally innocent people to die. The DDE would seem to prohibit this action, holding that it would violate conditions 2 and 3, or at least 2, doing a bad effect to bring about a good effect. It would seem to violate 3, given that the effect of turning the trolley onto the right sidetrack is so closely linked with the death of the worker because only a miracle could save him. The idea is that killing is worse than letting die. So, it would seem, according to DDE, Edward should not turn the trolley onto the sidetrack.

However, the proponent of DDE responds, "Edward has not formed an actual intention to kill the worker, so condition 3 is not violated. The trolley driver would not object if an angel rescued the worker while the trolley sped through the tunnel." The counterresponse is that turning the trolley onto the sidetrack is so closely and definitely linked with the death of the innocent worker that the intention is connected with the act. Otherwise, couldn't the terrorists on 9/11 argue that their destroying the Twin Towers of the World Trade Center was permitted by the DDE? Imagine such a defense: "We only meant to destroy the twin symbols of Corporate Greed (that is, capitalism) and foresaw that innocent lives would be lost as collateral damage. We would not have objected if an angel had rescued the lives of the passengers in the plane and the people in the Twin Towers."

Third, there is the problem of how to describe an act. Could I not redescribe abortion in which the woman's health or life is in danger as intending to improve the woman's health (or save her life) and only foreseeing that removing the fetus will result in its (unintended) death? Or, could I not steal some food from the grocery store, intending to feed the poor and foreseeing that the grocer will be slightly poorer? And, could I not redescribe Edward's trolley car dilemma as merely trying to save the lives of five people with the unintended consequence of allowing the trolley to run over one person?

Of course, the DDE must set limits to redescription; otherwise, almost any act can be justified by ingenious redescription. Eric D'Arcy has attempted to set such limits. He quotes the jingle "Imperious Caesar, dead and turned to clay, might stop a hole to keep the wind away" but adds that it would be ridiculous to describe killing Caesar as intending to block a windy draft. His own solution to this problem is that "certain kinds of acts are of such significance that the terms which denote them may not, special contexts apart, be elided into terms which (a) denote their consequences, and (b) conceal, or even fail to reveal, the nature of the act itself."[4]

This explanation may lend plausibility to the DDE, but it is not always possible to identify the exact nature of the act itself—it may have various interpretations. Furthermore, the absolutism of the doctrine will make it counterintuitive to many of us. It would seem to prohibit lying to save a life or breaking a promise to spare someone great suffering. Why should we accept a system that allows the destruction of many innocent people simply because we may have to override a normal moral precept? Aren't morals made for the human good? Doesn't the strong natural law tradition reverse things—requiring that humans serve rules for the rules' own sake? Furthermore, there may be more than a single right answer to every moral dilemma. The DDE seems *casuistic,* making hairsplitting distinctions that miss the point of morality. It gives us solutions to problems that seem to impose an artificial rigidity on human existence.

Fourth, there is one other difficulty with the absolute version of natural law: It is tied closely to a teleological view of human nature, a view that sees not only humanity but also each individual as having a plan designed by God or a godlike nature, so any deviation from the norm is morally wrong. Hence, because the plan of humanity includes procreation and sexuality is the means to that goal, only heterosexual intercourse (without artificial birth control devices) is morally permitted.

However, if Darwinian evolutionary theory is correct, there is no design. Human beings are animals who evolved from "lower" forms of life via the survival of the fittest. We are the product of chance in this struggle for existence. If this is so, then the ideas of a single human purpose and an absolute set of laws to serve that purpose are problematic. We may have many purposes, and our moral domain may include a certain relativity. For example, heterosexuality may serve one social purpose whereas homosexuality serves another, and both may be fulfilling for different types of individuals. Reason's task may not be to discover an essence of humanity or unchangeable laws but simply to help us survive and fulfill our desires.

However, even if this nonreligious account of evolution is inaccurate and there is a God who has guided evolution, it's still not obvious that the absolutist's way of looking at the world and morality is the best one available. Nonetheless, the DDE may remind us of two important moral truths: (1) Negative duties are typically more stringent than positive ones. Ordinarily, it is less wrong to allow an evil than to do evil; otherwise, a maniac, known to reliably execute his threats could get us to kill someone merely by threatening to kill five people unless we carried out the murder. (2) People have rights that must be respected, so we cannot simply decide what to do based on a crude utilitarian calculus.

If we give up the notion that a moral system must contain only absolute principles, duties that proceed out of a definite algorithm such as the DDE, what can we put in its place? One possibility is that there are valid rules of action that one should generally adhere to but in cases of moral conflict may be overridable by another moral principle. William D. Ross refers to these overridable moral rules as **prima facie duties.** That is, they are binding only initially, or on "first appearance," until overridden by a more urgent duty.[5] For example, even though a principle of justice may generally outweigh a principle of benevolence, there are times when one could do enormous good by sacrificing a small amount of justice; thus, an objectivist would be inclined to act according to the principle of benevolence.

There may be some absolute or nonoverrideable principles, but there need not be any (or many) for objectivism to be true. Renford Bambrough states this point nicely:

> To suggest that there is a *right* answer to a moral problem is at once to be accused of or credited with a belief in moral absolutes. But it is no more necessary to believe in moral absolutes in order to believe in moral objectivity than it is to believe in the existence of absolute space or absolute time in order to believe in the objectivity of temporal and spatial relations and of judgments about them.[6]

MODERATE OBJECTIVISM

What is central to moral objectivism, then, is not the absolutist position that moral principles are exceptionless and nonoverrideable. Rather, it is that there are universal and objective moral principles, valid for all people and social environments. If we can establish or show that it is reasonable to believe that there is, in some ideal sense, at least one objective moral principle that is binding on all people everywhere, then we will have shown that relativism probably is false and that a limited objectivism is true. Actually, I believe that many qualified general ethical principles are binding on all rational beings, but one principle will suffice to refute relativism:

A. It is morally wrong to torture people for the fun of it.

I claim that this principle is binding on all rational agents, so that if some agent, S, rejects A, we should not let that affect our intuition that A is a true principle; rather, we should try to explain S's behavior as perverse, ignorant, or irrational instead. For example, suppose Adolf Hitler doesn't accept A. Should that affect our confidence in the truth of A? Is it not more reasonable to infer that Hitler is morally deficient, morally blind, ignorant, or irrational than to suppose that his noncompliance is evidence against the truth of A?

Suppose further that there is a tribe of "Hitlerites" somewhere who enjoy torturing people. Their whole culture accepts torturing others for the fun of it. Suppose that Mother Teresa or Mohandas Gandhi tries unsuccessfully to convince these sadists that they should stop torturing people altogether, and the sadists respond by torturing her or him. Should this affect our confidence in A?

Would it not be more reasonable to look for some explanation of Hitlerite behavior? For example, we might hypothesize that this tribe lacks the developed sense of sympathetic imagination that is necessary for the moral life. Or we might theorize that this tribe is on a lower evolutionary level than most *Homo sapiens*. Or we might simply conclude that the tribe is closer to a Hobbesian state of nature than most societies, and as such probably would not survive very long—or if it did, the lives of its people would be largely "solitary, poor, nasty, brutish and short" as in the Ik culture in northern Uganda where the core morality has partly broken down. But we need not know the correct answer as to why the tribe is in such bad shape to maintain our confidence in A as a moral principle. If A is a basic or core belief for us, then we will be more likely to doubt the Hitlerites' sanity or ability to think morally than to doubt the validity of A.

Core Morality

We can perhaps produce other candidates for membership in our minimally basic objective moral set:

1. Do not kill innocent people.
2. Do not cause unnecessary pain or suffering.
3. Do not lie or deceive.
4. Do not steal or cheat.
5. Keep your promises and honor your contracts.
6. Do not deprive another person of his or her freedom.
7. Do justice, treating people as they deserve to be treated.

8. Reciprocate: Show gratitude for services rendered.

9. Help other people, especially when the cost to oneself is minimal.

10. Obey just laws.

These ten principles are examples of the *core morality,* principles necessary for the good life within a flourishing human community. They are not arbitrary, for we can give reasons that explain why they are constitutive elements of a successful society, necessary to social cohesion and personal well-being. Principles like the Golden Rule, (1) not killing innocent people, (3) telling the truth, (5) keeping promises, (6) respecting liberty, (7) rewarding or punishing people (whichever they deserve—justice), (9) helping those in need, and the like are central to the fluid progression of social interaction and the resolution of conflicts of interest that ethics bears on (at least minimal morality does, even though there may be more to morality than simply these concerns).

For example, regarding rule 1, the survival instinct causes us to place a high value on our lives so that any society that would survive must protect innocent life. Without the protection of innocent life, nothing would be possible for us. Rule 2, "Do not cause unnecessary pain or suffering," seems quite obvious. No normal person desires gratuitous pain or harm. We want to be healthy and successful and have our needs taken into consideration. The ancient code of medicine requiring that doctors "Above all, do no harm" is applicable to all of us.

Regarding rule 3, language itself depends on a general and implicit commitment to the principle of truth telling. Accuracy of expression is a primitive form of truthfulness. Hence, every time that we use words correctly (for example, "That is a book" or "My name is Sam"), we are telling the truth. Without a high degree of reliable matching between words and objects, language itself would be impossible. Likewise, regarding rule 5, without the practice of promise keeping, we could not rely on one another's words when they inform us about future acts. We could have no reliable expectations about their future behavior. Our lives are social, dependent on cooperation, so it is vital that when we make agreements, we fulfill them (for example, "I'll help you with your philosophy paper if you'll help me install a new computer program"). This rule borders on reciprocity, rule 8; we need to have confidence that the other party will reciprocate when we have done our part. Even chimpanzees follow the rule of reciprocity, *returning good for good* (*returning evil for evil* may not be as necessary for morality).

Regarding rule 4, without a prohibition against stealing and cheating, we could not claim property—not even ownership of our very limbs, let alone external goods. And, if freeloading and stealing became the norm, very little productive work would be done, so there would be little to steal and our lives would be impoverished. Anyone who has ever been confined to a small room or has had his limbs tied up should be able to see the need for rule 6, respect other people's liberty; for without freedom we could hardly attain our goals.

Sometimes, people question whether rule 7—that we do justice, treating people according to what they merit—implies that we should reward and punish on the basis of morally relevant criteria, not irrelevant ones like race, ethnicity, or gender. One part of justice advocates consistency. If a teacher gives Jack an A– for a certain quality of essay, she should give Jill the same grade if her essay is of the same quality. A stronger, more substantive principle of justice holds that we should "Give people what they deserve."

Rule 10, "Obey just laws," is necessary for harmonious social living. We may not always agree with the law, but in social situations we must make reasonable compromises and accept the decisions of the government. When we disagree with the law, we may work to convince the powers-that-be to change it; in extreme situations such as living in a society with racist laws, we may decide to engage in civil disobedience.

There may be other moral rules necessary or highly relevant to an objective core morality. Perhaps we should add something like "Cooperate with others for the common good," although I think that this is already included when we combine rules 2, 4, and 9. Perhaps you can think of other rules that are necessary to a flourishing community. In any case, although a moral code would be adequate if it contained a requisite set of these objective principles, there could be more than one adequate moral code that contained different rankings or different combinations of rules. Different specific rules may be required in different situations. For example, in a desert community, there may be a strict rule prohibiting the wasting of water, and in a community with a preponderance of females over males, there may be a rule permitting polygamy. A society where birth control devices are available may differ on the rule prescribing chastity from one that lacks such technology. Such moral flexibility does not entail moral relativism but simply a recognition that social situations can determine which rules are relevant to the flourishing of a particular community. Nevertheless, an essential core morality, such as that described above, will be practically necessary for human flourishing.

The core moral rules are analogous to the set of vitamins necessary for a healthy diet. We need an adequate amount of each vitamin—some need more of one than another—but in prescribing a nutritional diet we needn't set forth recipes, specific foods, place settings, or culinary habits. Gourmets will meet the requirements differently from ascetics and vegetarians, but all may obtain the basic nutrients without rigid regimentation or an absolute set of recipes.

Our Common Human Nature

In more positive terms, an objectivist bases his or her moral system on a common human nature with common needs and desires. There is more that unites all humanity than divides us. As Aristotle wrote, "One may also observe in one's travels to distant countries the feelings of recognition and affiliation that link every human being to every other human being." Think of all the things we humans have in common. We all must take in nutrition and water to live and to live a healthy life. We all want to have friends and family or some meaningful affiliation (for example, belonging to a fraternity, a church, or a club). Children in every culture must be nourished, cherished, and socialized to grow up into productive citizens. We are all vulnerable to disease, despair, and death. And we each must face our own death. There are many differences between human beings and cultures, but our basic nature is the same, and we have more in common than what separates us. Adopting this premise of our common human nature, we might argue for objectivism in the following manner:

(1) Human nature is relatively similar in essential respects, having a common set of basic needs and interests.

(2) Moral principles are functions of human needs and interests, instituted by reason to meet the needs and promote the most significant interests of human (or rational) beings.

(3) Some moral principles will meet needs and promote human interests better than other principles.

(4) Principles that will meet essential human needs and promote the most significant interests in optimal ways are objectively valid moral principles.

(5) Therefore, because there is a common human nature, there is an objectively valid set of moral principles, applicable to all humanity (or rational beings).

The argument assumes that there is a common human nature. In a sense, an objectivist accepts the view that morality depends on some social reality for its authentication; however, it isn't the reality of cultural acceptance but the reality of our common nature as rational beings, with needs, interests, and the ability to reason. There is only one large human framework to which all humans belong and to which all principles are relative. Relativists sometimes claim that the idea of a common human nature is an illusion, but our knowledge of human genetics, anthropology, and history provides overwhelming evidence that we are all related by common needs, interests, and desires. We all generally prefer to survive, to be happy, to experience love and friendship rather than hatred and enmity, to be successful in reaching our goals, and the like. We care for our children, feel gratitude for services rendered, and feel resentment for intentional harms done to us. We seek peace and security and, being social animals, want friends and family. Game theorists have performed decision-making experiments throughout the world, from tribes in the Amazon and New Guinea to Western societies. They confirm our judgment that all people value fairness and generosity and are willing to forego profit to punish freeloaders.[7] The core morality is requisite for the attainment of these goals.

Of course, these principles are prima facie, not absolutes. An absolute principle can never be overridden; it is exceptionless. Most moral principles, however, can be overridden when they conflict with other moral principles in some contexts.

For example, you may override the principle to keep your promise to meet me this afternoon if you come upon an accident victim in need of your help. Or you may override the principle forbidding lying when a murderer asks you where your friend, who the murderer wants to kill, is hiding, and you may steal in dire circumstances to feed your family. In general, though, these principles should be adhered to in order to give the maximal guarantee for the good life.

ETHICAL SITUATIONALISM

One of the reasons people believe in ethical relativism is that they confuse it with ethical situationalism, so we need to examine this concept. Ethical situationalism is given expression in the famous passage from the Old Testament:

> For everything there is a season, and a time for every matter under heaven: a time to be born, and a time to die; a time to plant, and a time to pluck up what is planted; a time to kill, and a time to heal; a time to break down, and a time to build up; a time to weep, and a time to laugh; a time to mourn, and a time to dance; a time to cast away stones, and a time to gather stones together; a time to embrace, and a time to refrain from embracing; a time to seek, and a time to lose; a time to keep, and a time to cast away; a time to rend, and a time to sew; a time to keep silence, and a time to speak; a time to love, and a time to hate; a time for war, and a time for peace.
>
> What gain has the worker from his toil? I have seen the business that God has given to the sons of men to be busy with. He has made everything beautiful in its time. (Ecclesiastes 3: 1–10)

Ethical situationalism states that objective moral principles are to be applied differently in different contexts, whereas **ethical relativism** denies universal ethical principles altogether. Let me illustrate the difference.

In the book (and David Lean's Academy Award–winning movie made after it) *The Bridge over the River Kwai*,[8] there is a marvelous example of ethical situationalism. During World War II, British prisoners in the jungle of Burma are ordered to work for their Japanese captors by building a railroad bridge across the River Kwai so that the Japanese can establish transportation between Rangoon and Bangkok. Their resourceful, courageous officer, Colonel Nicholson, sees this as a way of marshaling his soldiers' skills and establishing morale in a demoralizing situation. So, after some stubborn resistance and negotiations, Colonel Nicholson leads his men in building a first-rate bridge, one superior to what the Japanese had been capable of. However, the Allies discover that the bridge is soon to be used as a crucial link in the transport of Japanese soldiers and supplies to the war zone to fight the Allied forces, so a delegation of rangers is sent out to blow it up. As Major Warden, Lt. Joyce, and the American Spears lay their demolition onto the bridge, planning to explode it, Colonel Nicholson discovers a post with the lead wires attached to it, leading to the demolition device. Seeing Joyce about to blow up the bridge, Nicholson joins with the Japanese officer and charges the British lieutenant, killing him. Nicholson himself is then shot by Major Warden, but as he begins to die, he realizes his folly and falls on the demolition charge, setting off the explosive, and blowing up the bridge just as the Japanese train is crossing it.

Colonel Nicholson exemplifies the rigid rule-follower who loses sight of the purpose of building the bridge, which was to build morale for the Allied prisoners, not to aid the enemy. But when the time came to destroy his handiwork, Nicholson could not do it, having made the bridge a moral fetish.

Fortunately, as he was dying, he came to his senses and served his mission. The duty of the British soldiers was to aid in defeating their lethal enemy. As prisoners, they could best serve that goal by staying alive and healthy, and a means to that sub-goal was to keep their morale high by engaging in building the bridge. But when the situation altered, the main goal was served by destroying the bridge. In both situations, the same high purpose existed—working for victory over one's enemy, but the means changed as the circumstances changed.

A simpler example is that of Jesus breaking the Sabbath by picking food (work) to feed his disciples. When called to account by the Pharisees and charged with breaking the Sabbath law, he replied, "The Sabbath was made for man, not man for the Sabbath" (Mark 2: 23–27). The commandments were given to promote human flourishing, not for their own sake.

CONCLUSION

We have outlined a moderate objectivism, the thesis that a core set of moral principles is universally valid, applying to all people everywhere. Thus, we have answered the moral relativist and moral nihilist. The relativist holds that there are moral principles, but they are all relative to culture. The nihilist denies that there are any moral valid principles. We have argued that nihilism is false because valid moral principles exist, but we have acknowledged some relativity in ethics, especially as morality comes close to etiquette. We have also noted that morality is situational: Principles can be applied differently in different contexts. We have argued that a common human nature is the basis of our thesis that there is a set of universally valid moral rules. I have given a commonsense, functional account of objective morality following from the notion that morality serves specific human functions in promoting the human good. I have used a naturalist commonsense account to establish the core morality. Others may rely on direct intuitions or on religion to get to a similar conclusion.

Let's return now to the relativist question raised in Chapter 2: "Who's to judge what's right and wrong?" The correct reply is, "We all are—every rational being on Earth must make moral judgments and be prepared to be held responsible for one's own actions." As Ayn Rand said, "Judge and Be Prepared to Be Judged."[9] We are to judge based on the best reasoning that we can supply, in dialogue with other people of other cultures, and with sympathy and understanding. Virtually all moral theories recognize that morality serves the human good although they weight that idea differently.

NOTES

1. Kevin Bales, *Disposable People* (University of California Press, 2000), pp. 1–2. Seba eventually escaped to tell her story.

2. Aristotle, *Nicomachean Ethics* (Oxford University Press, 1925), Bk. 1, p. 7.

3. Thomas Aquinas, *Summa Theologica,* in *Basic Writings of St. Thomas Aquinas,* ed. A. C. Pegis (Random House, 1945), Q94.

4. Eric D'Arcy, *Human Acts* (Oxford University Press, 1963), Ch. 4.

5. William D. Ross, *The Right and the Good* (Oxford University Press, 1932), p. 18f.

6. Renford Bambrough, *Moral Skepticism and Moral Knowledge* (Routledge, Kegan & Paul, 1979), p. 33.

7. Karl Sigmund, Ernest Fehr, and Martin Nowak, "The Economics of Fair Play," *Scientific American* (January 2002).

8. Pierre Boulle, *The Bridge over the River Kwai* (Vanguard, 1954).

9. Ayn Rand, "How Does One Lead a Rational Life in an Irrational Society?" in *The Virtue of Selfishness* (New American Library, 1964).

FOR FURTHER REFLECTION

1. Analyze the story of Seba. What light does reflection on this illustration throw on the dispute between ethical relativism and objectivism?

2. What is the natural law position in morality? Evaluate it.

3. Discuss the doctrine of double effect (DDE). How valid is it?

4. Could terrorists use a version of the doctrine of double effect to justify their violent acts? Explain.

5. What is the difference between *moral absolutism* and *moral objectivism*? Which position is the correct one, and why?

6. What is the difference between *ethical relativism* and *ethical situationalism*?

7. Consider the quote by David Hume at the opening of this chapter. Does it support moral objectivism? Explain.

8. What is a *prima facie duty*? Give some examples.

FOR FURTHER READING

Cavanaugh, T. A. *Double-Effect Reasoning: Doing Good and Avoiding Evil.* New York: Oxford University Press, 2006.

Finnis, John. *Moral Absolutes: Tradition, Revision, and Truth.* Washington, D.C.: Catholic University of America Press, 1991.

Gómez-Lobo, Alfonso. *Morality and the Human Goods: An Introduction to Natural Law Ethics.* Washington, D.C.: Georgetown University Press, 2002.

Goyette, John, et al. *St. Thomas Aquinas and the Natural Law Tradition: Contemporary Perspectives.* Washington, D.C.: Catholic University of America Press, 2004.

Kainz, Howard P. *Natural Law: An Introduction and Re-Examination.* Chicago: Open Court, 2004.

Kreeft, Peter. *A Refutation of Moral Relativism: Interviews with an Absolutist.* San Francisco: Ignatius Press, 1999.

Woodward, P. A. *The Doctrine of Double Effect: Philosophers Debate a Controversial Moral Principle.* Notre Dame, Ind.: University of Notre Dame Press, 2001.

4

✳

Value and the Quest
for the Good

There is beauty in sky and cloud and sea, in lilies and in sunsets, in the
glow of bracken in autumn and in the enticing greenness of a leafy
spring. Nature, indeed, is infinitely beautiful, and she seems to wear her
beauty as she wears color or sound. Why then should her beauty belong
to us rather than to her? Human character and human dispositions have
value or worth, which belongs to them in the same sense as redness
belongs to the cherry.
JOHN LAIRD, *A STUDY IN REALISM*

We never strive for, wish for, long for, or desire anything, because we
deem it to be good, but, rather, we deem a thing good, because we strive
for it, wish for it, long for it, or desire it.
BENEDICT DE SPINOZA, *ETHICS*

What sorts of things are valuable? Some items that we value are rather trivial,
such as a new pair of shoes or one's preferred brand of soda. Yes we enjoy
them, but they have no real urgency. Other things, though, seem to be of ultimate
importance, and at the top of that list many of us would place the value of human
life. After all, it's hard to find value in anything unless we're alive to experience it.
Some of us might even claim to place an *absolute* value on human life. Now suppose
I told you that I had invented a marvelous Convenience Machine that would save
everyone an enormous amount of time and energy in our daily routines. However,
the downside of the Convenience Machine is that its use would result in the deaths
of over 75,000 Americans per year. Would you use this machine? Perhaps you'd
refuse on the grounds that the value of life exceeds any amount of convenience.

But suppose our economy centered on the use of this machine, and without it, the nation would be thrown into an unparalleled economic depression. Perhaps you'd still refuse to use it and insist that we change our economic expectations rather than continually sacrifice so many lives.

Well, we in fact have this Convenience Machine in several brands: Chevrolet, Ford, Chrysler, Toyota, Honda, Mercedes, and so on. Motor vehicle accidents in the United States result in about 45,000 deaths a year; another 30,000 deaths are caused by diseases brought on by automobile pollution. So how much do we *really* value life? Perhaps not as much as we often claim, and we certainly do not value life as an absolute. Some people say that it is the quality of life rather than life itself that is valuable. The ancient Greeks and Romans believed that when life became burdensome, one had the obligation to commit suicide, for it was not the quantity of life that counted but the quality. As one Stoic philosopher put it, "Mere living is not a good, but living well."

The human life is just one example of a wide range of things that we find valuable, and a complete list of them would probably be impossible to create. Nicholas Rescher, though, classifies some basic values into these eight categories:[1]

1. *Material and physical value:* health, comfort, physical security
2. *Economic value:* economic security, productiveness
3. *Moral value:* honesty, fairness, kindness
4. *Social value:* generosity, politeness, graciousness
5. *Political value:* freedom, justice
6. *Aesthetic value:* beauty, symmetry, grace
7. *Religious value:* piety, obedience, faith
8. *Intellectual value:* intelligence, clarity, knowledge

It's easy enough to devise a list of values like this: just think about what you do during the day and reflect on what is most important to you. What's less easy, though, is understanding why things are valuable to begin with and what, if anything, our various values have in common. In this chapter, we explore the notion of value and how value connects with issues of morality.

INTRINSIC AND INSTRUMENTAL VALUE

When we look at Rescher's list of basic values, we see that some seem to be valuable for their own sake, such as beauty and justice, while others are valuable because of their beneficial consequences, such as physical and economic security. The essential difference here is between intrinsic and instrumental goods. **Intrinsic goods** are good because of their nature and are not derived from other goods. By contrast,

instrumental goods are worthy of desire because they are effective means of attaining our intrinsic goods. Plato makes this distinction in his book, *The Republic,* where the characters Socrates and Glaucon are talking:

SOCRATES: Tell me, do you think there is a kind of good which we welcome not because we desire its consequences but for its own sake: joy, for example, and all the harmless pleasures which have no further consequences beyond the joy which one finds in them?

GLAUCON: Certainly, I think there is such a good.

SOCRATES: Further, there is the good which we welcome for its own sake and also for its consequences, knowledge, for example, and sight and health. Such things we somehow welcome on both accounts.

GLAUCON: Yes.

SOCRATES: Are you also aware of a third kind, such as physical training, being treated when ill, the practice of medicine, and other ways of making money? We should say that these are wearisome but beneficial to us; we should not want them for their own sake, but because of the rewards and other benefits which result from them.[2]

The question "What things are good or valuable?" is ambiguous. We need first to separate the kinds of values or goods there are. In the above, Socrates distinguishes three kinds of goods: (1) purely intrinsic goods (of which simple joys are an example), (2) purely instrumental goods (of which medicine and making money are examples), and (3) combination goods (such as knowledge, sight, and health), which are good in themselves *and* good as a means to further goods.

The essential difference is between intrinsic and instrumental goods. We consider some things good or worthy of desire (desirable) in themselves and other things good or desirable only because of their consequences. Intrinsic goods are good because of their nature. They are not derived from other goods, whereas instrumental goods are worthy of desire because they are effective means of attaining our intrinsic goods.

We may further distinguish an *instrumental good* from a *good instrument*. If something is an instrumental good, it is a means to attaining something that is intrinsically good; but merely to be a good instrument is to be an effective means to any goal, good or bad. For example, poison is a good instrument for murdering someone, but murder is not an intrinsically good thing; thus poison, in this use at least, is not an instrumental good.

Many things that we value are instrumental values. Socrates in our selection from *The Republic* mentions two instrumental values: medicine and money. Medicine is an instrumental good in that it can hardly be valued for its own sake. We can ask "What is medicine for?" The answer is, "It is to promote health." But, is health an intrinsic value or an instrumental one? Can we ask "What is health for?" Some will agree with Socrates that health is good for itself and for other things as well, such as happiness and creative activity. Others will dispute Socrates' contention and judge health to be wholly an instrumental good.

Money is Socrates' other example of an instrumental value. Few, if any, of us really value money for its own sake, but almost all of us value it for what it can buy. When we ask "What is money for?" we arrive at such goods as food and clothing, shelter and automobiles, and entertainment and education. But are any of these really intrinsic goods, or are they all instrumental goods? When we ask, for example, "What is entertainment for?" what answer do we come up with? Most of us would mention enjoyment or pleasure, Socrates' example of an intrinsic good. Can we further ask "What is enjoyment or pleasure for?" We examine this question in the next section, but, before we do, we need to ask whether the notion of intrinsic values makes any sense.

Are there any intrinsic values? Are there any entities whose values are not derived from something else—that is, that are sought for their own sake, that are *inherently good,* good in themselves? Or are all values relative to desirers— that is, instrumental to goals that are the creation of choosers? Those who espouse the notion of intrinsic value usually argue that pleasure is an example of an intrinsic value and pain an example of an intrinsic disvalue: It is good to experience pleasure and bad to experience pain. Naturally, these philosophers admit that individual experiences of pleasure can be bad (because they result in some other disvalue such as a hangover after a drinking spree) and individual painful experiences can be valuable (for example, having a painful operation to save one's life). The intrinsicalist affirms that pleasure is just better than pain. We can see this straight off. We do not need any arguments to convince us that pleasure is good or that gratuitous pain is intrinsically bad. Suppose we see a man torturing a child and order him to stop at once. If he replies, "I agree that the child is experiencing great pain, but why should I stop torturing her?" we would suspect some mental aberration on his part.

The nonintrinsicalist denies that the preceding arguments have any force. The notion that the experience itself could have any value is unclear. It is only by our choosing pleasure over pain that the notion of value begins to have meaning. In a sense, all value is extrinsic, or a product of choosing. Many existentialists, most notably Jean-Paul Sartre, believe that we invent our values by arbitrary choice. The freedom to create our values and thus to define ourselves is godlike and, at the same time, deeply frightening, for we have no one to blame for our failures but ourselves. "We are condemned to freedom.... Value is nothing else but the meaning that you choose. One may choose anything so long as it is done from the ground of freedom."[3]

But this seems false. We do not choose most of our values in the same way we choose between two different majors or whether to have soup or salad with our meal. We cannot help valuing pleasure, health, happiness, and love and disvaluing pain and suffering. With regard to the fundamental values, they choose us, not we them. Even Sartre's condition for choosing a value, *freedom,* is not a value that we choose but have thrust upon us by our nature. We could override our freedom for other values, but we can no more choose whether to value it or not value it than we can choose whether or not to be hungry or thirsty after being deprived of food or drink for days. It is as though God or evolution preprogrammed us to desire these basic goods. And when we find someone who does not value (or claims not to value) happiness, freedom, or love, we tend to explain this anomaly as a product of unfortunate circumstances.

THE VALUE OF PLEASURE

Philosophers divide into two broad camps: hedonists and nonhedonists. The hedonist (from *hedon,* Greek for "pleasure") asserts that all pleasure is good, that pleasure is the only thing good in itself, and that all other goodness is derived from this value. An experience is good in itself if and only if it provides some pleasure. Sometimes, this definition is widened to include the lessening of pain, pain being seen as the only thing bad in itself. For simplicity's sake, we will use the former definition, realizing that it may need to be supplemented by reference to pain.

Hedonists subdivide into two categories: (1) **sensualism,** the view that equates all pleasure with sensual enjoyment, and (2) **satisfactionism,** the view that equates all pleasure with satisfaction or enjoyment, which may not involve sensuality. Satisfaction is a pleasurable state of consciousness such as we might experience after accomplishing a successful venture or receiving a gift. The opposite of sensual enjoyment is physical pain; the opposite of satisfaction is displeasure or dissatisfaction.

The Greek philosopher Aristippus (ca. 435–366 BCE) espoused the sensualist position; that is, the only (or primary) good was sensual pleasure, and this goodness was defined in terms of its intensity.

This was also Mustapha Mond's philosophy in Aldous Huxley's *Brave New World.* The following dialogue is between Mustapha Mond, the genius technocrat who governs the brave new world, and the malcontent, "Savage," who believes that this hedonic paradise lacks something.

> SAVAGE: Yes, that's just like you. Getting rid of everything unpleasant instead of learning to put up with it. Whether 'tis better in the mind to suffer the slings and arrows of outrageous fortune, or to take arms against a sea of troubles and by opposing end them. . . . But you don't do either. Neither suffer nor oppose. You just abolish the slings and arrows. It's too easy. . . . Isn't there something in living dangerously?

> MUSTAPHA MOND: There's a great deal in it. . . . Men and women must have their adrenals stimulated from time to time. . . . It's one of the conditions of perfect health. That's why we've made the VPS treatment compulsory.

> SAVAGE: VPS?

> MUSTAPHA MOND: Violent Passion Surrogate. Regularly once a month. We flood the whole system with adrenin. It's the complete physiological equivalent of fear and rage . . . without any of the inconveniences.

SAVAGE: But I like the inconvenience.

MUSTAPHA MOND: In fact you're claiming the right to be unhappy.... Not to mention the right to grow old and ugly and impotent; the right to have syphilis and cancer; the right to have too little to eat; the right to live in constant apprehension of what may happen tomorrow; the right to be tortured by unspeakable pains of every kind.

SAVAGE (after a long silence): I claim them all.

MUSTAPHA MOND (shrugging his shoulders): You're welcome.[4]

The brave new world is a society of the future where people have been liberated from disease, violence, and crime through immunization, genetic engineering, and behavior modification. They are protected from depression and unhappiness through a drug, soma, that offers them euphoric sensations. Mustapha Mond, the brilliant manager of the society, defends this hedonistic utopia against one of the few remaining malcontents, the "Savage," who complains that something of value is missing in this "utopia."

All but sensuously deprived adolescents (or those in a similar psychological state) would probably agree that the brave new world is lacking something. The sensuous version of pleasure is too simple.

Most hedonists since the third century BCE follow Epicurus (342–270 BCE), who had a broader view of pleasure:

It is not continuous drinkings and revellings, nor the satisfaction of lusts, nor the enjoyment of fish and other luxuries of the wealthy table, which produce a happy life, but sober reasoning, searching out the motives for all choice and avoidance, and banishing mere opinions, to which are due the greatest disturbance of the spirit.[5]

The distinction between pleasure as satisfaction and as sensation is important, and failure to recognize it results in confusion and paradox. One example of this is the paradox of masochism. How can it be that the masochist enjoys (that is, takes pleasure in) pain, which is the opposite of pleasure? "Well," the hedonist responds, "because of certain psychological aberrations, the masochist enjoys (as satisfaction) what is painful (as sensation)." But he or she does not enjoy (as sensation) what is painful (as sensation). There is also a two-level analysis to explain the masochist's behavior: On a lower, or basic, level, he is experiencing either pain or dissatisfaction, but on a higher level, he approves and finds satisfaction from that pain or dissatisfaction.

Nonhedonists divide into two camps: monists and pluralists. *Monists* believe that there is a single intrinsic value, but it is not pleasure. Perhaps it is a transcendent value, "the Good," which we do not fully comprehend but which is the basis of all our other values. This seems to be Plato's view. *Pluralists* generally admit that pleasure or enjoyment is an intrinsic good, but they add that there are other intrinsic goods as well, such as knowledge, friendship, aesthetic beauty, freedom, love, moral goodness, and life itself.

Hedonists such as Jeremy Bentham (1748–1832) argue that although these qualities are good, their goodness is *derived* from the fact that they bring pleasure or satisfaction. Such hedonists ask of each of the previously mentioned values, "What is it for?" What is knowledge for? If it gave no one any satisfaction or enjoyment, would it really be good? Why do we feel there is a significant difference between knowing how many stairs there are in New York City and whether or not there is life after death? We normally do not value knowledge of the first kind, but knowledge of the second kind is relevant for our enjoyment.

The hedonist asks, "What are friendship and love for?" If we were made differently and got no satisfaction out of love and friendship, would they still be valuable? Are they not highly valuable, significant instrumental goods because they bring enormous satisfaction?

Even moral commitment or conscientiousness is not good in itself, argues the hedonist. Morality is not intrinsically valuable but is meant to serve human need, which in turn has to do with bringing about satisfaction.

And, life certainly is not intrinsically good. It is quality that counts. An amoeba or a permanently comatose patient has life but no intrinsic value. Only when consciousness appears does the possibility for value arrive. Consciousness is a necessary but not a sufficient condition for satisfaction.

The nonhedonist responds that this is counterintuitive. Consider, for example, the possibility of living in a Pleasure Machine. We have invented a complex machine into which people may enter to find pure and constant pleasure. Attached to their brains will be electrodes that send currents to the limbic area of the cerebral cortex and other parts of the brain, producing very powerful sensations of pleasure. When people get into the machine, they experience these wonderful feelings. Would you enter such a machine?

If all you want is pleasure or satisfaction, then the Pleasure Machine seems the right choice. You're guaranteed all the pleasure you've ever dreamed of—without frustration or competition from other people. But if you want to *do* something and *be* something (for example, have good character or a certain quality of personality) or experience reality (for example, friendship and competition), then you might think twice about this choice. Is the Pleasure Machine not just another addiction—like alcohol, heroin, cocaine, or crack? Once in the machine, would we become forever addicted to it? Furthermore, if all you want is pleasure, why not just hire someone to tickle you for a lifetime? Wouldn't we become tired of being passive blobs—even if it was pleasurable? Most of us would reject such an existence as equivalent to that of a drugged cockroach.

Or suppose there were two worlds with the same number of people and the same amount of total pleasure, but in World I the people were selfish and even evil, whereas in World II the people were deeply moral. Wouldn't it seem that World II was intrinsically better than World I?

Or imagine two lives, those of Suzy and Izzy. Suzy possesses 100 hedons (units of pleasure), even though she is severely retarded and physically disabled, whereas Izzy enjoys great mental acumen and physical prowess but has only 99 hedons.

Isn't it obvious that Izzy has the better life? But, hedonists are committed to saying that Suzy's life is better, which seems implausible.

It was these sorts of cases that led John Stuart Mill (1806–1873, to be examined in Chapter 7)—in his classic work, *Utilitarianism*—to modify the hedonic doctrine, admitting that "it is better to be a human dissatisfied than a pig satisfied; better to be Socrates dissatisfied than a fool satisfied."[6] He suggested that there were different qualities of pleasure and that those who had experienced the different kinds could distinguish among them. Whether the notion of *quality of pleasure* can save hedonism is a controversial matter, but many of us feel uneasy with the idea that pleasure alone is good. Some broader notion, such as *happiness* or *object of desire,* seems a more adequate candidate for what we mean by "value."

ARE VALUES OBJECTIVE OR SUBJECTIVE?

Do we desire the Good because it is good, or is the Good good because we desire it? The objectivist holds that values are worthy of desire whether or not anyone actually desires them; they are somehow independent of us. The subjectivist holds, to the contrary, that values are dependent on desirers, are relative to desirers.

The classic objectivist view on values (the absolutist version) was given by Plato (428–348 BCE), who taught that the Good was the highest form, ineffable, godlike, independent, and knowable only after a protracted education in philosophy. We desire the Good because it is good. Philosophers in the Platonic tradition hold to the independent existence of values apart from human or rational interest. For example, G. E. Moore claims that the Good is a simple, unanalyzable quality, such as the color yellow, but one that must be known through intuition. Moore believes that a world with beauty is more valuable than one that is a garbage dump, regardless of whether there are conscious beings in those worlds:

> Let us imagine one world exceedingly beautiful. Imagine it as beautiful as you can . . . and then imagine the ugliest world you can possibly conceive. Imagine it simply one heap of filth.[7]

Moore asks us whether, even if there were no conscious being who might derive pleasure or pain in either world, we would prefer the first world to exist rather than the second. Moore believes that it is obvious that the beautiful world is inherently better, but the objector asks, "What good is such a world if there is no one (even God) to enjoy it?"

Other, weaker objectivist versions treat values as *emergent* properties, or qualities in the nature of things. That is, just as the wetness of water is not in the H_2O molecules but in the interaction of our nervous system with millions of those molecules, and just as smoothness is not in the table that I am touching but in the relationship between the electrical charges of the subatomic particles of which the table is made up and my nervous system, so values (or good qualities) emerge in the relationship between conscious beings and physical and social existence. They are synergistic entities, depending on both our nature and their objective properties.

For example, if we were not beings with desires, we would not be in a position to appreciate values; but once there are such beings, certain things—such as pleasure, knowledge, freedom, friendship, and health—will be valuable, and others—such as pain, suffering, boredom, loneliness, disease, and death—will be disvalued or not valued for their own sake. This synergistic view recognizes both a subjective and an objective aspect to value.

Subjectivism treats values as merely products of conscious desire. The American pragmatist Ralph Barton Perry (1876–1957) states that a value is simply the object of interest.[8] Values are created by desires, and they are valuable just to that degree to which they are desired: The stronger the desire, the greater the value. The difference between the subjectivist and the weak objectivist position (or mixed view) is simply that the subjectivist makes no normative claims about "proper desiring," instead judging all desires as equal. Anything one happens to desire is, by definition, a value, a good.

The objectivist responds that we can separate the Good from what one desires. We can say, for example, that Joan desires more than anything else to get into the Pleasure Machine, but it is not good; or that John desires more than anything else to join the Satanic Society, where he will pursue evil for evil's sake, engaging in sado-masochistic behavior, but it is not good (not even for John). There is something just plain bad about the Pleasure Machine and the Satanic Society, even if Joan and John never experience any dissatisfaction on account of them.

On the other hand, suppose Joan does not want to have any friends and John does not want to know any history, literature, philosophy, or science (beyond whatever is necessary for his needs as a devotee of hardcore pornography or mud wrestling). The objectivist would reply that it really would be an objectively good thing if Joan did have friends and if John knew something about history, literature, philosophy, and science.

Perhaps a way to adjudicate the disagreement between the subjectivist and the objectivist is to imagine an Ideal Desirer, a person who is impartial and has maximal knowledge of the consequences of all actions. What the Ideal Desirer chooses is by definition the "good," and what he or she disdains is the "bad." If so, we can approximate such an ideal perspective by increasing our understanding and ability to judge impartially. The study of philosophy, especially moral philosophy, has as one of its main goals such an ability.

THE RELATION OF VALUE TO MORALITY

Typically, value theory is at the heart of moral theory. The question, however, is whether moral right and wrong are themselves intrinsic values (as Kant states, the moral law is "a jewel that shines in its own light") or whether rightness and wrongness are defined by their ability to further nonmoral values such as pleasure, happiness, health, and political harmony. To begin to understand this question and to get an overview view of the workings of morality, let me offer a schema of the moral process (Figure 4.1), which may help in locating the role of values in moral theory.

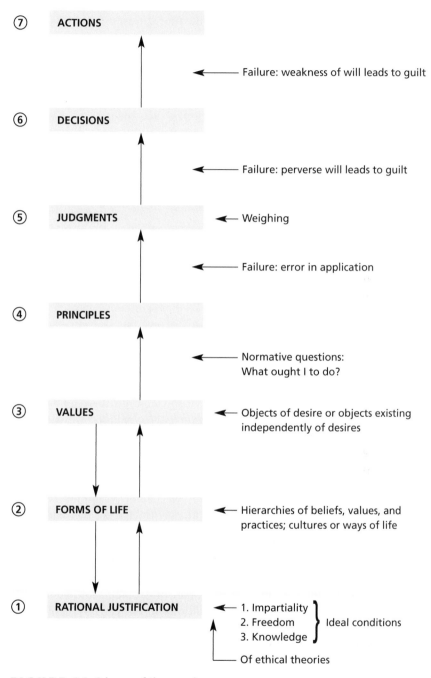

⑦ ACTIONS

← Failure: weakness of will leads to guilt

⑥ DECISIONS

← Failure: perverse will leads to guilt

⑤ JUDGMENTS   ← Weighing

← Failure: error in application

④ PRINCIPLES

← Normative questions:
What ought I to do?

③ VALUES   ← Objects of desire or objects existing
independently of desires

② FORMS OF LIFE   ← Hierarchies of beliefs, values, and
practices; cultures or ways of life

① RATIONAL JUSTIFICATION   ← 1. Impartiality ⎫
2. Freedom   ⎬ Ideal conditions
3. Knowledge ⎭
Of ethical theories

FIGURE 4.1 Schema of the moral process

The location of values in the schema of the moral process (box 3) indicates that values are central to the domain of morality. They are the source of principles (box 4) and rooted in the forms of life (box 2). Examples of values are life, loving relationships, freedom, privacy, happiness, creative activity, knowledge, health, integrity, and rationality. From our values, we derive principles (box 4), which we may call action-guiding value "instantiators" or "exemplifiers" (because they make clear the action-guiding or prescriptive force latent in values). From the value "life," we derive the principles "Promote and protect life" and/or "Thou shall not kill." From the value "freedom," we derive the principle "Thou shall not deprive another of his or her freedom." From the value "privacy," we derive the principle "Respect every person's privacy." From the value "happiness," we derive the principle "Promote human happiness," and so forth with all the other values.

This schema makes no judgment as to whether values are objective or subjective, intrinsic or instrumental. Neither does it take a stand on whether values or principles are absolute; they need not be absolute. Most systems allow that all or most values and principles are overridable. That is, they are considerations that direct our actions, and whenever they clash, an adjudication must take place to decide which principle overrides the other in the present circumstances.

We often find ourselves in moral situations in which one or more principles apply. We speak of making a judgment as to which principle applies to our situation or which principle wins out in the competition when two or more principles apply (box 5). The correct principle defines our duty. For example, we have the opportunity to cheat on a test and immediately judge that the principle of honesty (derived from the value integrity) applies to our situation. Or there might be an interpersonal disagreement in which two or more people differ on which of two values outweighs the other in importance, as when Mary argues that Jill should not have an abortion because the value of life outweighs Jill's freedom and bodily integrity, but John argues that Jill's freedom and bodily integrity outweigh the value of life.

Even after we judge which principle applies, we are not yet finished with the moral process. We must still *decide* to do the morally right act. Then finally, we must actually *do* the right act.

Note the possibilities for failure all along the way. We may fail to apply the right principle to the situation (the arrow between boxes 4 and 5). For example, we may simply neglect to bring to mind the principle against cheating. This is a failure of application. But even after we make the correct judgment, we may fail to make the right choice, deciding to cheat anyway. In this case, we have a perverse will (the arrow between boxes 5 and 6). Finally, we may make the correct choice but fail to carry out our decision (the arrow between boxes 6 and 7). We call this *weakness of will:* We mean to do the right act but simply are too morally weak to accomplish it. In our example, we meant to refrain from cheating but couldn't control ourselves. "The good that I would, I do not, but the evil that I would not, that I do."[9]

A more controversial matter concerns the deep structure in which values are rooted. Some theories deny that there is any deep structure but assert instead that values simply exist in their own right—independently, as it were. More often, however, values are seen as rooted in whole forms of life (box 2) that can be actual or ideal, such as Plato's hierarchical society or Aristotle's aristocracy or the Judeo-Christian notion of the kingdom of God (the ideal synagogue or church). Ways of life or cultures are holistic and hierarchical combinations of beliefs, values, and practices.

The deepest question about morality is whether and how these forms of life are justified (box 1). Are some forms of life better or more justified than others? If so, how does one justify a form of life? Candidates for justification are ideas such as God's will, human happiness, the flourishing of all creation, the canons of impartiality and knowledge, a deeply rational social contract (Hobbes and Rawls), and the like. For example, a theist might argue that the ideal system of morality (that is, the ideal form of life) is justified by being commanded by God. A utilitarian would maintain that the ultimate criterion is the promotion of welfare or utility. A naturalist or secular humanist might argue that the ideal system is justified by the fact that it best meets human need or promotes human flourishing or that it would be the one chosen by ideally rational persons. Some ethicists would make level 2 the final source of justification, denying that there is any ideal justification at all. These are the ethical relativists, who contend that each moral system is correct simply by being chosen by the culture or individual.

The main point of the schema, however, is not to decide on the exact deep structure of morality but to indicate that values are rooted in cultural constructs and are the foundation for moral principles upon which moral reasoning is based. We could also devise a similar schema for the relationship between values and virtues (to be discussed in Chapter 9). Each virtue is based on a value and each vice on a disvalue.

THE GOOD LIFE

Finally, we want to ask what kind of life is most worth living. Aristotle (384–322 BCE) wrote long ago that what all people seek is happiness:

> There is very general agreement; for both the common person and people of superior refinement say that it is happiness, and identify living well and doing well with being happy; but with regard to what happiness is they differ, and the many do not give the same account as the wise. For the former think it is some plain and obvious thing, like pleasure, wealth or honor.[10]

What is happiness? Again, the field divides up among objectivists, subjectivists, and combination theorists. The objectivists, following Plato and Aristotle, distinguish happiness from pleasure and speak of a single ideal for human nature; if we do not reach that ideal, then we have failed. Happiness (from the Greek *eudaimonia,* literally meaning "good demon") is not merely a subjective state of pleasure or contentment but the kind of life we would all want to live if we understood our essential nature. Just as knives and forks and wheels have functions, so do species, including the human species. Our function (sometimes called our "essence") is to live according to reason and thereby to become a certain sort of highly rational, disciplined being. When we fulfill the ideal of living the virtuous life, we are truly happy.

Plato speaks of happiness as "harmony of the soul." Just as the body is healthy when it is in harmony with itself and the political state is a good state when it is functioning harmoniously, so the soul is happy when all its features are functioning in harmonious accord, with the rational faculty ruling over the spirited and emotional elements. Although we no doubt know when we are happy and feel good about ourselves, the subjective feeling does not itself define happiness, for people who fail to attain human excellence can also feel happy via self-deception or ignorance.

The objectivist view fell out of favor with the rise of the evolutionary account of human nature, which undermined the sense of a preordained essence or function. Science cannot discover any innate *telos,* or goal, to which all people must strive. The contemporary bias is in favor of value pluralism—that is, the view that there are many ways of finding happiness: "Let a thousand flowers bloom." This leads to subjectivism.

The subjectivist version of happiness states that happiness is in the eyes of the beholder. You are just as happy as you think you are—no more, no less. The concept is not a descriptive one but a first-person evaluation. I am the only one who decides or knows whether I am happy. If I feel happy, I am happy, even though everyone else despises my lifestyle. Logically, happiness has nothing to do with virtue although—due to our social nature—it usually turns out that we will feel better about ourselves if we are virtuous.

The combination view tries to incorporate aspects of both the objectivist and the subjectivist views. One version is John Rawls's "plan of life" conception of happiness: There is a plurality of life plans open to each person, and what is important is that the plan be an integrated whole, freely chosen by the person, and that the person be successful in realizing his or her goals. This view is predominantly subjective in that it recognizes the person as the autonomous chooser of goals and a plan. Even if a person should choose a life plan

> whose only pleasure is to count blades of grass in various geometrically shaped areas such as park squares and well-trimmed lawns, . . . our definition of the good forces us to admit that the good for this man is indeed counting blades of grass.[11]

However, Rawls recognizes an objective element in an otherwise subjective schema. There are primary goods that are necessary to any worthwhile life plan: "rights and liberties, powers and opportunities, income and wealth, . . . self-respect, . . . health and vigor, intelligence and imagination."[12] The primary goods function as the core (or the hub of the wheel) from which may be derived any number of possible life plans (the spokes). But unless these primary goods (or most of them) are present, the life plan is not an authentic manifestation of an individual's autonomous choice of his or her own selfhood. Thus, it is perfectly possible that people believe themselves to be happy when they really are not.

Although subjectivist and plan-of-life views dominate the literature today, there is some movement back to an essentialist, or Aristotelian, view of happiness as a life directed toward worthwhile goals. Some lifestyles are more worthy than others, and some may be worthless. Philosopher Richard Kraut asks us to imagine a man who has as his idea of happiness the state of affairs of being loved, admired, or respected by his friends and who would hate to have his "friends" only pretend to care for him. Suppose his "friends" really do hate him but "orchestrate an elaborate deception, giving him every reason to believe that they love and admire him, though in fact they don't. And he is taken in by the illusion."[13] Can we really call this man happy?

Or suppose a woman centers her entire life around an imaginary Prince Charming. She refuses to date—let alone marry—perfectly eligible young men; she turns down educational travel opportunities lest they distract her from this wonderful future event; for ninety-five years, she bores all her patient friends with tales of the prince's imminent appearance. As death approaches at age ninety-six, after a lifetime of disappointment, she discovers that she's been duped; she suddenly realizes that what appeared to be a happy life was a stupid, self-deceived, miserable existence. Would we say that our heroine was happy up until her deathbed revelation? Do these thought experiments not indicate that our happiness depends, at least to some extent, on reality and not simply on our own evaluation?

Or suppose we improve on our Pleasure Machine, turning it into a Happiness Machine. This machine is a large tub that is filled with a chemical solution. Electrodes are attached to many more parts of your brain. You work with the technician to program all the "happy experiences" that you have ever wanted. Suppose that includes wanting to be a football star, a halfback who breaks tackles like a dog shakes off fleas and who has a fondness for scoring last-minute game-winning touchdowns. Or perhaps you've always wanted to be a movie star and to bask in the public's love and admiration. Or maybe you've wanted to be the world's richest person, living in the splendor of a magnificent castle, with servants faithfully at your beck and call. In fact, with the Happiness Machine you can have all of these plus passionate romance and the love of the most beautiful (or handsome) people in the world. All these marvelous adventures would be simulated, and you would truly believe you were experiencing them. Would you enter the Happiness Machine?

What if I told you that once you were unplugged, you could either stay out or go in for another round but that no one who entered the machine ever chose to leave of his or her own accord, having become addicted to its pleasures and believing that reality could never match its ecstasy. Now you have an opportunity to enter the Happiness Machine for the first time. Will you enter? If not, are you not voting against making the subjectivist view (or even the plan-of-life view) the sole interpretation of happiness?

When I ask this question in class, I get mixed responses. Many students say they would enter the Happiness Machine; most say they would not. I myself would not, for the same reason that I do not use drugs and rarely watch television or spectator sports—because some very important things are missing that are necessary for the happy life. What are these vital missing ingredients?

1. *Action.* We are entirely passive in the machine, a mere spectator. But the good life requires participation in our own destiny. We don't just want things to happen to us; we want to accomplish things, even at the risk of failure.

2. *Freedom.* Not only do we want to do things, but we want to make choices. In the Happiness Machine, we are entirely determined by a preordained plan—we cannot do otherwise. In fact, we cannot do anything but react to what has been programmed into the machine.

3. *Character.* Not only do we want to do things and act freely, but we also want to *be* something and someone. To have character is to be a certain kind of person, ideally one who is trustworthy, worthy of respect, and responsible for one's actions. In the machine, we lose our identity. We are defined only by our experience but have no character. We are not persons who act out of set dispositions, for we never act at all. We are mere floating blobs in a glorified bathtub.

4. *Relationships.* There are no real people in our Happiness Machine life. We subsist in splendid solipsism. All the world is a figment of our imagination as dictated by the machine; our friends and loved ones are mere products of our fancy. But we want to love and be loved by real people, not by phantasms.

In sum, the Happiness Machine is a myth, all *appearance* and no *reality*—a bliss bought at too high a price, a deception! If this is so and if reality is a necessary condition for the truly worthwhile life, then we cannot be happy in the Happiness Machine. But neither can we be happy outside of the Happiness Machine when the same necessary ingredients are missing: activity, freedom, moral character, loving relationships, and a strong sense of reality.

The objective and subjective views of happiness assess life from different perspectives, with the objectivist assuming that there is some kind of independent standard of assessment and the subjectivist denying it. Even though there seems to be an immense variety of lifestyles that could be considered intrinsically worthwhile or happy and even though some subjective approval or satisfaction seems necessary before we are willing to attribute the adjective "happy" to a life, there do seem to be limiting conditions on what may count as happy. We have a notion of *fittingness* for the good life, which would normally *exclude* being severely retarded, being a slave, or being a drug addict (no matter how satisfied) and which would *include* being a deeply fulfilled, autonomous, healthy person. It is better to be Socrates dissatisfied than to be the pig satisfied, but only the satisfied Socrates is happy.

This moderate objectivism is set forth by John Stuart Mill. Happiness, according to Mill, is

> not a life of rapture; but moments of such, in an existence made up of few and transitory pains, many and various pleasures, with a decided

predominance of the active over the passive, and having as the foundation of the whole, not to expect more from life than it is capable of
bestowing.[14]

This conception of happiness is worth pondering. It includes activity, freedom,
and reality components, which exclude being satisfied by the passive experience
in the Happiness Machine, and it supposes (the context tells us this) that some
pleasing experiences are better than others. I would add to Mill's definition the
ingredients of moral character and loving relations. A closer approximation
might go like this:

> Happiness is a life in which there exists free action (including meaningful
> work), loving relations, and moral character and in which the individual
> is not plagued by guilt and anxiety but is blessed with peace and
> satisfaction.

The *satisfaction* should not be confused with complacency; rather, it means contentment with one's lot—even as one strives to improve it. Whether this neo-
objectivist, Millian view of happiness is adequate, you must decide.

CONCLUSION

In this chapter, we've seen that there is a range of ways to dissect the notion of
moral goodness. Some goods are intrinsic because of their nature and are not
derived from other goods, and others are instrumental because they are effective
means of attaining intrinsic goods. Goods are often connected with pleasure; sensualism equates all pleasure with sensual enjoyment whereas the satisfactionism
identifies all pleasure with satisfaction or enjoyment, which may not involve sensuality. There is a debate whether values are objective or subjective. Plato held the
former position, maintaining that goods have an independent existence of values
apart from human or rational interest; Perry held the latter view that values are
merely products of conscious desire. Although value theory is at the center of
moral theory, there is dispute about whether the moral notions of right and
wrong are themselves intrinsic values. Finally, there is the issue of how values
are connected with human happiness and the good life, particularly whether
there is a human purpose, or *telos*, that defines our capacity for happiness in
terms of specific values.

NOTES

1. Nicholas Rescher, *Introduction to Value Theory* (Prentice Hall, 1969), p. 16.
2. Plato's *The Republic,* Bk. II, trans. G. M. A. Grube (Hackett, 1980).
3. Jean-Paul Sartre, *Existentialism and Human Emotions,* trans. Bernard Frechtman
   (Philosophical Library, 1957), pp. 23, 48–49.

4. Adapted from Aldous Huxley, *Brave New World* (Harper & Row, 1932), pp. 286–287.

5. Epicurus, "Letter to Menoeceus," trans. C. Bailey, in *The Stoics and Epicurean Philosophers,* ed. W. J. Oates, (Random House, 1940), p. 32.

6. From John Stuart Mill, *Utilitarianism* (1863); reprinted in *Ethical Theory,* ed. Louis Pojman (Wadsworth, 1989), p. 165.

7. G. E. Moore, *Principia Ethica* (Cambridge University Press, 1903), pp. 83ff.

8. R. B. Perry, *Realms of Value* (Harvard University Press, 1954).

9. Paul, in Romans 7:15.

10. Aristotle, *Nicomachean Ethics,* trans. William D. Ross (Oxford University Press, 1925), Bk. I: 4, p. 1095.

11. John Rawls, *A Theory of Justice* (Harvard University Press, 1971), p. 432. See Paul Taylor's discussion in his *Principles of Ethics* (Wadsworth, 1989), Ch. 6.

12. Rawls, *A Theory of Justice,* p. 62.

13. Richard Kraut, "Two Concepts of Happiness," *Philosophical Review* (1979); reprinted in *Ethical Theory,* ed. Louis Pojman.

14. John Stuart Mill, *Utilitarianism* (1863), Ch. 2; reprinted in *Ethical Theory,* ed. Louis Pojman.

FOR FURTHER REFLECTION

1. Look at Rescher's list of basic values at the opening of this chapter. Which of the eight types of value are the most important, and why?

2. List five values that you think are intrinsic (as opposed to instrumental) and explain why.

3. The section in this chapter on value and pleasure describes a Pleasure Machine. If you could, would you live your life in the pleasure machine?

4. Are values objective or subjective? That is, do we desire the Good because it is good, or is the Good good because we desire it?

5. The section in this chapter on the good life describes a Happiness Machine—an improved version of the Pleasure Machine. If you could, would you live your life in the Happiness Machine?

6. The section in this chapter on the good life discusses several theories of happiness. Which one seems closest to the truth?

FOR FURTHER READING

Audi, Robert. *Moral Value and Human Diversity.* New York: Oxford University Press, 2007.

Bond, E. J. *Reason and Value.* Oxford, Engl.: Cambridge University Press, 1983.

Brandt, Richard B. *A Theory of the Good and the Right*. New York: Oxford University Press, 1979.

Feldman, Fred. *Pleasure and the Good Life: Concerning the Nature, Varieties and Plausibility of Hedonism*. Oxford, Engl.: Clarendon Press, 2004.

Perry, Ralph B. *Realms of Value*. Cambridge, Ma.: Harvard University Press, 1954.

Rescher, Nicholas. *Introduction to Value Theory*. Englewood Cliffs, N.J.: Prentice Hall, 1982.

Rønnow-Rasmussen, Toni, and Michael J. Zimmerman. *Recent Work on Intrinsic Value*. Dordrecht: Springer, 2005.

Von Wright, G. H. *The Varieties of Goodness*. London: Routledge & Kegan Paul, 1963. A rich analysis of values.

Zimmerman, Michael J. *The Nature of Intrinsic Value*. Lanham, Md.: Rowman & Littlefield, 2001.

5

✳

Social Contract Theory and the Motive to Be Moral

> The question [why be moral] is on a par with the hazards of love; indeed, it is simply a special case. Those who love one another, or who acquire strong attachments to persons and to forms of life, at the same time become liable to ruin: their love makes them hostages to misfortune and the injustice of others. Friends and lovers take great chances to help each other; and members of families willingly do the same once we love we are vulnerable.
>
> JOHN RAWLS, *A THEORY OF JUSTICE*

Carl owns a very profitable car dealership, and he attributes its success to long hours, talented workers, and, most important, using every trick in the book to manipulate buyers. The cars themselves are not particularly well constructed or fuel efficient, but he claims the exact opposite in his advertisements. Once customers are on his lot, his sales staff takes over, buttering up prospective buyers and seeking out their psychological vulnerabilities. Because they work on commission, it's in their best interests to charge the highest possible price for vehicles, so they budge little from the retail sticker price and secretly add on extra expenses for useless features. They especially inflate prices for women, racial minorities, and the elderly, who frequently end up spending a thousand dollars more on exactly the same vehicle that other customers buy. They coax low-income customers into purchasing luxury vehicles well beyond their price range; as long as loan companies are willing to foot the bill, it's no loss to Carl's dealership if the customers default on loan payments. And when cars come in for repair, the mechanics, who also work on commission, trick customers into paying for expensive repairs that they don't need. At the end of the day, Carl and his workers go home to their families, giving little thought to the morality of their conduct during business hours.

Although Carl is a fictitious character, all these abuses are well documented among car dealerships. By breaking the rules of morality in seemingly undetectable ways, car dealers and mechanics routinely pad their pockets at the expense of unsuspecting customers. Attempts to cheat the system are clearly not confined to the business world. Over half of all college students cheat on exams, essays, or homework. One in five taxpayers thinks it is okay to cheat on taxes. With more serious offenses, 3 percent of adult Americans are currently behind bars, on probation, or on parole—and those are just the ones who have been caught.[1]

With human self-interest as strong as it is, what can motivate us to always follow the rules of morality? Asked more simply, "Why be moral?" Among the more common answers are these:

- Behaving morally is a matter of self-respect.
- People won't like us if we behave immorally.
- Society punishes immoral behavior.
- God tells us to be moral.
- Parents need to be moral role models for their children.

These are all good answers, and each may be a powerful motivation for the right person. With religious believers, for example, having faith in God and divine judgment might prompt them to act properly. With parents, the responsibility of raising another human being might force them to adopt a higher set of moral standards than they would otherwise. However, many of these answers won't apply to every person: nonbelievers, nonparents, people who don't respect themselves, people who think that they can escape punishment.

One of the more universal motivations to be moral is explained in a philosophical view known as **social contract theory.** The central idea is that people collectively agree to behave morally as a way to reduce social chaos and create peace. Through this agreement—or "contract"—I set aside my own individual hostilities toward others, and in exchange they set aside their hostilities toward me. Life is then better for all of us when we collectively follow basic moral rules.

There are two distinct components to the question "Why be moral?":

1. Why does society need moral rules?
2. Why should I be moral?

The first question asks for a justification for the institution of morality within our larger social framework. The second asks for reasons why I personally should be moral even when it does not appear to be in my interest. This chapter explores social contract theory's answers to both of these questions. We should note that social contract theory is also an important political concept insofar as it explains where governments get their authority: Citizens agree to give governments power as a means of keeping society peaceful. However, our focus here is on social contract theory's answer to the uniquely ethical question "Why be moral?"

WHY DOES SOCIETY NEED MORAL RULES?

Why does society need moral rules? What does morality do for us that no other social arrangement does? Social contract theory's answer is forcefully presented in the book *Leviathan* (1651) by English philosopher Thomas Hobbes (1588–1679).

Hobbes and the State of Nature

Hobbes believed that human beings always act out of perceived self-interest; that is, we invariably seek gratification and avoid harm. His argument goes like this. Nature has made us basically equal in physical and mental abilities so that, even though one person may be somewhat stronger or smarter than another, each has the ability to harm and even kill the other, if not alone then in alliance with others. Furthermore, we all want to attain our goals such as having sufficient food, shelter, security, power, wealth, and other scarce resources. These two facts, equality of ability to harm and desire to satisfy our goals, lead to social instability:

> From this equality of ability arises equality of hope in the attaining of our ends. And therefore if any two people desire the same thing, which nevertheless they cannot both enjoy, they become enemies; and in the way to their end, which is principally their own preservation and some-times their enjoyment only, endeavor to destroy or subdue one another. And from hence it comes to pass, that where an invader hath no more to fear, than another man's single power; if one plant, sow, build, or possess a convenient seat, others may probably be expected to come prepared with forces united, to dispossess, and deprive him, not only of the fruit of his labor, but also of his life or liberty. And the invader again is in the like danger of another.[2]

Given this state of insecurity, people have reason to fear one another. Hobbes calls this a **state of nature,** in which there are no common ways of life, no enforced laws or moral rules, and no justice or injustice, for these concepts do not apply. There are no reliable expectations about other people's behavior, except that they will follow their own inclinations and perceived interests, tending to be arbitrary, violent, and impulsive. The result is a war of all against all:

> Hereby it is manifest, that during the time men live without a common power to keep them all in awe, they are in that condition which is called war; and such a war, as is for *every man, against every man.* For war consists

not in battle only or in the act of fighting; but in a tract of time, wherein the will to contend in battle is sufficiently known: and therefore the notion of *time,* is to be considered in the nature of war; as it is in the nature of weather. For as the nature of foul weather lies not in the shower or two of rain, but in an inclination thereto of many days together; so the nature of war consists not in actual fighting, but in the known disposition thereto, during all the time there is no disposition to the contrary.

Hobbes described the consequence of this warring state of nature here:

> In such a condition, there is no place for industry; because the fruit thereof is uncertain: and consequently no cultivating of the earth; no navigation, nor use of the comfortable buildings; no instruments of moving, and removing, such things as require much force; no knowledge of the face of the earth; no account of time; no arts; no literature; no society; and which is worst of all, continual fear, and danger of violent death; and the life of man solitary, poor, nasty, brutish and short.

But this state of nature, or more exactly, state of anarchy and chaos, is in no one's interest. We can all do better if we compromise, give up some of our natural liberty—to do as we please—so that we will all be more likely to get what we want: security, happiness, power, prosperity, and peace. So, selfish yet rational people that we are, according to Hobbes, we give up some of our liberty and agree to a *social contract,* or *covenant.* This agreement sets up both rules and a governing force: The rules create an atmosphere of peace, and the government ensures that we follow the rules out of fear of punishment. Only within this contract does morality arise and do justice and injustice come into being. Where there is no enforceable law, there is neither right nor wrong, justice nor injustice.

Thus, morality is a form of social control. We all opt for an enforceable set of rules such that if most of us obey them most of the time, then most of us will be better off most of the time. Perhaps a select few people may actually be better off in the state of nature, but the vast majority will be better off in a situation of security and mutual cooperation. Some people may cheat and thus go back on the social contract, but as long as the majority honors the contract most of the time, we will all flourish.

Hobbes does not claim that a pure state of nature ever existed or that humanity ever really formally entered into such a contract, although he notes that such a state actually exists among nations, so a "cold war" keeps us all in fear. Rather, Hobbes explains the function of morality. He answers the question "Why do we need morality?" Why? Because without it, existence would be an unbearable hell in which life is "solitary, poor, nasty, brutish and short."

Hobbesian Morality and *Lord of the Flies*

William Golding's classic novel *Lord of the Flies* (1954)[3] brilliantly portrays the Hobbesian account of morality. In this work, a group of boys, ages 6 to 12 years old, from an English private school, have been cast adrift on an uninhabited Pacific island and have created their own social system. For a while, the constraints of civilized society keep things peaceful, but soon their system unravels into brutal chaos. The title *Lord of the Flies* comes from a translation of the Greek "Beelzebub," which is a name for the devil. Golding's point is that we need no external devil to bring about evil but that we have found the devil and he is *us*. Ever-present, ever-waiting for a moment to strike, the devil emerges from the depths of the subconscious whenever there is a conflict of interest or a moment of moral laziness. Let's consider some main themes of Golding's story, which illustrate how the dominance of the devil within us proceeds through fear, hysteria, violence, and ultimately leads to death.

In the novel, all the older boys recognize the necessity of procedural rules. During an assembly, only the boy who has the white conch shell, the symbol of authority, may speak. They choose the leader democratically and invest him with limited powers. Even the evil Roger, while taunting little Henry by throwing stones near him, manages to keep the stones from harming the child:

> Here, invisible yet strong, was the taboo of the old life. Round the squatting child was the protection of parents and school and policemen and the law. Roger's arm was conditioned by a civilization that knew nothing of him and was in ruins.

After some initial euphoria in being liberated from the adult world of constraints and entering an exciting world of fun in the sun, the children come up against the usual irritations of social existence: competition for power and status, neglect of social responsibility, failure of public policy, and escalating violence. Two boys, Ralph and Jack, vie for leadership, and a bitter rivalry emerges between them. As a compromise, a division of labor ensues in which Jack's choirboy hunters refuse to help the others in constructing shelters. Freeloading soon becomes common because most of the children leave their tasks to play on the beach. Neglect of duty results in their failure to be rescued by a passing airplane.

Civilization's power is weak and vulnerable to primitive, explosive passions. The sensitive Simon, the symbol of religious consciousness, is slaughtered by the group in a wild fury. Only Piggy and Ralph, mere observers of the homicide, feel sympathetic pangs of guilt at this atrocity.

Piggy (the incarnation of philosophy and culture) with his broken spectacles and asthma becomes ever more pathetic as the chaos increases. He reaches the depths of his ridiculous position after the rebels, led by Jack, steal his spectacles to harness the sun's rays for starting fires. Ralph, the emblem of not-too-bright but morally good civilized leadership, fails to persuade Jack to return the glasses, and Piggy then asserts his moral right to them:

> You're stronger than I am and you haven't got asthma. You can see. . . . But I don't ask for my glasses back, not as a favor. I don't ask you to be a sport . . . not because you're strong, but because what's right's right. Give me my glasses. . . . You got to.

Piggy might as well have addressed the fire itself, for in this state of moral anarchy moral discourse is a foreign tongue that only incites the worst elements to greater immorality. Roger, perched on a cliff above, responds to moral reasoning by dislodging a huge rock that hits Piggy and flings him to his death forty feet below.

A delegation starts out hunting pigs for meat. Then they find themselves enjoying the kill. To drown the initial shame over bloodthirstiness and take on a persona more compatible with their deed, the children paint themselves with colored mud. Being liberated from their social selves, they kill without remorse whoever gets in their way. The deaths of Simon and Piggy (the symbols of the religious and the philosophical, the two great fences blocking the descent to hell) and the final hunt with the "spear sharpened at both ends" signal for Ralph the depths of evil in the human heart.

Ironically, it is the British navy that finally comes to the rescue and saves Ralph (civilization) just when all seems lost. But, the symbol of the navy is a two-faced warning. On the one hand, it symbolizes that a military defense is unfortunately sometimes needed to save civilization from the barbarians (Hitler's Nazis or Jack and Roger's allies), but on the other hand it symbolizes the quest for blood and vengeance hidden in contemporary civilization. The children's world is really only a stage lower than the adult world from whence they come, and that shallow adult civilization could very well regress to tooth and claw if it were scratched too sharply. The children were saved by the adults, but who will save the adults who put so much emphasis on military enterprises and weapons systems in the name of so-called defense?

The fundamental ambiguity of human existence is visible in every section of the book, poignantly mirroring the human condition. Even Piggy's spectacles, the sole example of modern technology on the island, become a curse for the island as Jack uses them to ignite a forest fire that will smoke out their prey, Ralph, and burn down the entire forest and destroy the island's animal life. It is a symbol both of our penchant for misusing technology to vitiate the environment and our ability to create weapons that will lead to global suicide.

Social Order and the Benefits of Morality

We learn from *Lord of the Flies* that rules formed over the ages and internalized within us hold us back and hopefully defeat the devil in society, wherever that devil might reside. Again, from Hobbes's perspective, morality consists of a set of rules such that, if nearly everyone follows them, then nearly everyone will flourish. These rules restrict our freedom but promote greater freedom and well-being. More specifically, the five social benefits of establishing and following moral rules accomplish the following:

1. Keep society from falling apart.
2. Reduce human suffering.
3. Promote human flourishing.
4. Resolve conflicts of interest in just and orderly ways.
5. Assign praise and blame, reward and punishment, and guilt.

All these benefits have in common the fact that morality is a social activity: It has to do with society, not the individual in isolation. If only one person exists on an island, no morality exists; indeed, some behavior would be better for that person than others—such as eating coconuts rather than sand—but there would not be morality in the full meaning of that term. However, as soon as a second person appears on that island, morality also appears. *Morality* is thus a set of rules that enable us to reach our collective goals. Imagine what society would be like if we did whatever we pleased without obeying moral rules. I might promise to help you with your homework tomorrow if you wash my car today. You believe me. So you wash my car, but you are angered when I laugh at you tomorrow while driving off to the beach instead of helping you with your homework. Or you loan me money, but I run off with it. Or I lie to you or harm you when it is in my interest or even kill you when I feel the urge.

Under such circumstances, society would completely break down. Parents would abandon children, and spouses would betray each other whenever it was convenient. No one would have an incentive to help anyone else because cooperative agreements would not be recognized. Great suffering would go largely unhindered, and people would not be very happy. We would not flourish or reach our highest potential.

I once visited the country of Kazakhstan shortly after the collapse of the Soviet Union, when it was undergoing a difficult shift from communism to democracy. During this transition with the state's power considerably withdrawn, crime was increasing and distrust was prevalent. At night, trying to navigate my way up the staircases in the apartment building where I was staying, I was in complete darkness. I asked why there were no light bulbs in the stairwells, only to be told that the residents stole them, believing that, if they did not take them, their neighbors would. Absent a dominant authority, the social contract had eroded, and everyone had to struggle in the darkness—both literally and metaphorically.

We need moral rules to guide our actions in ways that light up our paths and prevent and reduce suffering, enhance human well-being (and animal well-being, for that matter), resolve our conflicts of interests according to recognizably fair rules, and assign responsibility for actions so that we can praise, blame, reward, and punish people according to how their actions reflect moral principles. In a world becoming ever more interdependent, with the threats of terrorism and genocide, we need a sense of global cooperation and a strong notion of moral responsibility. If the global community is to survive and flourish, we need morality as much now as we ever have in the past.

WHY SHOULD I BE MORAL?

Let's agree with Hobbes's social contract theory that moral rules are needed for social order: Morality serves as an important antidote to the state of nature, and unless there is general adherence to the moral point of view, society will break down. There remains, though, a nagging question: "Why should *I* join in?" If I'm sly enough, I can break moral rules when they benefit me but never get caught and thus avoid being punished. What motivation is there for me to accept the moral viewpoint at all? This question was raised over two millennia ago by Plato in his dialogue, *The Republic,* where he tells the story of Gyges.

The Story of Gyges

In Plato's story, Gyges is a shepherd who stumbles upon a ring that at his command makes him invisible and, while in that state, he can indulge in his greed to the fullest without fear of getting caught. He can thus escape the restraints of society, its laws, and punishments. So, he kills the king, seduces his wife, and becomes king himself. The pertinent question raised by the story is this: Wouldn't we all do likewise if we too had this ring?

To sharpen this question, let's recast the Gyges story in contemporary terms. Suppose there were two brothers, Jim and Jack. Jim was a splendid fellow, kind and compassionate, almost saintly, always sacrificing for the poor, helping others. In fact, he was too good to be true. As a young man, he was framed by Jack for a serious crime, was imprisoned, and was constantly harassed and tortured by the guards and prisoners. When released, he could not secure employment and was forced to beg for his food. Now he lives as a street-person in a large city, in poor health, without a family, and without shelter. People avoid him whenever they can because he looks dangerous. Yet, in truth, his heart is as pure as the driven snow.

Jack, the older brother who framed Jim, is as evil as Jim is good. He also is as "successful" as Jim is "unsuccessful." He is the embodiment of respectability and civic virtue. He is a rising and wealthy corporate executive who is praised by all for his astuteness and appearance integrity (the latter of which he lacks completely). He is married to the most beautiful woman in the community, and his children all go to the best private schools. Jack's wife is completely taken in by his performance, and his children, who hardly know him, love him unconditionally. He is an elder in his church, on the board of directors of various charity groups, and he was voted the Ideal Citizen of his city. Teachers use him as an example of how one can be both morally virtuous and a successful entrepreneur. He is honored and admired by all. Yet he has attained all his success and wealth by ruthlessly destroying people who trusted him. He is in reality an evil man.

So, the question posed by the story of Gyges is this: If you had to make a choice between living either of these lives, which life would you choose? That of the unjust brother Jack who is incredibly successful or that of the just brother Jim who is incredibly unsuccessful?

Let's consider two reasons for opting to live the life of Jim, the good man who through no fault of his own is a social outcast. Plato argued that we should choose the life of the "unsuccessful" just person because it's to our advantage to be moral. He draws attention to the idea of the harmony of the soul and argues that immorality corrupts the inner person, whereas virtue purifies the inner person, so one is happy or unhappy in exact proportion to one's moral integrity. Asking to choose between being morally good and immoral is like asking to choose between being healthy and sick. Even if the immoral person has material benefits, he cannot enjoy them in his awful state, whereas the good person may find joy in the simple pleasures despite poverty and ill fortune.

Is Plato correct? Is the harm that Jim suffers compensated by the inner goodness of his heart? Is the good that Jack experiences outweighed by the evil of his heart? Perhaps we don't know enough about the hearts of people to be certain who is better off, Jim or Jack. But perhaps we can imagine people like Jack who seem to flourish despite their wickedness. They may not fool us completely, but they seem satisfied with the lives they are living, moderately happy in their business and personal triumphs. And perhaps we know of some people like Jim who are really very sad despite their goodness. They wish they had meaningful work, a loving family, friends, and shelter; but they don't, and their virtue is insufficient to produce happiness. Some good people are unhappy, and some bad people seem to be happy. Hence, the Socratic answer on the health–sickness analogy may not be correct.

Plato's second answer is a religious response: God will reward or punish people on the basis of their virtue or vice. The promise is of eternal bliss for the virtuous and hard times for the vicious. God sees all and rewards with absolute justice according to individual moral merit. Accordingly, despite what may be their differing fates here on earth, Jim is infinitely better off than Jack. If religious ethics of this sort is true, it is in our self-interest to be moral. The good is really good for us. The religious person has good reason to choose the life of the destitute saint.

We'll take up the relationship of religion to morality in a later chapter, but we can say this much about the problem: Unfortunately, we do not know for certain whether there is a God or life after death. Many sincere people doubt or disbelieve religious doctrines, and it is not easy to prove them wrong. Even the devout have doubts and probably cannot be sure of the truth of the doctrine of life after death and the existence of God. In any case, millions of people are not religious, and the question of the relationship between self-interest and morality is a pressing one. Can a moral philosopher give a nonreligious answer as to why they should choose to be moral all of the time?

MORALITY, SELF-INTEREST, AND GAME THEORY

Attempting to prove that we should always be moral is an uphill battle because, as we've seen, countless situations may arise in which it's in our best interests to break the rules of morality as long as we don't get caught. Social contract theorists have recently attempted to resolve the conflict between morality and self-interest by drawing from a field of study called **game theory.** The idea behind game theory is to present situations in which players make decisions that will bring each of them the greatest benefit; these games then provide easy models for understanding more complex situations of social interaction in the real world. A simple game like Monopoly, for example, models the real dog-eat-dog world of business in which you need to kill the competition before the competition kills you. At the same time, Monopoly shows the devastating results on society when a single person succeeds in owning everything. The most common game theory scenario in philosophy is the Prisoner's Dilemma, and this is frequently used to illuminate the tension between morality and self-interest.

Game 1: The Prisoner's Dilemma

The Prisoner's Dilemma scenario is this. The secret police in another country have arrested two of our spies, Sam and Sue. Prior to being caught, Sam and Sue have agreed to keep silent during interrogation if they are ever arrested. Now that they are in the hands of the enemy, they both know that if they adhere to their agreement to keep silent the police will be able to hold them for four months; but if they violate their agreement and both confess that they are spies, they will each get six years in prison. However, if one adheres and the other violates, the one who adheres will get nine years, and the one who confesses will be let go immediately. We might represent their plight with the following matrix. The figures on the left represent the amount of time Sam will spend in prison under the various alternatives, and the figures on the right represent the amount of time that Sue will spend in prison under those alternatives.

		Sue	
		Adheres	*Violates*
Sam	*Adheres*	4 months, 4 months	0 time, 9 years
	Violates	9 years, 0 time	6 years, 6 years

Initially, Sam reasons in this manner. Either Sue will adhere to the agreement or she will violate it. If Sue adheres, then Sam should violate because it's better for him to spend zero time in prison than four months. On the other hand, if Sue violates, then Sam should violate because it's better for him to spend six years in prison than nine years. Therefore, no matter what Sue does, it's in Sam's best interest to violate their agreement. However, Sue reasons exactly the same way about Sam and will conclude that it is in her best interest to violate the agreement. Here's the catch: If both reason in this way, they will obtain the second-worst position—six years each, which we know to be pretty awful. If they could only stick to their original agreement and stay silent, they could each do better—getting only four months. But how can they confidently do that without magically reading each other's minds to see the other's true intentions? They can't and thus each will be forced to look out for his or her own best interests and violate their original agreement.

In a nutshell, here's the lesson that the Prisoner's Dilemma teaches us about violating the rules of morality. It's better for me to secretly violate society's rules, regardless of what other people do. It would be nice if the Prisoner's Dilemma told us that adhering to morality was the best thing for me, but unfortunately it shows the opposite. What do we do now? Remember that the point of games like the Prisoner's Dilemma is to provide an easy model for understanding complex social situations such as how I might benefit by adhering to the rules of morality. The Prisoner's Dilemma, though, might not be a very good model for this. In particular, it inaccurately depicts moral choices as a one-shot event: Sam and Sue are in a single situation in which they must make a single choice about whether to adhere to or violate their initial agreement to stay silent. But, morality is not a single-issue decision. On a daily basis, we decide whether or not to violate society's moral rules when we might benefit from deception. Should I cheat on my taxes? Should I rack up charges on a bogus credit card? Should I defraud a trusting buyer on eBay? Morality is more like a game in which each player takes several turns, so we need to consider a different game model.

Game 2: Cooperate or Cheat

Consider this alternative game theory scenario called Cooperate or Cheat.[4] In it there are two players and a banker who pays out money or fines to the players. Each player has two cards, labeled "Cooperate" and "Cheat." Each move consists of both players simultaneously laying down one of their cards. Suppose you and I are playing against one another. There are four possible outcomes:

Outcome 1. We both play Cooperate. The banker pays each of us $300. We are rewarded nicely.

Outcome 2. We both play Cheat. The banker fines each of us $10. We are punished for mutual defection.

Outcome 3. You play Cooperate and I play Cheat. The banker pays me $500 (Temptation money) and you are fined $100 (a Sucker fine).

Outcome 4. I play Cooperate and you play Cheat. The banker fines me $100 and pays you $500. This is the reverse of Outcome 3.

The game continues until the banker calls it quits. Theoretically, I could win a lot of money by always cheating. After twenty moves, I could hold the sum of $10,000—that is, if you are sucker enough to continue to play Cooperate, in which case you will be short $2,000. If you are rational, you won't do that. If we both continually cheat, we'll each end up minus $200 after twenty rounds.

Suppose we act on the principle "Always cooperate if the other fellow does and cheat only if he cheats first." If we both adhere to this principle, we'll each end up with $6,000 after our twenty rounds—not a bad reward! And, we have the prospects of winning more if we continue to act rationally.

We may conclude that rational self-interest over the long run would demand that you and I cooperate. While I might gain greater rewards by cheating, it comes at a high risk of winning much less. As contemporary social contractarian David Gauthier puts it, "Morality is a system of principles such that it is advantageous for everyone if everyone accepts and acts on it, yet acting on the system of principles requires that some persons perform disadvantageous acts."[5] The game of Cooperate or Cheat illustrates that morality is the price that we each have to pay to keep the minimal good that we have in a civilized society. We have to bear some disadvantage in loss of freedom (analogous to paying membership dues in an important organization) so that we can have both protection from the onslaughts of chaos and promotion of the good life. Because an orderly society is no small benefit, even a selfish person who is rational should allow his or her freedom to be limited.

The answer, then, to the question "Why should I be moral" is that I allow some disadvantage for myself so that I may reap an overall, long-run advantage.

THE MOTIVE TO ALWAYS BE MORAL

The game of Cooperate or Cheat informs us that even the amoralist must generally adhere to the moral rule because it will give him or her some long-term advantage. There remains, however, a serious problem: The clever person will still break a moral rule whenever he or she can do so without getting detected and unduly undermining the whole system. This clever amoralist takes into account his overall impact on the social system and cheats whenever a careful cost–benefit analysis warrants it. Reaping the rewards of his clever deceit, he may even encourage moral education so that more people will be more dedicated to the moral rule, which in turn will allow him to cheat with greater confidence.

The Paradox of Morality and Advantage

Gauthier describes this problem of the clever amoralist through what he calls the **paradox of morality and advantage;** he writes,

> If it is morally right to do an act, then it must be reasonable to do it. If it is reasonable to do the act, then it must be in my interest to do it. But sometimes the requirements of morality are incompatible with the requirements of self-interest. Hence, we have a seeming contradiction: It both must be reasonable and need not be reasonable to meet our moral duties.[6]

Laid out more formally, the argument is this:

(1) If an act is morally right, then it must be reasonable to do it.

(2) If it is reasonable to do the act, then it must be in my interest to do it.

(3) But sometimes the requirements of morality are incompatible with the requirements of self-interest.

(4) Hence, a morally right act must be reasonable and need not be reasonable, which is a contradiction.

The problematic premise seems to be the second one claiming that our reasons for acting have to appeal to self-interest. For simplicity, let's call this the *principle of rational self-interest*.

Might we not doubt this principle of rational self-interest? Could we not have good reasons for doing something that goes against our interest? Suppose Lisa sees a small boy about to get run over by a car and, intending to save the child, hurls herself at the youngster, fully aware of the danger to herself. Lisa's interest is in no way tied up with the life of that child, but she still tries to save his life at great risk to her own. Isn't this a case of having a reason to go against one's self-interest?

I think that it is such a reason. The principle of rational self-interest seems unduly based on the position that people always act to satisfy their perceived best interest—a view called psychological egoism, which we will critically examine in a later chapter. Sometimes, we have reasons to do things that go against our perceived self-interest. We find this, for example, when a poor person gives away money to help another poor person; so too with the student who refrains from cheating when she knows that she could easily escape detection. Being faithful, honest, generous, and kind often requires us to act against our own interest.

But you may object to this reasoning by saying, "It is perhaps against our immediate or *short-term* interest to be faithful, honest, generous, or kind; but in the long run, it really is likely to be in our best interest because the moral and altruistic life promises benefits and satisfactions that are not available to the immoral and stingy."

There seems to be merit in this response. The basis of it seems to be a plausible view of moral psychology that stipulates that character formation is not like a bathroom faucet that you can turn on and off at will. To have the benefits of the moral life—friendship, mutual love, inner peace, moral pride or satisfaction, and freedom from moral guilt—one has to have a certain kind of reliable character. All in all, these benefits are very much worth having. Indeed, life without them may not be worth living. Thus, we can assert that for every person (insofar as he or she is rational) the deeply moral life is the best sort of life that he or she can live. Hence, it follows that it is reasonable to develop such a deeply moral character—or to continue to develop it because our upbringing partly forms it for most of us.

Those raised in a normal social context will feel deep distress at the thought of harming others or doing what is immoral and feel deep satisfaction in being moral. For such people, the combination of internal and external sanctions may well bring prudence and morality close together. This situation may not apply, however, to people not brought up in a moral context. Should this dismay us? No. As Gregory Kavka says, we should not perceive "an immoralist's gloating that it does not pay him to be moral . . . as a victory over us. It is more like the pathetic boast of a deaf person that he saves money because it does not pay him to buy opera records."[7] The immoralist is a Scrooge who takes pride in not having to buy Christmas presents because he has no friends.

The Modified Principle of Rational Self-Interest

We want to say, then, that the choice of the moral point of view is not an arbitrary choice but a rational one. Some kinds of lives are better than others: A human life without the benefits of morality is not an ideal or fulfilled life; it lacks too much that makes for human flourishing. The occasional acts through which we sacrifice our self-interest within the general flow of a satisfied life are unavoidable risks that reasonable people will take. Although you can lose by betting on morality, you are almost certain to lose if you bet against it.

Therefore, the principle of rational self-interest must be restated in a modified form:

> *Modified principle of rational self-interest.* If it is reasonable to choose a life plan L, which includes the possibility of doing act A, then it must be in my interest (or at least not against it) to choose L, even though A itself may not be in my self-interest.

Now there is no longer anything paradoxical in doing something not in one's interest because, although the individual moral act may occasionally conflict with one's self-interest, the entire life plan in which the act is embedded and from which it flows is not against the individual's self-interest. For instance, although you might be able to cheat a company or a country out of some money that would leave you materially better off, it would be contrary to the *form of life* to which you have committed yourself and that has generally been rewarding.

Furthermore, character is important and habits force us into predictable behavior. Once we obtain the kind of character necessary for the moral life— once we become *virtuous*—we will not be able to turn morality on and off like a faucet. When we yield to temptation, we will experience alienation in going against this well-formed character. The guilt will torment us, greatly diminishing any ill-gotten gains.

The modified principle of rational self-interests answers several moral questions raised throughout this chapter. Should I act immorally if I wear the ring of Gyges? Should I break the social contract if I can get away with it? The answer in both cases is no. First, it is sometimes reasonable to act morally even when those actions do not immediately involve our self-interest. Second, and more important, a life without spontaneous and deliberate moral kindness may not be worth living. This helps explain why Carl and his employees at the car dealership should behave morally, even if it means risking fewer sales with less profit. If they adopted a moral form of life that's not overburdened with a desire for private financial gain, they may feel more rewarded in their business lives by not cheating their customers.

Of course, there's no guarantee that morality will produce success and happiness. Jim—the moral yet unsuccessful brother discussed earlier in this chapter—is not happy. In a sense, morality is a rational gamble. It doesn't guarantee success or happiness. Life is tragic. The good fail and the bad—the Jacks of life—seem to prosper. Yet the moral person is prepared for this eventuality. John Rawls sums up the vulnerability of the moral life this way:

> A just person is not prepared to do certain things, and so in the face of evil circumstances he may decide to chance death rather than to act unjustly. Yet although it is true enough that for the sake of justice a man may lose his life where another would live to a later day, the just man does what all things considered he most wants; in this sense he is

not defeated by ill fortune, the possibility of which he foresaw. The question is on a par with the hazards of love; indeed, it is simply a special case. Those who love one another, or who acquire strong attachments to persons and to forms of life, at the same time become liable to ruin: their love makes them hostages to misfortune and the injustice of others. Friends and lovers take great chances to help each other; and members of families willingly do the same.... Once we love we are vulnerable.[8]

We can, however, take steps to lessen the vulnerability by working together for a more moral society, by bringing up our children to have keener moral sensitivities and good habits so that there are fewer Jacks around. We can establish a more just society so that people are less tempted to cheat and more inclined to cooperate, once they see that we are all working together for a happier world, a mutual back-scratching world, if you like. In general, the more just the political order, the more likely it will be that the good will prosper, and the more likely that self-interest and morality will converge.

CONCLUSION

In this chapter, we've examined social contract theory's explanation of moral motivation as expressed in two questions: "Why does society need moral rules?" and "Why should I be moral?" Hobbes argues that because humans always act out of perceived self-interest people are naturally driven into conflict with everyone—the state of nature. The solution is for us to create a social contract: By giving up some of our liberty and adopting moral rules, we gain peace. Thus, the answer to the first question ("Why does society need moral rules?") is that morality is a much needed mechanism of social control.

Social contract theory's answer to the second question ("Why should I be moral?") is more complicated as the game Cooperate or Cheat shows. Ultimately, I should be moral because, by occasionally allowing some disadvantage for myself, I may obtain an overall, long-term advantage. Even when it seems as though I can break moral rules without getting caught, I still need to consistently follow them because, although an individual moral act may sometimes be at odds with my self-interest, the complete moral form of life in which the act is rooted is not against my self-interest.

NOTES

1. Donald McCabe, "Cheating in Academic Institutions: A Decade of Research," *Ethics & Behavior* 11, no. 3 (2001): 219–232; "Cheating on Spouse or Taxes Morally Acceptable for Many" in LiveScience (www.livescience.com), March 28, 2006; James Vicini, "US Has the Most Prisoners in the World," Reuters, December 9, 2006.

2. Thomas Hobbes, *Leviathan* (1642). A recent edition is by Edwin Curly (Indianapolis: Hackett, 1994). All quoted material in this section is from this work.

3. William Golding, *Lord of the Flies* (New York: Putnam, 1954). All quoted material in this section is from this work.

4. Robert Axelrod, *The Evolution of Cooperation* (New York: Basic Books, 1984); Robert Axelrod and William Hamilton, "The Evolution of Cooperation," *Science* 211 (1981): 1390–1396. The game of Cooperate or Cheat is sometimes called the Iterated Prisoner's Dilemma.

5. David Gauthier, "Morality and Advantage," *Philosophical Review* 76 (1967): 460–475.

6. Ibid.

7. Gregory Kavka, "Reconciliation Project," in *Morality, Reason and Truth,* ed. D. Copp and D. Zimmerman (Totowa, N.J.: Rowman & Allenheld, 1984).

8. John Rawls, *A Theory of Justice* (Cambridge, Ma.: Harvard University Press, 1971), p. 573.

FOR FURTHER REFLECTION

1. Consider the following situation proposed by John Hospers in *Human Conduct* (Harcourt Brace Jovanovich, 1961), p. 174: "Suppose you tell a blind news vendor that it's a five-dollar bill you are handing him, and he gives you four dollars and some coins in change, whereas actually you handed him only a one-dollar bill. Almost everyone would agree that such an act is wrong. But some people who agree may still ask, 'Tell me why I shouldn't do it just the same.'" What would you say to such people?

2. Explain the Hobbesian account of the state of nature and discuss whether you agree with it.

3. Hospers believes that the question "Why should I be moral?" can only be answered by the response "Because it's right." Self-interested answers just won't do because they come down to asking for self-interested reasons for going against my self-interest, which is a self-contradiction. Is Hospers correct about this, or is there something more we can say about being moral?

4. Many students over the years have cheated their ways into medical school. Would you want to be a patient of one of these doctors? What does this tell you about the reasons to be moral?

5. At the Website serendip.brynmawr.edu/playground/pd.html, there is an online version of the game Cooperate or Cheat. Play the game for a few minutes, trying different strategies, and discuss whether your experience confirms that in the long run cooperating is better for you than cheating.

6. Whether you believe that there are always self-interested reasons for being moral will largely depend on whether and to what degree you believe that some forms of life are better than others. Is there an objective standard by which we can judge the quality of one form of life over another?

FOR FURTHER READING

Binmore, Ken. *Game Theory and the Social Contract, Vol. 1: Playing Fair.* Cambridge, Ma.: MIT Press, 1994.

Darwall, Stephen L., ed. *Contractarianism, Contractualism.* Malden, Ma : Blackwell, 2003.

Gauthier, David, ed. *Morality and Rational Self-Interest.* Englewood Cliffs, N.J.: Prentice Hall, 1970.

Gauthier, David. *Morals by Agreement.* Oxford, Engl.: Clarendon Press, 1986.

Kavka, Gregory. *Hobbesian Moral and Political Theory.* Princeton, N.J.: Princeton University Press 1986.

Nielsen, Kai. *Why Be Moral?* Buffalo, N.Y.: Prometheus, 1989.

Poundstone, William. *The Prisoner's Dilemma.* New York: Doubleday, 1992.

6

Egoism, Self-Interest, and Altruism

Nice guys finish last.
LEO DUROCHER, FORMER MANAGER OF THE BROOKLYN DODGERS

The achievement of his own happiness is man's highest moral purpose.
AYN RAND, *THE VIRTUE OF SELFISHNESS*

One of the most notorious examples of selfishness in the business world is that of Nestlé's infant formula. During the 1970s and 1980s, Nestlé launched a marketing strategy in developing countries that lured countless poor mothers into infant formula dependency. Wearing uniforms that resembled those of legitimate nurses, Nestlé's sales force infiltrated hospitals, praised the health benefits of their infant formula, and left mothers with free samples that would last a few weeks—just long enough to diminish the mothers' abilities to produce breast milk. Left with no choice, mothers purchased the formula. However, proper use of it required up to 70 percent of a family's income, and unable to pay, mothers diluted the formula, often with contaminated local water. The result was the death of millions of infants from disease and malnutrition. After a decade-long worldwide boycott against Nestlé, in 1984 the company changed their marketing practices. However, even today some activist groups charge that infant formula companies, including Nestlé, are still marketing to poor mothers, resulting in 4,000 babies dying each day.[1]

Even the worst corporations don't intentionally set out to kill people. Rather, they are continually driven by the need to make a profit, which overrides all other considerations. If people are harmed or die in the course of doing business, that's not an issue for them unless it seriously harms sales through fines, bad publicity, or boycotts. One lesson that we might learn from the Nestlé story is that corporations are chronically selfish: Every decision is made in a way that ultimately serves the best interest of the company and *only* that company. Even when corporations donate to charities, it's invariably done as a public relations effort to improve public image and in turn improve sales. Considering that corporations are composed of nothing but human beings, this raises serious questions about whether selfishness is the driving force behind all human conduct—in our private as well as business lives.

What is the place of self-regard, self-interest, or self-love in the moral life? Is everything that we do really done out of the motive of self-interest so that morality is necessarily egoistic? Is some form of egoism the best moral theory? Or is egoism really diametrically opposed to true morality? Is selflessness possible, and if so, is it rational? These are the questions that we discuss in this chapter. There are many different kinds of egoism, but the two main types that interest moral philosophers are psychological egoism and ethical egoism.

Psychological egoism is the position that we always do that act that we perceive to be in our own best self-interest. That is, we have no choice but to be selfish. We cannot be motivated by anything other than what we believe will promote our interests. I always try to promote my self-interest, and you always try to promote your self-interest.

Ethical egoism, by contrast, holds that everyone ought always to do those acts that will best serve his or her own best self-interest. Whereas psychological egoism is a theory about how we *do* behave as human beings, ethical egoism is a theory about how we *ought* to behave. That is, our moral obligation is to seek one's own self-interest, and the rightness or wrongness of our conduct depends on us fulfilling our self-interest. Let's begin our investigation with psychological egoism.

PSYCHOLOGICAL EGOISM

Again, psychological egoism is the theory that we always do that act that we perceive to be in our own best self-interest. This view claims to be a description of human nature; that is, it maintains that all people are in fact psychologically designed to act only in those ways that advance their perceived individual self-interest. It makes no difference what action I perform: donating to charity, rescuing someone from drowning, or volunteering for a disaster-relief organization. At bottom, all my actions are selfishly motivated. Perhaps I do these seemingly selfless actions to improve my reputation or just to make me feel good. The bottom line, though, is that I do them all for *me*. Because psychological egoism purports to be a factual theory of human nature, we may rightfully ask what proof there is for that view. One such defense is the argument from self-satisfaction.

The Argument from Self-Satisfaction

Stated most simply, the argument from self-satisfaction is this:

S.   Everyone is an egoist because everyone always tries to do what will bring him or her satisfaction.

This argument is most famously given by Abraham Lincoln in the following anecdote:

> Mr. Lincoln once remarked to a fellow-passenger on an old-time mudcoach that all men were prompted by selfishness in doing good. His fellow-passenger was antagonizing this position when they were passing over a corduroy bridge that spanned a slough. As they crossed this bridge they espied an old razorbacked sow on the bank making a terrible noise because her pigs had got into the slough and were in danger of drowning.
>
> As the old coach began to climb the hill, Mr. Lincoln called out, "Driver, can't you stop just a moment?" Then Mr. Lincoln jumped out, ran back and lifted the little pigs out of the mud and water and placed them on the bank. When he returned, his companion remarked: "Now Abe, where does selfishness come in on this little episode?" "Why, bless your soul, Ed, that was the very essence of selfishness. I should have had no peace of mind all day had I gone on and left that suffering old sow worrying over those pigs. I did it to get peace of mind, don't you see?"[2]

Is S true? Well, at first sight it seems ambiguous. On the one hand, it might mean this:

S1. For any act A, everyone does A *in order* to obtain satisfaction.

Satisfaction is the goal. From this interpretation, it may be inferred that we all always act in such a way as to maximize our own self-interest—self-interest being interpreted in terms of satisfaction of wants. But S could conceivably mean this as well:

S2. We all do the act that we most want to do, and as a consequence, we are satisfied by the success of carrying out the act.

Although the first interpretation (S1) reflects the view of psychological egoism, the second (S2) does not. Thus, let's set the second one aside and focus on the first. Enlarged, this first interpretation reads as follows:

> We all want to be happy—to find satisfaction in life—and everything that we do we consciously do toward that end.

Abe Lincoln, in the story quoted at the beginning of this section, claimed to help the piglets out of the slough to relieve his conscience, sheerly out of selfish motivation.

Consider a variation on the Lincoln story: The situation is the same, only it is Ed who calls to the driver to halt and who spontaneously jumps out to save the piglets. He returns from the ordeal, pleased. Lincoln now greets him with these words:

> "Ed, you know that what you did was the very essence of selfishness. You couldn't have lived with yourself had you not tried to help those piglets."

But Ed replies,

> "Abe, I wasn't aware of seeking my own happiness in trying to help those piglets. I did it because I believe that suffering should be alleviated. Of course, I feel satisfaction for having succeeded, but satisfaction is an automatic accompaniment of any successful action. Even if I had failed to help them, I would have felt a measure of satisfaction in that I succeeded in *trying* to help them."

Lincoln seems wrong and Ed seems right in his assessment of the relation of motivation to success. We do not always consciously seek our own satisfaction or happiness when we act. In fact, some people seem to seek their own unhappiness, as masochists and self-destructive people do, and we all sometimes seem to act spontaneously without consciously considering our happiness. Ed's position approximates the second interpretation of the motivation statement S:

S2. We all do the act that we most want to do, and as a *consequence,* we are satisfied by the success of carrying out the act.

Actually, S2 doesn't seem quite right either because it is doubtful whether we always do what we most want to do. When I am on a diet, I most want to refrain from eating delicious chocolate cakes and rich ice cream, but I sometimes find myself yielding to the temptation. Alcoholics and addicts have even more poignant experiences of doing what they don't want to do. Such experiences of weakness of will count heavily against S2. Let's therefore attempt one more interpretation of S:

S3. We always try to do what we most want to do and, as a consequence of success in carrying out the act, experience satisfaction.

S3 takes weakness of will into account and so seems closer to the truth. It also seems better for the following reason: We usually are not conscious of any concern for satisfaction when we seek some goal, but satisfaction seems to follow naturally on accomplishing any task. When I reach out to grab a child who is about to be hit by a car, pulling her back from danger, I feel satisfaction at my success, but I didn't save her to feel satisfied. To conclude that, because I feel satisfaction after saving her, I must have had satisfaction as my purpose is to confuse a consequence of an act with a purpose. This is as fallacious as reasoning that because a car constantly consumes gasoline during driving the purpose of such driving is to consume gasoline. In short, as we push for greater clarity in the psychological egoist's position, the initial argument from self-satisfaction disappears.

The Paradox of Hedonism

Another problem with the argument from self-satisfaction centers on what is called the **paradox of hedonism.** Suppose a super-psychologist who could reliably predict outcomes told you that two courses of actions were open to you: (1) You would perform a perfect robbery, kill the bank president and the only person who knew your whereabouts—namely, your best friend or mother—and flee to Argentina to live a happy life; or (2) you would refrain from crime and live a simple but decent middle-class life as a teacher. Suppose further that he convinced you that option (1) would yield 1,000 units of happiness or satisfaction (call these units "hedons"), whereas option (2) would yield only 500 hedons. Which would you choose? If you would choose (2), then this is evidence that psychological egoism is false.

This seems to show that we act out of our overall value schemas and find satisfaction in achieving our goals, but that satisfaction is not the only goal. This is what John Stuart Mill meant when he said, "Better Socrates dissatisfied, than the pig satisfied." Likewise, "Better a discontented good person than a blissful bad person." Seeking satisfaction for its own sake and nothing else seems to merit Mill's undesirable "pig philosophy." We all want to be happy, but we don't want happiness at any price or to the exclusion of certain other values.

Moreover, happiness itself seems a peculiar kind of goal. As the paradox of hedonism asserts, the best way to get happiness is to forget it. That is, you'll have a higher probability of attaining happiness if you aim at accomplishing worthy goals that will indirectly bring about happiness:

I sought the bird of bliss, she flew away.
I sought my neighbor's good, bliss flew my way.

Happiness seems to be an elusive goal as long as we desire it alone and for its own sake. It is in the process of reaching other intrinsically worthy goals that happiness comes into being. Joel Feinberg puts the paradox of hedonism this way:

Imagine a person, Jones, who is, first of all, devoid of intellectual curiosity. He has no desire to acquire any kind of knowledge for its own sake, and thus is utterly indifferent to questions of science, mathematics, and philosophy. Imagine further that the beauties of nature leave Jones cold: he is unimpressed by the autumn foliage, the snow-capped mountains, and the rolling oceans. Long walks in the country on spring mornings and skiing forays in the winter are to him equally a bore. Moreover, let us suppose that Jones can find no appeal in art. Novels are dull, poetry a pain, paintings nonsense and music just noise. Suppose further that Jones has neither the participant's nor the spectator's passion for baseball, football, tennis, or any other sport. Swimming to him is a cruel aquatic form of calisthenics, the sun only a cause of sunburn. Dancing is coeducational idiocy, conversation a waste of time, the other sex an unappealing mystery. Politics is a fraud, religion mere superstition; and the misery of millions of underprivileged human beings is nothing to be concerned with or excited about. Suppose finally that Jones has no talent for any kind of handicraft, industry, or commerce, and that he does not regret that fact.

What then is Jones interested in? He must desire something. To be sure, he does. Jones has an overwhelming passion for, a complete preoccupation with, his own happiness. The one exclusive desire of his life is to be happy. It takes little imagination at this point to see that Jones's one desire is bound to be frustrated.[3]

The paradox of hedonism seems to suggest that psychological egoism has severe problems.

The Argument from Self-Deception

Suppose the psychological egoist alters his interpretation of S to include subconscious motivations. The thesis now states that sometimes we are self-deceived about our motivation, but whenever we overcome self-deception and really look deep into our motivational schemes, we find an essential selfishness.

Is the self-deception argument sound? One problem with it is that it seems to be an unfalsifiable dogma, for what evidence could ever count against it? Suppose you look within your motivational structure and do not find a predominant egoistic motive. What does the egoist say to this? The egoist responds that you just haven't looked deep enough. But how, you may wonder, do you know when you have looked deep enough? The egoist answers: When you discover the selfish motive. For example, suppose Lincoln's friend Ed introspects about his motivational scheme in pulling the piglets out of the slough and fails to find a selfish motive. Abe might then respond, "Ed, I don't mean that the selfishness is always conscious. Self-deception is very deep in humans, so you just haven't looked deep enough."

This contention may show that we can never disprove psychological egoism. But it doesn't offer comfort to the egoist thesis either. Quite the contrary. If we look as deep as we can and still don't come up with a selfish motive, then we're justified in believing that not all action is motivated by agent—utility considerations. The burden of proof is on the egoist to convince us that we are still self-deceived. The egoist seems to be guilty of committing the fallacy of unwarranted generalization. Just because we are *sometimes* self-deceived about our motives, she reasons, we must *always* be deceived. But this doesn't follow at all.

Suppose humans are predominantly psychological egoists, that we are very often motivated by self-regarding motives. This does not imply that we are entirely egoists, nor does it mean that we are necessarily selfish. *Webster's Dictionary* defines *selfish* as "seeking or concentrating on one's own advantage, pleasure, or well-being without regard for others." But, we may find that our values are such that we incorporate the good of others as part of our happiness. A friend's or a lover's happiness is so bound up with the good of the other that the two cannot be separated. So if psychological egoism is interpreted as selfishness, it is surely false. If it is simply a statement of how we are motivated, then it probably still is false. Something like it—predominant psychological egoism—may be true, but this does not rule out the possibility of disinterested action.

ETHICAL EGOISM

Ethical egoism is the moral view that everyone ought always to do those acts that will best serve his or her own best self-interest. That is, morally right actions are those that maximize the best interest of oneself, even when it conflicts with the interests of others. It's important to recognize that the moral theory of ethical egoism does not maintain that every person ought to serve the best interests of *me* specifically (or the speaker). We could imagine, for example, that a tyrannical king might think that moral actions are those which serve specifically the king's best interest. The position of ethical egoism is more universal than that. It urges everyone to maximize his or her best interests. John, Mary, Bill, and Sue should each act in ways that serve their own interests. We next consider four common arguments in defense of ethical egoism.

The Argument from Strict Psychological Egoism

One argument for ethical egoism follows immediately from the theory of psychological egoism, which we examined in the previous section. If I am psychologically programmed to act only in my own best interest, then I can never be obligated to perform altruistic (that is, selfless) acts toward others. More formally the argument is this:

(1) We all always seek to maximize our own self-interest (definition of psychological egoism).

(2) If one cannot do an act, one has no obligation to do that act (*ought* implies *can*).

(3) Altruistic acts involve putting other people's interests ahead of our own (definition of **altruism**).

(4) But, altruism contradicts psychological egoism and so is impossible (by premises 1 and 3).

(5) Therefore, altruistic acts are never morally obligatory (by premises 2 and 4).

Premise 1 is the theory of psychological egoism itself. Premise 2 stipulates a basic moral principle that we can never be under an obligation to do what is impossible. If I am obligated to perform some action, at minimum it must first be within my power to perform that action. For example, I'm under no obligation to cure cancer because it's completely beyond my ability to do so. This basic position is encapsulated in the expression "*ought* implies *can*." Premise 3 defines altruistic actions as those that are selfless. Premise 4 states that by definition altruistic actions are in direct opposition to psychological egoism's claim that all actions aim to maximize one's self-interest. It follows from this that we can never be morally obligated to perform obligatory acts.

Does this argument succeed? If we accept the criticisms of psychological egoism in the previous section, then we must reject premise 1, and the whole argument crumbles. For the sake of argument, though, let's grant the truth of premise 1 and assume that psychological egoism accurately describes human nature. Does this argument now prove ethical egoism? Not necessarily. The above argument only entitles us to reject the contention that altruistic acts are morally obligatory. However, it does not follow from this that we *ought* to perform egoistic acts. For that matter, the above argument doesn't show that we are morally obligated to perform any acts whatsoever. As such, the argument fails.

Hobbes's Argument from Predominant Psychological Egoism

Let's now consider an alternative argument from psychological egoism that we find in the writings of Thomas Hobbes. His argument goes like this: Suppose we existed outside of any society, without laws or agreed-on morality, in a "state of nature." There are no common ways of life, no means of settling conflicts of interest except violence, no reliable expectations of how other people will behave. Further, people are inherently selfish; they will follow their own inclinations and perceived interests, tending to act and react and overreact in fearful, capricious, and violent ways. The result of life in the state of nature is chaotic anarchy where life is "solitary, poor, nasty, brutish, and short."

According to Hobbes, we are driven to survive at all costs, and we see that it would be better for all of us, individually and collectively, if we adopted certain minimal rules that would override immediate self-interest whenever self-interest was a threat to others. Thus, the notion of a mutually agreed-on moral code arises from a situation of rational self-interest. But, of course, the moral code will not work if only some obey it. To prevent violations, Hobbes proposes a strong central government with a powerful police force and a sure and effective system of punishment. The threat of being caught and punished should function as a deterrence to crime. People must believe that offenses against the law are not in their overall interest.[4]

The engine that drives Hobbes's entire theory is psychological egoism: Selfishness forces us into chaos, and selfishness forces us to solve the problem through mutually agreed-on moral codes. Although Hobbes undoubtedly endorses psychological egoism, some scholars argue that he does so in a more moderate way.[5] For Hobbes, human action is *predominantly* motivated by self-interest. That is, human nature causes us to be heavily biased toward our own self-interest over that of others' interest. Because we cannot act altruistically without unreasonable effort, it follows that it is morally permissible to act entirely out of self-interest. Further, the approach that Hobbes takes in developing our self-interested moral obligations is rather sophisticated and ultimately leads us to adopt familiar moral principles. Enlightened common sense tells us that we should aim at fulfilling our *long-term* versus our short-term interests, so we need to refrain from immediate gratification of our senses—from doing those things that would break down the social conditions that enable us to reach our goals. We should even, perhaps, generally obey the Golden Rule, "Do to others as you would have them do to you," for doing good to others will help ensure that they do good to us.

Does Hobbes's argument for ethical egoism succeed? On the one hand, it seems to overcome both of the limitations of the above argument from strict psychological egoism. First, by advocating a more moderate version of psychological egoism, he sidesteps at least some of the attacks on psychological egoism that we previously examined. Second, Hobbes does more than just rule out the possibility of morally obligatory acts of altruism: He seeks to establish a concrete moral obligation toward maximizing our long-term individual self-interest. Specifically, for Hobbes, we are morally permitted to perform egoistic acts that lead to our individual survival.

Although Hobbes's argument for ethical egoism is plausible, it still seems to rest too heavily on psychological egoism. It assumes that we cannot do any better than be egoists, so we should be as strategic about our egoism as possible. But if, as we argued earlier, psychological egoism is false, there is no reason to rule out the possibility of nonegoistic behavior. Maybe we all should just try harder to act altruistically. Because Hobbes is advancing a more moderate view of psychological egoism, we need not of necessity become ethical egoists. In short, Hobbes's theory is plausible but not foolproof.

Smith's Economic Argument

Eighteenth-century economist Adam Smith defended an egoistic approach toward morality based on the economic benefits that this would bring to society. According to Smith, individual self-interest in a competitive marketplace produces a state of optimal goodness for society at large. Competition, he argues, causes each individual to produce a better product and sell it at a lower price than competitors. For example, if I'm a car manufacturer and hope to survive against the competition, I will need to find ways of making my car better and selling it at a cheaper price in an effort to get more customers. I gain but so too does the customer. Thus, my self-interest leads to the best overall situation for society. Smith picturesquely describes this benefit as the result of an "invisible hand," which almost magically directs the economy when we pursue our self-interest.

Does this argument succeed? Essentially, Smith's economic argument is not an argument for ethical egoism. It is really an argument for utilitarianism, which makes use of self-interest to attain the good of all. The goal of this theory is social benefit, but it places its faith in an invisible hand inherent in the free-enterprise system that guides enlightened self-interest to reach that goal. We might say that it is a two-tier system: On the highest level, it is utilitarian, but on a lower level of day-to-day action, it is practical egoism.

> Tier 2   *General goal:* social utility
>
> Tier 1   *Individual motivation:* egoistic

The economic argument as a two-tier system suggests that we not worry about the social good but only about our own good, and in that way we will attain the highest social good possible.

There may be some truth in such a two-tier system. But, first, it is unclear whether you can transpose the methods of economics (which are debatable) into the realm of personal relations, which may have a logic that differs from that of economic relations. The best way to maximize utility in an ethical sense may be to give one's life for others rather than kill another person, as an egoist might maintain. Second, it is not clear that classical laissez-faire capitalism works. Since the 1929 depression, most economists have altered their faith in classical capitalism, and most Western nations have supplemented capitalism with some governmental intervention. Likewise, although self-interest often leads to greater social utility, it may get out of hand and need to be supplemented by a concern for others. Classical capitalism has been altered to allow governmental intervention—resulting in a welfare system for the worst-off people, public education, Social Security, and Medicare. Similarly, an adequate moral system may need to draw attention to the needs of others and direct us to meeting those needs even when we do not consider it to be in our immediate self-interest.

Rand's Argument for the Virtue of Selfishness

The contemporary writer whose name is most associated with ethical egoism is Ayn Rand. In her book *The Virtue of Selfishness,* she argues that selfishness is a virtue and altruism a vice, a totally destructive idea that leads to the undermining of individual worth. Rand defines *altruism* as the view that

> Any action taken for the benefit of others is good, and any action taken for one's own benefit is evil. Thus, the *beneficiary* of an action is the only criterion of moral value—and so long as the beneficiary is anybody other than oneself, anything goes.[6]

As such, altruism is suicidal:

> If a man accepts the ethics of altruism, his first concern is not how to live his life, but how to sacrifice it. . . . Altruism erodes men's capacity to grasp the value of an individual life; it reveals a mind from which the reality of a human being has been wiped out. . . . Altruism holds death as its ultimate goal and standard of value—and it is logical that renunciation, resignation, self-denial, and every other form of suffering, including self-destruction, are the virtue of its advocates.

But, a person ought to profit from his own action. As Rand says, "Man's proper values and interests, that concern with his own interests, is the essence of a moral existence, and that man must be the beneficiary of his own moral actions." We all really want to be the beneficiary, but society has deceived us into thinking egoism is evil and altruism good, that collectivist mediocrity is virtuous and bold creativity is a vice.

We have an inalienable right to seek our own happiness and fulfillment, Rand argues, regardless of its effects on others. Altruism would deny us this right, so it is the "creed of corruption." Since finding our ego-centered happiness is the highest goal and good in life, altruism, which calls on us to sacrifice our happiness for the good of others, is contrary to our highest good. Her argument goes something like this:

(1) The perfection of one's abilities in a state of happiness is the highest goal for humans. We have a moral duty to attempt to reach this goal.

(2) The ethics of altruism prescribes that we sacrifice our interests and lives for the good of others.

(3) Therefore, the ethics of altruism is incompatible with the goal of happiness.

(4) Ethical egoism prescribes that we seek our own happiness exclusively, and as such it is consistent with the happiness goal.

(5) Therefore, ethical egoism is the correct moral theory.

Rand seems to hold that every individual has a duty to seek his or her own good first, regardless of how it affects others. She seems to base this duty on the fact that the actions of every living organism are "directed to a single goal: the mainte- nance of the organism's life." From this, she infers that the highest value is the organism's self-preservation. Ultimately, each of us should take care of Number One, the "I-god," letting the devil take care of anyone not strong enough to look after himself.

What should we think about Rand's argument for the virtue of selfishness? In a nutshell, it appears to be flawed by the fallacy of a false dilemma. It simplistically assumes that absolute altruism and absolute egoism are the only alternatives. But, this is an extreme view of the matter. There are plenty of options between these two positions. Even a predominant egoist would admit that (analogous to the par- adox of hedonism) sometimes the best way to reach self-fulfillment is for us to forget about ourselves and strive to live for goals, causes, or other persons. Even if altruism is not required as a duty, it may be permissible in many cases. Furthermore, self-interest may not be incompatible with other-regarding motiva- tion. Self-interest and self-love are morally good things but not at the expense of other people's legitimate interests. When there is a moral conflict of interests, a fair process of adjudication needs to take place.

Another problem with this argument is that, in her writings, Rand slides back and forth between advocating selfishness and self-interest. These are, however, dif- ferent concepts. *Self-interest* means we are concerned to promote our own good, although not necessarily at any cost. I want to succeed, but I recognize that some- times I will justly fail to do so. I accept the just outcome even though it is frustrat- ing. *Selfishness* entails that I sacrifice the good of others for my own good, even when it is unjust to do so. Self-interest is a legitimate part of our nature whereas selfishness is an aberration, a failure to accept the moral point of view.

Thus, Rand's thesis that ethics requires "that the actor must always be the beneficiary of his action" is not supported by good argument, and it is further contradicted by our common moral experience.

ARGUMENTS AGAINST ETHICAL EGOISM

When examining a theory like ethical egoism, the first step is to evaluate argu- ments supporting it; we've just done this in the previous section and seen that none of the arguments are compelling although Hobbes's argument may be plausible. The second step is to consider arguments that attempt to refute the theory. Accordingly, we look at five arguments against ethical egoism.

The Inconsistent Outcomes Argument

Brian Medlin argues that ethical egoism cannot be true because it fails to meet a necessary condition of morality—namely, being a guide to action. He claims that it would be like advising people to do inconsistent things based on incompatible desires.[7] His argument goes like this:

(1) Moral principles must be universal and categorical.

(2) I must universalize my egoist desire to come out on top over Tom, Dick, and Harry.

(3) But, I must also prescribe Tom's egoist desire to come out on top over Dick, Harry, and me (and so on).

(4) Therefore, I have prescribed incompatible outcomes and have not provided a way of adjudicating conflicts of desire. In effect, I have said nothing.

The proper response to this is that of Jesse Kalin who argues that we can separate our beliefs about ethical situations from our desires.[8] He likens the situation to a competitive sports event in which you believe that your opponent has a right to try to win as much as you, but you desire that you, not he, will in fact win. An even better example is that of the chess game in which you recognize that your opponent ought to move her bishop to prepare for checkmate, but you hope she won't see the move. Belief that A ought to do Y does not commit you to wanting A to do Y.

The Publicity Argument

The publicity argument against ethical egoism states that an egoist cannot publicly advertise his egoistic project without harming that very project. On the one hand, for something to be a moral theory, it seems necessary that its moral principles be publicized. Unless principles are put forth as universal prescriptions that are accessible to the public, they cannot serve as guides to action or as aids in resolving conflicts of interest. But on the other hand, it is not in the egoist's self-interest to publicize them. Egoists would rather that the rest of us be altruists. For example, we might ask why did Rand write books announcing their positions? Was the money that she received from her book by announcing ethical egoism worth the price of letting the cat out of the bag?

Thus, it would be self-defeating for the egoist to argue for her position—and even worse that she should convince others of it. But, it is perfectly possible to have a private morality that does not resolve conflicts of interest. Thus, the egoist should publicly advocate standard principles of traditional morality—so that society doesn't break down—while adhering to a private, nonstandard, solely self-regarding morality. So, if you're willing to pay the price, you can accept the solipsistic-directed norms of egoism.

If the egoist is prepared to pay the price, egoism could be a consistent system that has some limitations. Although the egoist can cooperate with others in limited ways and perhaps even have friends—as long as their interests don't conflict with his—he has to be very careful about preserving his isolation. The egoist can't give advice or argue about his position—not sincerely at least. He must act alone, atomistically or solipsistically in moral isolation, for to announce his adherence to the principle of egoism would be dangerous to his project. He can't teach his children the true morality or justify himself to others or forgive others.

The Paradox of Ethical Egoism

The situation may be even worse than the sophisticated, self-conscious egoist supposes. Could the egoist have friends? If limited friendship is possible, could he or she ever be in love or experience deep friendship? Suppose the egoist discovers that in the pursuit of the happiness goal, deep friendship is in her best interest. Can she become a friend? What is necessary to establish deep friendship? A true friend is one who is not always preoccupied about his or her own interest in the relationship but who forgets about herself altogether, at least sometimes, to serve or enhance the other person's interest. "Love seeks not its own." It is an altruistic disposition, the very opposite of egoism. And, yet we recognize that it is in our self-interest to have friends and loving relations, without which life lacks the highest joy and meaning. Thus, the **paradox of ethical egoism** is that to reach the goal of egoism one must give up egoism and become (to some extent) an altruist, the very antithesis of egoism.

We may once again appeal to a level distinction. On the *highest, reflective* level, I conclude that I want to be happy. But, I also conclude that the best way to find happiness is to have friends and good relations in a community where we all act justly and lovingly. Because having friends and acting justly requires having dispositions to act justly and altruistically, I determine that on a *lower*, or *first order*, level I must live *justly* and *altruistically* rather than *egoistically*.

The Argument from Counterintuitive Consequences

A fourth argument against ethical egoism is that it is an absolute moral system that not only permits egoistic behavior but also demands it. Helping others at one's own expense is not only not required but also morally wrong. Whenever I do not have good evidence that my helping you will end up to my advantage, I must refrain from helping you. If I can save the whole of Europe and Africa from destruction by pressing a button, then as long as there is nothing for me to gain by it, it is wrong for me to press that button. The Good Samaritan was, by this logic, morally wrong in helping the injured victim and not collecting payment for his troubles. It is certainly hard to see why the egoist should be concerned about environmental matters if he or she is profiting from polluting the environment. Suppose, for example, that the egoist gains 40 units of pleasure in producing chemical solvent. This causes pollution that in turn causes others 1,000 units of suffering; the egoist himself, though, experiences only 10 units of suffering. Thus, according to an agent-maximizing calculus, he is morally obligated to produce the polluting chemical.

The Problem of Future Generations

A final problem with ethical egoism is that there is no obligation to preserve scarce natural resources for future generations. "Why should I do anything for posterity?" the egoist asks. "What has posterity ever done for me?" The egoist gains nothing by preserving natural resources for future generations that do not yet exist and thus can give no benefit to the egoist. Garrett Hardin tells the story of how he spent $1 to plant a redwood seedling that would take 2,000 years to reach its full economic value of $14,000. He confesses that, as an "economic man," he was being stupid in planting it, but he did so anyway. "It is most unlikely that any of my direct descendants will get [the value of the tree]. The most I can hope for is that an anonymous posterity will benefit by my act. . . . Why bother?" His answer is an admission of the failure of egoistic and economic reasoning—or of his own rationality. He writes, "I am beginning to suspect that rationality—as we now conceive it—may be insufficient to secure the end we desire, namely, taking care of the interests of posterity."[9]

Consider also the reasoning of an economist at the London School of Economics:

> Suppose that, as a result of using up all the world's resources, human life did come to an end. So what? What is so desirable about an indefinite continuation of the human species, religious conviction apart? It may well be that nearly everybody who is already here on earth would be reluctant to die, and that everybody has an instinctive fear of death. But one must not confuse this with the notion that, in any meaningful sense, generations who are yet unborn can be said to be better off if they are born than if they are not.[10]

This seems a consistent egoist answer. Another economist from MIT puts the matter this way:

> Geological time [has been] made comprehensible to our finite human minds by the statement that the 4.5 billion years of the earth's history [are] equivalent to once around the world in a Supersonic jet. . . . Man got on eight miles before the end, and industrial man got on six feet before the end. . . . Today we are having a debate about the extent to which man ought to maximize the length of time that he is on the airplane.
>
> According to what the scientists think, the sun is gradually expanding and 12 billion years from now the earth will be swallowed up by the sun. This means that our airplane has time to go round three more times. Do we want man to be on it for all three times around the world? Are we interested in man being on for another eight miles? Are we interested in man being on for another six feet? Or are we only interested in man for a fraction of a millimeter—our lifetimes?

> That led me to think: Do I care what happens a thousand years from
> now?...Do I care when man gets off the airplane? I think I basically
> [have come] to the conclusion that I don't care whether man is on the
> airplane for another eight feet, or if man is on the airplane another
> three times around the world.[11]

But most of us do find it intuitively obvious that we have obligations to future
people, even if they cannot reciprocate. If this is so, ethical egoism cannot be a
sufficient ethical theory. It may be part of a larger theory, but it must be supplemented by other theories.

In conclusion, we see that ethical egoism has a number of serious problems. It
cannot consistently publicize itself, nor often argue its case. It tends toward solipsism and the exclusion of many of the deepest human values such as love and deep
friendship. It violates the principle of fairness, and, most of all, it entails an absolute prohibition on altruistic behavior, which we intuitively sense as morally
required (or at least permissible).

EVOLUTION AND ALTRUISM

If sheer unadulterated ethical egoism is an inadequate moral theory, does that
mean we ought to aim at complete altruism, total selflessness for the sake of
others? An interesting place to start answering this question is with the new
field of **sociobiology,** which theorizes that social structures and behavioral patterns, including morality, have a biological base explained by evolutionary
theory.

In the past, linking ethics to evolution meant justifying exploitation.
Nineteenth-century social Darwinism applied the notion of "survival of the
fittest" to virtually all aspects of social life, often leading to the position that
"might makes right": The most powerful force in society is the one that domi-
nates and makes all the rules. This in turn justified imperialistic rule of preindus-
trial societies around the globe. This philosophy lent itself to a promotion of
ruthless egoism: This is nature's law, "nature red in tooth and claw." In more
recent times, though, animal scientists have argued for a more gentle view of
the animal kingdom in which animals often survive by cooperating with other
members of their species—a social behavior that is at least as important as competition. The goal for these animals is not so much survival for them individually
but survival of their genes. Indeed, in his book *The Selfish Gene,* Richard Dawkins
argues that behavior is determined evolutionarily by strategies set to replicate our
genes. This is not done consciously, of course, but by the invisible hand that drives
consciousness. We are essentially gene-perpetuating machines.[12]

Morality—that is, successful morality—can be seen as an evolutionary strategy for gene replication. That is, groups who adopted morality increased their
chances of surviving, and those that didn't eventually died out. Here's a good
example from the animal world. Birds are afflicted with life-endangering parasites.
Because they lack limbs to enable them to pick the parasites off their heads,

they—like much of the animal kingdom—depend on the ritual of mutual grooming. It turns out that nature has evolved two basic types of birds in this regard: those who are disposed to groom anyone and those who refuse to groom anyone but others who present themselves for grooming. The former type of bird Dawkins calls "Suckers" and the latter "Cheaters."

In a geographical area containing harmful parasites and where there are only Suckers or Cheaters, Suckers will do fairly well, but Cheaters will not survive for lack of cooperation. However, in a Sucker population in which a mutant Cheater arises, the Cheater will prosper, and the Cheater-gene type will multiply. As the Suckers are exploited, they will gradually die out. But, if and when they become too few to groom the Cheaters, the Cheaters will start to die off too and eventually become extinct.

Why don't birds all die off, then? Well, somehow nature has come up with a third type, call them "Grudgers." Grudgers groom only those who reciprocate in grooming them. They groom one another and Suckers, but not Cheaters. In fact, once caught, a Cheater is marked forever. There is no forgiveness. It turns out then that unless there are a lot of Suckers around, Cheaters have a hard time of it—harder even than Suckers. However, it is the Grudgers that prosper. Unlike Suckers, they don't waste time messing with unappreciative Cheaters, so they are not exploited and have ample energy to gather food and build better nests for their loved ones.

The point of the bird example is this: Showing reciprocal altruism to others (you scratch my back, I'll scratch yours) is a good strategy for survival. Pure altruism is a failure, as is pure egoism. Elliott Sober and David Sloan Wilson illustrate this point about reciprocal altruism through the system of distributing socially beneficial rewards and punishments. They take the case of the hunter who spends an enormous amount of time hunting at great risk to himself but distributes food to the entire group, hunters and nonhunters alike. This seemingly altruistic, group-enhancing behavior, it turns out, is rewarded by the group:

> It turns out that women think that good hunters are sexy and have more children with them, both in and out of marriage. Good hunters also enjoy a high status among men, which leads to additional benefits. Finally, individuals do not share meat the way Mr. Rogers and Barney and Dinosaur would, out of the goodness of their heart. Refusing to share is a serious breach of etiquette that provokes punishment. In this way sharing merges with taking. These new discoveries make you feel better, because the apparently altruistic behavior of sharing meat that would have been difficult to explain now seems to fit comfortably within the framework of individual selection theory.[13]

So, although hunting might at first sight appear an example of pure altruism, the rule of reciprocity comes into play, rewarding the hunter for his sacrifice and contribution to the group. Sober and Wilson call activities like hunting, which increase the relative fitness of the hunter, primary behavior, and the rewards and punishment that others confer on the hunters, secondary behavior. "By itself, the primary behavior increases the fitness of the group and decreases the relative fitness of the hunters within the group. But the secondary behaviors off-set the hunters' sacrifice and promote altruistic behavior, so that they may be called the amplification of altruism."[14]

This primitive notion of reciprocity seems to be necessary in a world like ours. One good deed deserves another, and similarly, one bad deed deserves another. Reciprocity is the basis of desert—good deeds should be rewarded and bad deeds punished. We are grateful for favors rendered and thereby have an impulse to return the favor; we resent harmful deeds and seek to pay the culprit back in kind ("an eye for an eye, a tooth for a tooth, a life for a life").

What lessons can we learn from sociobiology's account of morality? There is indeed a difference between pure altruism and reciprocal altruism, but, to a degree, we have duties to both of these kinds of altruism. On the one hand, we seem to have a special duty of pure altruism toward those in the close circle of our concern—namely, our family and friends. Our behavior toward them should be as selfless as possible. On the other hand, we have duties to cooperate and reciprocate but no duty to serve those who manipulate us, nor any obvious duty to sacrifice ourselves for people outside our domain of special responsibility. The larger lesson to be drawn is that we should provide moral training so that children grow up to be spontaneously altruistic in a society that rewards such socially useful behavior. In this way, what is legitimate about egoism can be merged with altruism in a manner that produces deep individual flourishing. Through our efforts to instill altruistic behavior in our children, we increasingly expand the circle of our moral concerns, wider and wider, eventually reaching all humanity, and, possibly, the animal kingdom.

CONCLUSION

Martin Luther, the Protestant reformer, once said that humanity is like a man who, when mounting a horse, always falls off on the opposite side, especially when he tries to overcompensate for his previous exaggerations. So it is with ethical egoism. Trying to compensate for an irrational, guilt-ridden, Sucker altruism of the morality of self-effacement, it falls off the horse on the other side, embracing a Cheater's preoccupation with self-exaltation that robs the self of the deepest joys in life. Only the person who mounts properly, avoiding both extremes, is likely to ride the horse of happiness to its goal.

NOTES

1. See Mike Muller, *The Baby Killer* (London: War on Want, 1974); Nestlé's Website, www.babymilk.nestle.com/History/, and www.babymilkaction.org.
2. Quoted from the *Springfield Monitor*, in F. C. Sharp, *Ethics* (Appleton-Century, 1928), p. 28.

3. Joel Feinberg, "Psychological Egoism," in *Reason and Responsibility* (Wadsworth, 1985).

4. Thomas Hobbes, *Leviathan* (London: Dutton, 1931), Ch. 13.

5. See Gregory S. Kavka, *Hobbesian Moral and Political Theory* (Princeton, N.J.: Princeton University Press, 1986), pp. 64–82.

6. Ayn Rand, *The Virtue of Selfishness* (New American Library, 1964), pp. vii, 27–32, 80 ff. All quoted material in this section is from this work.

7. Brian Medlin, "Ultimate Principles and Ethical Egoism," *Australasian Journal of Philosophy* (1957): 111–118; reprinted in *Ethical Theory: Classical and Contemporary Issues,* ed. Louis Pojman (Belmont, Calif.: Wadsworth, 2007), pp. 81–85.

8. Jesse Kalin, "In Defense of Egoism," in *Morality and Rational Self-Interest,* ed. David Gauthier (Englewood Cliffs, N.J.: Prentice Hall, 1970).

9. Garrett Hardin, "Who Cares for Posterity," in *The Limits of Altruism* (Bloomington: Indiana University Press, 1977).

10. Quoted in Robert Heilbroner, "What Has Posterity Ever Done for Me?" *New York Times Magazine,* January 19, 1975.

11. Ibid.

12. Richard Dawkins, *The Selfish Gene* (Oxford University Press, 1976), Ch. 10.

13. Elliott Sober and David Sloan Wilson, *Unto Others: The Evolution and Psychology of Unselfish Behavior* (Harvard University Press, 1998), pp. 142–143.

14. Ibid.

FOR FURTHER REFLECTION

1. Evaluate whether this statement is true or false: "Everyone is an egoist, for everyone always tries to do what will bring himself or herself satisfaction."

2. Chapter 1 began with the story of the killing of Kitty Genovese. Review that story, and discuss how an ethical egoist would respond to the plight of Kitty Genovese. Would egoists admit that they have a duty to come to the aid of Genovese?

3. Discuss the four arguments in favor of ethical egoism. Which of these is the most compelling, and why?

4. Discuss the five arguments against ethical egoism. Which of these is the most compelling, and why?

5. Egoists often argue that most moral systems fail to recognize adequately that morality should be in our best interest. In this light, ethical egoism could be seen as an attempt to compensate for the inadequacies of other ethical views that emphasize doing duty for duty's sake or for the sake of others. Explain whether this argument has merit.

6. The central ethical message of sociobiology is that morality is grounded upon the survival-enhancing principle of reciprocity. Is there anything more to morality than this?

FOR FURTHER READING

Dugatkin, Lee Alan. *The Altruism Equation: Seven Scientists Search for the Origins of Goodness.* Princeton, N.J.: Princeton University Press, 2006.

Gauthier, David, ed. *Morality and Rational Self-Interest.* Englewood Cliffs, N.J.: Prentice Hall, 1970.

Gauthier, David. *Morals by Agreement.* Oxford, Engl.: Clarendon Press, 1986.

Joyce, Richard. *The Evolution of Morality.* Cambridge, Mass.: MIT Press, 2006.

Nagel, Thomas. *The Possibility of Altruism.* Oxford, Engl.: Clarendon Press, 1970.

Peikoff, Lonard. *Objectivism: The Philosophy of Ayn Rand.* New York: Dutton, 1991.

Singer, Peter. *The Expanding Circle: Ethics and Sociobiology.* Oxford, Engl.: Oxford University Press, 1983.

Singer, Peter. *A Darwinian Left: Politics, Evolution, and Cooperation.* New Haven, Conn.: Yale University Press, 2000.

Wilson, Edward O. *Sociobiology: The New Synthesis.* Cambridge, Mass.: Harvard University Press, 1976.

7

✳

Utilitarianism

> That action is best, which procures the greatest happiness
> for the greatest numbers.
> FRANCIS HUTCHESON, *AN INQUIRY CONCERNING MORAL GOOD AND EVIL*

Suppose you are on an island with a dying millionaire. With his final words, he begs you for one final favor: "I've dedicated my whole life to baseball and for fifty years have gotten endless pleasure rooting for the New York Yankees. Now that I am dying, I want to give all my assets, $2 million, to the Yankees." Pointing to a box containing money in large bills, he continues: "Would you take this money back to New York and give it to the Yankees' owner so that he can buy better players?" You agree to carry out his wish, at which point a huge smile of relief and gratitude breaks out on his face as he expires in your arms. After traveling to New York, you see a newspaper advertisement placed by your favorite charity, World Hunger Relief Organization (whose integrity you do not doubt), pleading for $2 million to be used to save 100,000 people dying of starvation in Africa. Not only will the $2 million save their lives, but it will also purchase equipment and the kinds of fertilizers necessary to build a sustainable economy. You decide to reconsider your promise to the dying Yankee fan, in light of this advertisement.

What is the right thing to do in this case? Consider some traditional moral principles and see if they help us come to a decision. One principle often given to guide action is "Let your conscience be your guide." I recall this principle with fondness, for it was the one my father taught me at an early age, and it still echoes in my mind. But does it help here? No, since conscience is primarily a function of upbringing. People's consciences speak to them in different ways according to how they were brought up. Depending on upbringing, some people feel no qualms about committing violent acts, whereas others feel the torments of conscience over stepping on a gnat. Suppose your conscience tells you to give the money to the Yankees and my conscience tells me to give the money to the World Hunger Relief Organization. How can we even discuss the matter? If conscience is the end of it, we're left mute.

Another principle urged on us is "Do whatever is most loving"; Jesus in particular set forth the principle "Love your neighbor as yourself." Love is surely a wonderful value. It is a more wholesome attitude than hate, and we should overcome feelings of hate if only for our own psychological health. But is love enough to guide our actions when there is a conflict of interest? "Love is blind," it has been said, "but reason, like marriage, is an eye-opener." Whom should I love in the case of the disbursement of the millionaire's money—the millionaire or the starving people? It's not clear how love alone will settle anything. In fact, it is not obvious that we must always do what is most loving. Should we always treat our enemies in loving ways? Or is it morally permissible to feel hate for those who have purposely and unjustly harmed us, our loved ones, or other innocent people? Should the survivors of Auschwitz love Adolph Hitler? Love alone does not solve difficult moral issues.

A third principle often given to guide our moral actions is the Golden Rule: "Do to others as you would have them do to you." This, too, is a noble rule of thumb, one that works in simple, commonsense situations. But it has problems. First, it cannot be taken literally. Suppose I love to hear loud heavy-metal music. Since I would want you to play it loudly for me, I reason that I should play it loudly for you—even though I know that you hate the stuff. Thus, the rule must be modified: "Do to others as you would have them do to you if you were in their shoes." However, this still has problems. If I were the assassin of Robert Kennedy, I'd want to be released from the penitentiary; but it's not clear that he should be released. If I put myself in the place of a sex-starved individual, I might want to have sex with the next available person; but it's not obvious that I (or anyone else) must comply with that wish. Likewise, the Golden Rule doesn't tell me to whom to give the millionaire's money.

Conscience, love, and the Golden Rule are all worthy rules of thumb to help us through life. They work for most of us, most of the time, in ordinary moral situations. But, in more complicated cases, especially when there are legitimate conflicts of interests, they are limited.

A more promising strategy for solving dilemmas is that of following definite moral rules. Suppose you decided to give the millionaire's money to the Yankees to keep your promise or because to do otherwise would be stealing. The principle you followed would be "Always keep your promise." Principles are important in life.

All learning involves understanding a set of rules; as R. M. Hare says, "Without principles we could not learn anything whatever from our elders. . . . Every generation would have to start from scratch and teach itself."[1] If you decided to act on the principle of keeping promises, then you adhered to a type of moral theory called **deontology.** In Chapter 1, we saw that deontological systems maintain that the center of value is the act or kind of act; certain features in the act itself have intrinsic value. For example, a deontologist would see something intrinsically wrong in the very act of lying.

If, on the other hand, you decided to give the money to the World Hunger Relief Organization to save an enormous number of lives and restore economic solvency to the region, you sided with a type of theory called **teleological ethics.** Sometimes, it is referred to as *consequentialist ethics.* We also saw in Chapter 1 that the center of value here is the outcome or consequences of the act. For example, a teleologist would judge whether lying was morally right or wrong by the consequences it produced.

We have already examined one type of teleological ethics: *ethical egoism,* the view that the act that produces the most amount of good for the agent is the right act. Egoism is teleological ethics narrowed to the agent himself or herself. In this chapter, we will consider the dominant version of teleological ethics— *utilitarianism.* Unlike ethical egoism, utilitarianism is a universal teleological system. It calls for the maximization of goodness in society—that is, the greatest goodness for the greatest number—and not merely the good of the agent.

CLASSIC UTILITARIANISM

In our normal lives we use utilitarian reasoning all the time; I might give money to charity when seeing that it would do more good to needy people than it would for me. In time of war, I might join the military and risk dying because I see that society's needs at that time are greater than my own. One of the earliest examples of utilitarian reasoning is found in Sophocles' *Antigone* (ca. 440 BCE) in which we find King Creon faced with the tragic task of sacrificing his beloved niece, Antigone, who has violated the law by performing funeral rites over her brother, Polynices. Creon judges that it is necessary to sacrifice one person rather than expose his society to the dangers of rebelliousness— regardless of that person's innocence or social standing:

> And whoever places a friend above the good of his own country, I have no use for him. . . . I could never stand by silent, watching destruction march against our city, putting safety to rout, nor could I ever make that man a friend of mine who menaces our country. Remember this: our country is our safety.[2]

As a formal ethical theory, the seeds of utilitarianism were sewn by the ancient Greek philosopher Epicurus (342–270 BCE) who stated that "pleasure is the goal that nature has ordained for us; it is also the standard by which we judge everything good." According to this view, rightness and wrongness are determined by pleasure or pain that something produces. Epicurus's theory focused largely on the individual's personal experience of pleasure and pain, and to that extent he advocated a version of ethical egoism. Nevertheless, Epicurus inspired a series of eighteenth-century philosophers who emphasized the notion of general happiness—that is, the pleasing consequences of actions that impact others and not just the individual. Francis Hutcheson (1694–1746) stated that "that action is best, which procures the greatest happiness for the greatest numbers." David Hume (1711–1776) introduced the term *utility* to describe the pleasing consequences of actions as they impact people.

The classical expressions of utilitarianism, though, appear in the writings of two English philosophers and social reformers Jeremy Bentham (1748–1832) and John Stuart Mill (1806–1873). They were the nonreligious ancestors of the twentieth-century secular humanists, optimistic about human nature and our ability to solve our problems without recourse to God. Engaged in a struggle for legal as well as moral reform, they were impatient with the rule-bound character of law and morality in eighteenth- and nineteenth-century Great Britain and tried to make the law serve human needs and interests.

Jeremy Bentham

There are two main features of utilitarianism, both of which Bentham articulated: the consequentialist principle (or its teleological aspect) and the utility principle (or its hedonic aspect). The *consequentialist principle* states that the rightness or wrongness of an act is determined by the goodness or badness of the results that flow from it. It is the end, not the means, that counts; the end justifies the means. The *utility,* or *hedonist, principle* states that the only thing that is good in itself is some specific type of state (for example, pleasure, happiness, welfare). Hedonistic utilitarianism views pleasure as the sole good and pain as the only evil. To quote Bentham, "Nature has placed mankind under the governance of two sovereign masters, pain and pleasure. It is for them alone to point out what we ought to do, as well as what we shall do."[3] An act is right if it either brings about more pleasure than pain or prevents pain, and an act is wrong if it either brings about more pain than pleasure or prevents pleasure from occurring.

Bentham invented a scheme for measuring pleasure and pain that he called the **hedonic calculus:** The quantitative score for any pleasure or pain experience is obtained by summing the seven aspects of a pleasurable or painful experience: its intensity, duration, certainty, nearness, fruitfulness, purity, and extent. Adding up the amounts of pleasure and pain for each possible act and then comparing the scores would enable us to decide which act to perform. With regard to our example of deciding between giving the dying man's money to the Yankees or to the African famine victims, we would add up the likely pleasures to all involved, for all seven qualities. If we found that giving the money to the famine victims would cause at least 3 million *hedons* (units of happiness) but that giving the money to the Yankees would cause less than 1,000 hedons, we would have an obligation to give the money to the famine victims.

There is something appealing about Bentham's utilitarianism. It is simple in that there is only one principle to apply: Maximize pleasure and minimize suffering. It is commonsensical in that we think that morality really is about reducing suffering and promoting benevolence. It is scientific: Simply make quantitative measurements and apply the principle impartially, giving no special treatment to ourselves or to anyone else because of race, gender, personal relationship, or religion.

However, Bentham's philosophy may be too simplistic in one way and too complicated in another. It may be too simplistic in that there are values other than pleasure (as we saw in Chapter 6), and it seems too complicated in its artificial hedonic calculus. The calculus is encumbered with too many variables and has problems assigning scores to the variables. For instance, what score do we give a cool drink on a hot day or a warm shower on a cool day? How do we compare a 5-year-old's delight over a new toy with a 30-year-old's delight with a new lover? Can we take your second car from you and give it to Beggar Bob, who does not own a car and would enjoy it more than you? And if it is simply the overall benefits of pleasure that we are measuring, then if Jack or Jill would be "happier" in the Pleasure Machine or the Happiness Machine or on drugs than in the real world, would we not have an obligation to ensure that these conditions obtain? Because of such considerations, Bentham's version of utilitarianism was, even in his own day, referred to as the "pig philosophy" because a pig enjoying his life would constitute a higher moral state than a slightly dissatisfied Socrates.

John Stuart Mill

It was to meet these sorts of objections and save utilitarianism from the charge of being a pig philosophy that Bentham's successor, John Stuart Mill, sought to distinguish happiness from mere sensual pleasure. His version of the theory is often called **eudaimonistic utilitarianism** (from the Greek *eudaimonia,* meaning "happiness"). He defines happiness in terms of certain types of higher-order pleasures or satisfactions such as intellectual, aesthetic, and social enjoyments, as well as in terms of minimal suffering. That is, there are two types of pleasures. The lower, or elementary, include eating, drinking, sexuality, resting, and sensuous titillation. The higher include high culture, scientific knowledge, intellectuality, and creativity. Although the lower pleasures are more intensely gratifying, they also lead to pain when overindulged in. The higher pleasures tend to be more long term, continuous, and gradual.

Mill argued that the higher, or more refined, pleasures are superior to the lower ones: "A being of higher faculties requires more to make him happy, is capable probably of more acute suffering, and certainly accessible to it at more points, than one of an inferior type," but still he is qualitatively better off than the person without these higher faculties. "It is better to be a human being dissatisfied than a pig satisfied; better to be Socrates dissatisfied than a fool satisfied."[4]

Humans are the kind of creatures who require more to be truly happy. They want the lower pleasures, but they also want deep friendship, intellectual ability, culture, the ability to create and appreciate art, knowledge, and wisdom.

But one may object, "How do we know that it really is better to have these higher pleasures?" Here, Mill imagines a panel of experts and says that of those who have had a wide experience of pleasures of both kinds almost all give a decided preference to the higher type. Because Mill was an *empiricist*—one who believed that all knowledge and justified belief was based in experience—he had no recourse but to rely on the composite consensus of human history. By this view, people who experience both rock music and classical music will, if they appreciate both, prefer Bach and Beethoven to the Rolling Stones or the Dancing Demons. That is, we generally move up from appreciating simple things (for example, nursery rhymes) to more complex and intricate things (for example, poetry that requires great talent) rather than the other way around.

Mill has been criticized for not giving a better reply—for being an elitist and for unduly favoring the intellectual over the sensual. But he has a point. Don't we generally agree, if we have experienced both the lower and the higher types of pleasure, that even though a full life would include both, a life with only the for-mer is inadequate for human beings? Isn't it better to be Socrates dissatisfied than the pig satisfied—and better still to be Socrates satisfied?

The point is not merely that humans wouldn't be satisfied with what satisfies a pig but that somehow the quality of the higher pleasures is *better*. But what does it mean to speak of better pleasure? The formula he comes up with is this:

> Happiness . . . [is] not a life of rapture; but moments of such, in an exis-tence made up of few and transitory pains, many and various pleasures, with a decided predominance of the active over the passive, and having as the foundation of the whole, not to expect more from life than it is capa-ble of bestowing.[5]

Mill is clearly pushing the boundaries of the concept of "pleasure" by empha-sizing higher qualities such as knowledge, intelligence, freedom, friendship, love, and health. In fact, one might even say that his litmus test for happiness really has little to do with actual pleasure and more to do with a nonhedonic cultivated state of mind.

ACT- AND RULE-UTILITARIANISM

There are two classical types of utilitarianism: act- and rule-utilitarianism. In applying the principle of utility, act-utilitarians, such as Bentham, say that ideally we ought to apply the principle to all of the alternatives open to us at any given moment. We may define act-utilitarianism in this way:

Act-utilitarianism: An act is right if and only if it results in as much good as any available alternative.

One practical problem with act–utilitarianism is that we cannot do the necessary calculations to determine which act is the correct one in each case, for often we must act spontaneously and quickly. So rules of thumb are of practical importance—for example, "In general, don't lie," and "Generally, keep your promises." However, the right act is still that alternative that results in the most utility.

A second problem with act-utilitarianism is that it seems to fly in the face of fundamental intuitions about minimally correct behavior. Consider Richard Brandt's criticism of act-utilitarianism:

> It implies that if you have employed a boy to mow your lawn and he has finished the job and asks for his pay, you should pay him what you promised only if you cannot find a better use for your money. It implies that when you bring home your monthly paycheck you should use it to support your family and yourself only if it cannot be used more effectively to supply the needs of others. It implies that if your father is ill and has no prospect of good in his life, and maintaining him is a drain on the energy and enjoyments of others, then, if you can end his life without provoking any public scandal or setting a bad example, it is your positive duty to take matters into your own hands and bring his life to a close.[6]

The alternative to act-utlitarianism is a view called rule-utilitarianism—elements of which we find in Mill's theory. Most generally, the position is this:

> **Rule-utilitarianism:** An act is right if and only if it is required by a rule that is itself a member of a set of rules whose acceptance would lead to greater utility for society than any available alternative.

Human beings are rule-following creatures. We learn by adhering to the rules of a given subject, whether it is speaking a language, driving a car, dancing, writing an essay, rock climbing, or cooking. We want to have a set of action-guiding rules by which to live. The act-utilitarian rule, to do the act that maximizes utility, is too general for most purposes. Often, we don't have time to decide whether lying will produce more utility than truth telling, so we need a more specific rule prescribing truthfulness that passes the test of rational scrutiny. Rule-utilitarianism asserts that the best chance of maximizing utility is by following the *set of rules* most likely to give us our desired results. Because morality is a social and public institution, we need to coordinate our actions with others so that we can have reliable expectations about other people's behavior.

For the most sophisticated versions of rule-utilitarianism, three levels of rules will guide actions. On the lowest level is a set of utility-maximizing rules of thumb, such as "Don't lie" and "Don't cause harm," that should always be followed unless there is a conflict between them. If these first-order rules conflict, then a second-order set of conflict-resolving rules should be consulted, such as "It's more important to avoid causing serious harm than to tell the truth." At the top of the hierarchy is a third-order rule sometimes called the *remainder rule,* which is the principle of act-utilitarianism: When no other rule applies, simply do what your best judgment deems to be the act that will maximize utility.

An illustration of this might be the following: Two of our first-order rules might be "Keep your promises" and "Help those in need when you are not seriously inconvenienced in doing so." Suppose you promised to meet your teacher at 3 p.m. in his office. On your way there, you come upon an accident victim stranded by the wayside who desperately needs help. It doesn't take you long to decide to break the appointment with your teacher because it seems obvious in this case that the rule to help others overrides the rule to keep promises. We might say that there is a second-order rule prescribing that the first-order rule of helping people in need when you are not seriously inconvenienced in doing so overrides the rule to keep promises. However, there may be some situation where no obvious rule of thumb applies. Say you have $50 that you don't really need now. How should you use this money? Put it into your savings account? Give it to your favorite charity? Use it to throw a party? Here and only here, on the third level, the general act-utility principle applies without any other primary rule; that is, do what in your best judgment will do the most good.

Debates between act- and rule-utilitarians continue today. Kai Nielsen, a staunch act-utilitarian, attacks what he calls *moral conservatism*, which is any normative ethical theory that maintains that there is a privileged moral principle, or cluster of moral principles, prescribing determinate actions that it would always be wrong not to act in accordance with no matter what the consequences. For Nielsen, no rules are sacred; differing situations call forth different actions, and potentially any rule could be overridden.

Nielsen argues further that we are responsible for the consequences of not only the actions that we perform but also the nonactions that we fail to perform. He calls this "negative responsibility." To illustrate, suppose you are the driver of a trolley car and suddenly discover that your brakes have failed. You are just about to run over five workers on the track ahead of you. However, if you act quickly, you can turn the trolley onto a sidetrack where only one man is working. What should you do? One who makes a strong distinction between *allowing* versus *doing* evil would argue that you should do nothing and merely allow the trolley to kill the five workers. But one who denies that this is an absolute distinction would prescribe that you do something positive to minimize evil. Negative responsibility means that you are going to be responsible for someone's death in either case. Doing the right thing, the utilitarian urges, means minimizing the amount of evil. So you should actively cause the one death to save the other five lives.[7] Critics of utilitarianism contend either that negative responsibility is not a strict duty or that it can be worked into other systems besides utilitarianism.

The Strengths of Utilitarianism

Utilitarianism has three very positive features. The first attraction or strength is that it is a single principle, an absolute system with a potential answer for every situation: Do what will promote the most utility! It's good to have a simple, action-guiding principle that is applicable to every occasion—even if it may be difficult to apply (life's not simple).

Its second strength is that utilitarianism seems to get to the substance of morality. It is not merely a formal system that simply sets forth broad guidelines for choosing principles but offers no principles—such as the guideline "Do whatever you can universalize." Rather it has a material core: We should promote human (and possibly animal) flourishing and reduce suffering. The first virtue gives us a clear decision procedure in arriving at our answer about what to do. The second virtue appeals to our sense that morality is made for people and that morality is not so much about rules as about helping people and alleviating the suffering in the world.

As such, utilitarianism seems commonsensical. For instance, it gives us clear and reasonable guidance in dealing with the Kitty Genovese case discussed in Chapter 1: We should call the police or do what is necessary to help her, as long as helping her does not create more disutility than leaving her alone. And, in the case of deciding what to do with the $2 million of the dead millionaire, something in us says that it is absurd to keep a promise to a dead person when it means allowing hundreds of thousands of famine victims to die. Far more good can be accomplished by helping the needy than by giving the money to the Yankees!

A third strength of utilitarianism is that it is particularly well suited to address the **problem of posterity**—namely, why we should preserve scarce natural resources for the betterment of future generations of humans that do not yet exist. Expressed rhetorically, the question is "Why should I care about posterity; what has posterity ever done for me?" In Chapter 6, we saw that the theory of ethical egoism failed to give us an adequate answer to this problem. That is, the egoist gains nothing by preserving natural resources for future generations that do not yet exist and thus can give no benefit to the egoist. However, utilitarians have one overriding duty: to maximize general happiness. As long as the quality of life of future people promises to be positive, we have an obligation to continue human existence, to produce human beings, and to take whatever actions are necessary to ensure that their quality of life is not only positive but high.

It does not matter that we cannot identify these future people. We may look upon them as mere abstract placeholders for utility and aim at maximizing utility. Derek Parfit explains this using the following utilitarian principle: "It is bad if those who live are worse off than those who might have lived." He illustrates his principle this way. Suppose our generation has the choice between two energy policies: the "Safe Energy Policy" and the "Risky Energy Policy."[8] The Risky Policy promises to be safe for us but is likely to create serious problems for a future generation, say, 200 years from now. The Safe Policy won't be as beneficial to us but promises to be stable and safe for posterity—those living 200 years from now and beyond. We must choose and we are responsible for the choice that we make. If we choose the Risky Policy, we impose harms on our descendants, even if they don't now exist. In a sense, we are responsible for the people who will live because our policy decisions will generate different causal chains, resulting in different people being born. But more important, we are responsible for their quality of life because we could have caused human lives to have been better off than they are.

What are our obligations to future people? If utilitarians are correct, we have an obligation to leave posterity to as good a world as we can. This would mean radically simplifying our lifestyles so that we use no more resources than are necessary, keeping as much top soil intact as possible, protecting endangered species, reducing our carbon dioxide emissions, preserving the wilderness, and minimizing our overall deleterious impact on the environment in general while using technology wisely.

CRITICISM OF UTILITARIANISM

Utilitarianism has been around for several centuries, but so too have been its critics, and we need to address a series of standard objections to utilitarianism before we can give it a "philosophically clean bill of health."

Problems with Formulating Utilitarianism

The first set of problems occurs in the very formulation of utilitarianism: "The greatest happiness for the greatest number." Notice that we have two "greatest" things in this formula: "happiness" and "number." Whenever we have two variables, we invite problems of determining which of the variables to rank first when they seem to conflict. To see this point, consider the following example: I am offering a $1,000 prize to the person who runs the longest distance in the shortest amount of time. Three people participate: Joe runs 5 miles in 31 minutes, John runs 7 miles in 50 minutes, and Jack runs 1 mile in 6 minutes. Who should get the prize? John has fulfilled one part of the requirement (run the longest distance), but Jack has fulfilled the other requirement (run the shortest amount of time).

This is precisely the problem with utilitarianism. On the one hand, we might concern ourselves with spreading happiness around so that the greatest number obtain it (in which case, we should get busy and procreate a larger population). On the other hand, we might be concerned that the greatest possible amount of happiness obtains in society (in which case, we might be tempted to allow some people to become far happier than others, as long as their increase offsets the losers' diminished happiness). So should we worry more about total happiness or about highest average?

Utilitarians also need to be clear about specifically whose happiness we are talking about: all beings that experience pleasure and pain, or all human beings, or all rational beings. One criterion might exclude mentally deficient human beings, and another might include animals. Finally, utilitarians need to indicate how we measure happiness and make interpersonal comparisons between the happiness of different people. We've seen Mill's efforts to address this problem with his notion of higher pleasures; we've also seen the additional complications that his solution creates.

None of the above problems defeat utilitarianism as a workable theory, but they do place a heavy burden on utilitarians to clarify the objectives of their theory.

The Comparative Consequences Objection

Another crucial problem with utilitarianism is that it seems to require a superhuman ability to look into the future and survey a mind-boggling array of consequences of actions. Of course, we normally do not know the long-term consequences of our actions because life is too complex and the consequences go on into the indefinite future. One action causes one state of affairs, which in turn causes another state of affairs, indefinitely, so that calculation becomes impossible. Recall the nursery rhyme:

> For want of a nail, the shoe was lost;
> For want of a shoe, the horse was lost;
> For want of a horse, the rider was lost;
> For want of a rider, the battle was lost;
> For want of a battle, the kingdom was lost;
> And all for the want of a horseshoe nail.

Poor, unfortunate blacksmith; what utilitarian guilt he must bear all the rest of his days!

But it is ridiculous to blame the loss of one's kingdom on the poor, unsuccessful blacksmith, and utilitarians are not so foolish as to hold him responsible for the bad situation. Instead, following C. I. Lewis, utilitarians distinguish two kinds of consequences: (1) actual consequences of an act and (2) consequences that could reasonably have been expected to occur.[9] Based on these two kinds of consequences, there are two corresponding right actions. An act is *absolutely* right if it has the best actual consequences (as per consequence 1). An act is *objectively* right if it is reasonable to expect that it will have the best consequences (as per consequence 2).

Only *objective rightness,* that based on reasonable expectations, is central here. *Actual rightness,* based on actual consequences, is irrelevant because this can only be determined after an action is performed and we sit back and watch the series of actual consequences unfold. But when an agent is trying to determine in advance how to act, the most that she can do is to use the best information available and do what a reasonable person would expect to produce the best overall results. Suppose, for example, that while Hitler's grandmother was carrying little Adolph up the stairs to her home, she slipped and had to choose between either dropping infant Adolph and allowing him to be fatally injured or breaking her arm. According to the formula just given, it would have been *absolutely* right for her to let him be killed because history would have turned out better. But, it would not have been within her power to know that. She did what any reasonable person would do—she saved the baby's life at the risk of injury to herself. She did what was *objectively* right. The utilitarian theory holds that by generally doing what reason judges to be the best act based on likely consequences, we will, in general, actually promote the best consequences.

The Consistency Objection to Rule-Utilitarianism

An often-debated question about rule-utilitarianism is whether, when pushed to its logical limits, it must either become a deontological system or transform itself into act-utilitarianism. As such, it is an inconsistent theory that offers no truly independent standard for making moral judgments. Briefly, the argument goes like this: Imagine that following the set of general rules of a rule-utilitarian system yields 100 hedons (positive utility units). We could always find a case where breaking the general rule would result in additional hedons without decreasing the sum of the whole. So, for example, we could imagine a situation in which breaking the general rule "Never lie" to spare someone's feelings would create more utility (for example, 102 hedons) than keeping the rule would. It would seem that we could always improve on any version of rule-utilitarianism by breaking the set of rules whenever we judge that by doing so we could produce even more utility than by following the set.

To illustrate more fully, consider this example. Suppose a disreputable former convict Charley has been convicted of a serious crime and sentenced to a severe punishment. You, the presiding judge, have just obtained fresh evidence that if brought into court would exonerate Charley of the crime. But you also have evidence, not admissible in court, that Charley is guilty of an equally heinous crime for which he has not been indicted. The evidence suggests that Charley is a dangerous man who should not be on the streets of our city. What should you do? An act-utilitarian would no doubt suppress the new evidence in favor of protecting the public from a criminal. A rule-utilitarian has a tougher time making the decision. On the one hand, he has the rule "Do not permit innocent people to suffer for crimes they didn't commit." On the other hand, he has the rule "Protect the public from unnecessary harm." The rule-utilitarian may decide the matter by using the *remainder principle,* which yields the same result as that of the act-utilitarian. This seems, however, to give us a counterintuitive result. Why not just be an act-utilitarian and forgo the middle steps if that is what we are destined to reach anyway?

There may be other ways for the rule-utilitarian to go. He or she may opt for a different remainder principle, one that appeals to our deepest intuitions: "Whenever two rules conflict, choose the one that fits your deepest moral intuition." Thus, the judge may very well decide to reveal the evidence exonerating Charley, holding to the rule not to allow people to suffer for crimes for which there is insufficient evidence to convict them. The rule-utilitarian argues that, in the long run, a *rule* that protects such legally innocent but morally culpable, people will produce more utility than following an act-utilitarian principle. If we accept the second intuitionist version of the remainder principle, we may be accused of being deontological intuitionists and not utilitarians at all.

How might we respond to this criticism of inconsistency? It may be more accurate to see moral philosophy as complex and multidimensional so that both striving for the goal of utility and the method of consulting our intuitions are part of moral deliberation and action. Thus, even if rule-utilitarianism involves consulting moral intuitions, both of these elements may be intertwined and equally legitimate parts of moral reasoning. What at first appears to be a problem of consistency is really just an indicator of the multilayered nature of morality.

The No-Rest Objection

According to utilitarianism, one should always do that act that promises to promote the most utility. But there is usually an infinite set of possible acts to choose from, and even if I can be excused from considering all of them, I can be fairly sure that there is often a preferable act that I could be doing. For example, when I am about to go to the cinema with a friend, I should ask myself if helping the homeless in my community wouldn't promote more utility. When I am about to go to sleep, I should ask myself whether I could at that moment be doing something to help save the ozone layer. And, why not simply give all my assets (beyond what is absolutely necessary to keep me alive) to the poor to promote utility? Following utilitarianism, I should get little or no rest, and, certainly, I have no right to enjoy life when by sacrificing I can make others happier. Peter Singer actually advocates an act-utilitarian position similar to this. According to Singer, middle-class people have a duty to contribute to poor people (especially in undeveloped countries) more than one-third of their income, and all of us have a duty to contribute every penny above $30,000 we possess until we are only marginally better off than the worst-off people on earth.

The problem with approaches like Singer's is that this makes morality too demanding, creates a disincentive to work, and fails to account for different levels of obligation. Thus, utilitarianism must be a false doctrine. But rule-utilitarians have a response to this no-rest objection: A rule prescribing rest and entertainment is actually the kind of rule that would have a place in a utility-maximizing set of rules. The agent should aim at maximizing his or her own happiness as well as other people's happiness. For the same reason, it is best not to worry much about the needs of those not in our primary circle. Although we should be concerned about the needs of poor people, it actually would promote disutility for the average person to become preoccupied with these concerns. Singer represents a radical act-utilitarian position that fails to give adequate attention to the rules that promote human flourishing, such as the right to own property, educate one's children, and improve one's quality of life, all of which probably costs more than $30,000 per year in many parts of North America. However, the utilitarian would remind us, we can surely do a lot more for suffering humanity than we now are doing—especially if we join together and act cooperatively. And we can simplify our lives, cutting back on unnecessary consumption, while improving our overall quality.

The Publicity Objection

It is usually thought that moral principles must be known to all so that all may freely obey the principles. But utilitarians usually hesitate to recommend that everyone act as a utilitarian, especially an act-utilitarian, because it takes a great deal of deliberation to work out the likely consequences of alternative courses of action. It would be better if most people acted simply as deontologists.[10] Thus, utilitarianism seems to contradict our requirement of publicity.

There are two responses to this objection. First, at best this objection only works against act-utilitarianism, which at least in theory advocates sitting down and calculating the good and bad consequences of each action that we plan to perform. Rule-utilitarianism, by contrast, does not focus on the consequences of particular actions but on the set of rules that are likely to bring about the most good. These rules indeed are publicized by rule-utilitarians.

A second response is one that act-utilitarians themselves might offer: The objection shows a bias only toward publicity (or even democracy). It may well be that publicity is only a rule of thumb to be overridden whenever there is good reason to believe that we can obtain more utility by not publicizing act-utilitarian ideas.

However, this response places an unacceptably low value on the benefits of publicity. Since we need to coordinate our actions with other people, moral rules must be publicly announced, typically through legal statutes. I may profit from cutting across the grass to save a few minutes in getting to class, but I also value a beautiful green lawn. We need public rules to ensure the healthy state of the lawn. So we agree on a rule to prohibit walking on the grass—even when it may have a utility function. There are many activities that may bring about individual utility advancement or even communal good, which if done regularly would be disastrous, such as cutting down trees to build houses or make newspapers or paper for books, valuable as it is. So we regulate the lumber industry so that every tree cut down is replaced with a new one and large forests are kept intact. So moral rules must be publicly advertised, often made into laws, and enforced. In short, while the publicity objection does not affect rule-utilitarianism, it appears to be a serious obstacle to act-utilitarianism.

The Relativism Objection

Sometimes people accuse rule-utilitarianism of being relativistic because it seems to endorse different rules in different societies. In one society, it may uphold polygamy, whereas in our society it defends monogamy. In a desert society, it upholds a rule "Don't waste water," whereas in a community where water is plentiful no such rule exists. But this is not really conventional relativism because the rule is not made valid by the community's choosing it but by the actual situation. In the first case, it is made valid by an imbalance in the ratio of women to men and, in the second case, by the environmental factors concerning the availability of water. Situationalism is different from relativism and consistent with objectivism because it really has to do with the application of moral principles—in this case, the utility principle.

But there is a more serious worry about rule-utilitarianism's tendency toward relativism—namely, that it might become so plastic that it justifies any moral rule. Asked why we support benevolence as a moral rule, it seems too easy to respond, "Well, this principle will likely contribute to the greater utility in the long run." The fear is that the act-utilitarian could give the same answer to rules that we consider malevolent, such as torture. Shifting conceptions of general happiness will generate shifting moral rules.

How might the rule-utilitarian respond to this? David Hume, an early defender of utilitarian moral reasoning, argued that human nature forces consistency in our moral assessments. Specifically, he argues, there are "universal principles of the human frame" that regulate what we find to be agreeable or disagreeable in moral matters. Benevolence, for example, is one such type of conduct that we naturally find agreeable.[11] Following Hume's lead, the rule-utilitarian might ground the key components of happiness in our common human psychological makeup rather than the result of fluctuating personal whims. This would give utilitarianism a more objective foundation and thus make it less susceptible to the charge of relativism.

CRITICISM OF THE ENDS JUSTIFYING IMMORAL MEANS

Chief among the criticisms of utilitarianism is that utilitarian ends might justify immoral means. There are many dastardly things that we can do in the name of maximizing general happiness: deceit, torture, slavery, even killing off ethnic minorities. As long as the larger populous benefits, these actions might be justified. The general problem can be laid out in this argument:

(1) If a moral theory justifies actions that we universally deem impermissible, then that moral theory must be rejected.

(2) Utilitarianism justifies actions that we universally deem impermissible.

(3) Therefore, utilitarianism must be rejected.

Let's look at several versions of this argument.

The Lying Objection

William D. Ross has argued that utilitarianism is to be rejected because it leads to the counterintuitive endorsement of lying when it serves the greater good. Consider two acts, A and B, that will both result in 100 hedons (units of pleasure of utility). The only difference is that A involves telling a lie and B involves telling the truth. The utilitarian must maintain that the two acts are of equal value. But this seems implausible; truth seems to be an intrinsically good thing.

Similarly, in Arthur Koestler's *Darkness at Noon*, we find this discussion of Communist philosophy in the former Soviet Union:

> History has taught us that often lies serve her better than the truth; for man is sluggish and has to be led through the desert for forty years before each step in his development. And he has to be driven through the desert with threats and promises, by imaginary terrors and imaginary consolations, so that he should not sit down prematurely to rest and divert himself by worshipping golden calves.[12]

According to this interpretation, orthodox Soviet communism justified its lies through utilitarian ideas. Something in us revolts at this kind of value system. Truth is sacred and must not be sacrificed on the altar of expediency.

In response to this objection, utilitarians might agree that there is something counterintuitive in the calculus of equating an act of lying with one of honesty; but, they argue, we must be ready to change our culturally induced moral biases. What is so important about truth telling or so bad about lying? If it turned out that lying really promoted human welfare, we'd have to accept it. But that's not likely. Our happiness is tied up with a need for reliable information (that is, truth) on how to achieve our ends, so truthfulness will be a member of the rule-utility's set. But where lying will clearly promote utility without undermining the general adherence to the rule, we simply ought to lie. Don't we already accept lying to a gangster or telling white lies to spare people's feelings?

The Integrity Objection

Bernard Williams argues that utilitarianism violates personal integrity by commanding that we violate our most central and deeply held principles. He illustrates this with the following example:

> Jim finds himself in the central square of a small South American town. Tied up against the wall are a row of twenty Indians, most terrified, a few defiant, in front of them several armed men in uniform. A heavy man in a sweat-stained khaki shirt turns out to be the captain in charge and, after a good deal of questioning of Jim which establishes that he got there by accident while on a botanical expedition, explains that the Indians are a random group of inhabitants who, after recent acts of protest against the government, are just about to be killed to remind other possible protesters of the advantages of not protesting. However, since Jim is an honored visitor from another land, the captain is happy to offer him a guest's privilege of killing one of the Indians himself. If Jim accepts, then as a special mark of the occasion, the other Indians will be let off. Of course, if Jim refuses, then there is no special occasion, and Pedro here will do what he was about to do when Jim arrived, and kill them all. Jim, with some desperate recollection of schoolboy fiction, wonders whether if he got hold of a gun, he could hold the captain, Pedro and the rest of the soldiers to threat, but it is quite clear from the set-up that nothing of that kind is going to work: any attempt of that sort of thing will mean that all the Indians will be killed, and himself. The men against the wall, the other villagers, understand the situation, and are obviously begging him to accept. What should he do?[13]

Williams asks rhetorically,

> How can a man, as a utilitarian agent, come to regard as one satisfaction among others, and a dispensable one, a project or attitude round which

he has built his life, just because someone else's projects have so struc-
tured the causal scene that *that* is how the utilitarian sum comes out?[14]

In response to this criticism, the utilitarian can argue that integrity is not an
absolute that must be adhered to at all costs. Some alienation may be necessary
for the moral life, and the utilitarian can take this into account in devising strategies of action. Even when it is required that we sacrifice our lives or limit our
freedom for others, we may have to limit or sacrifice something of what Williams
calls our integrity. We may have to do the "lesser of evils" in many cases. If the
utilitarian doctrine of negative responsibility is correct, we need to realize that
we are responsible for the evil that we knowingly allow, as well as for the evil
we commit.

The Justice Objection

With both of the above problems, the utilitarian response was that we should
reconsider whether truth telling and personal integrity are values that should
never be compromised. The situation is intensified, though, when we consider
standards of justice that most of us think should never be dispensed with. Let's
look at two examples, each of which highlights a different aspect of justice.

First, imagine that a rape and murder is committed in a racially volatile community. As the sheriff of the town, you have spent a lifetime working for racial harmony. Now, just when your goal is being realized, this incident occurs. The crime
is thought to be racially motivated, and a riot is about to break out that will very
likely result in the death of several people and create long-lasting racial antagonism.
You see that you could frame a tramp for the crime so that a trial will find him
guilty and he will be executed. There is every reason to believe that a speedy
trial and execution will head off the riot and save community harmony. Only
you (and the real criminal, who will keep quiet about it) will know that an innocent
man has been tried and executed. What is the morally right thing to do? The utilitarian seems committed to framing the tramp, but many would find this appalling.

As a second illustration, imagine that you are a utilitarian physician who has
five patients under your care. One needs a heart transplant, one needs two lungs,
one needs a liver, and the last two each need a kidney. Now into your office
comes a healthy bachelor needing an immunization. You judge that he would
make a perfect sacrifice for your five patients. Through a utility-calculus, you determine that, without a doubt, you could do the most good by injecting the healthy
man with a fatal drug and then using his organs to save your five other patients.[15]

These careless views of justice offend us. The very fact that utilitarians even
consider such actions—that they would misuse the legal system or the medical
system to carry out their schemes—seems frightening. It reminds us of the medieval Roman Catholic bishop's justification for heresy hunts and inquisitions and
religious wars:

> When the existence of the Church is threatened, she is released from the
> commandments of morality. With unity as the end, the use of every

means is sanctified, even cunning, treachery, violence, simony, prison, death. For all order is for the sake of the community, and the individual must be sacrificed to the common good.[16]

Similarly, Koestler argues that this logic was used by the Communists in the Soviet Union to destroy innocent people whenever it seemed to the Communist leaders that torture and false confessions served the good of the state because "you can't make an omelet without breaking eggs."

How can the utilitarian respond to this? It won't work this time to simply state that justice is not an absolute value that can be overridden for the good of the whole society. The sophisticated rule–utilitarian insists it makes good sense to have a principle of justice to which we generally adhere. That is, general happiness is best served when we adopt the value of justice. Justice should not be overridden by current utility concerns because human rights themselves are outcomes of utility consideration and should not be lightly violated. That is, because we tend subconsciously to favor our own interests and biases, we institute the principle of rights to protect ourselves and others from capricious and biased acts that would in the long run have great disutility. Thus, we must not undermine institutional rights too easily. Thus, from an initial rule–utilitarian assessment, the sheriff should not frame the innocent tramp, and the doctor should not harvest organs from the bachelor.

However, the utilitarian cannot exclude the possibility of sacrificing innocent people for the greater good of humanity. Wouldn't we all agree that it would be right to sacrifice one innocent person to prevent an enormous evil? Suppose, for example, a maniac is about to set off a nuclear bomb that will destroy New York City. He is scheduled to detonate the bomb in one hour. His psychiatrist knows the lunatic well and assures us that there is one way to stop him—torture his 10-year-old daughter and televise it. Suppose for the sake of the argument that there is no way to simulate the torture. Would you not consider torturing the child in this situation? As the rule–utilitarian would see it, we have two moral rules that are in conflict: the rule to prevent widespread harm and the rule against torture. To resolve this conflict, the rule–utilitarian might appeal to this second-level conflict-resolving rule: We may sacrifice an innocent person to prevent a significantly greater social harm. Or, if no conflict-resolving rule is available, the rule–utilitarian can appeal to this third-level remainder rule: When no other rule applies, simply do what your best judgment deems to be the act that will maximize utility. Using this remainder rule, the rule–utilitarian could justify torturing the girl.

Thus, in such cases, it might be right to sacrifice one innocent person to save a city or prevent some wide-scale disaster. In these cases, the rule–utilitarian's approach to justice is in fact the same as the above approach to lying and compromising one's integrity: Justice is just one more lower-order principle within utilitarianism. The problem, clearly, is determining which kinds of wide-scale disasters warrant sacrificing innocent lives. This question invariably comes up in wartime: In every bombing raid, especially in the dropping of the atomic bomb on Hiroshima and Nagasaki, the noncombatant–combatant distinction is overridden. Innocent civilian lives are sacrificed with the prospect of ending the war. We seem to be making this judgment call in our decision to drive auto-mobiles and trucks even though we are fairly certain the practice will result in the death of thousands of innocent people each year. Judgment calls like these high-light utilitarianism's difficulty in handling issues of justice.

CONCLUSION

We've seen that multilevel rule-utilitarianism satisfies the purposes of ethics, gives a clear decision procedure for moral conduct, and focuses on helping people and reducing suffering in the world. It also offers a compelling solution to the prob-lem of posterity. Further, rule-utilitarianism has responses to all the criticisms directed toward it. Whether the responses are adequate is another story. Perhaps it would be better to hold off making a final judgment about utilitarianism until considering the next two chapters, in which two other types of ethical theory are discussed.

NOTES

1. R. M. Hare, *The Language of Morals* (Oxford: Oxford University Press, 1952), p. 60.

2. Sophocles, *Antigone,* trans. Robert Eagles (Penguin Classics, 1982), lines 204–214.

3. Jeremy Bentham, *An Introduction to the Principles of Morals and Legislation* (1789), Ch. 1.

4. J. S. Mill, *Utilitarianism* (1861), Ch. 2.

5. Ibid.

6. Richard Brandt, "Towards a Credible Form of Utilitarianism," in *Morality and the Language of Conduct,* ed. H. Castaneda and G. Naknikian (Wayne State University Press, 1963), pp. 109–110.

7. Kai Nielsen, "Against Moral Conservatism," *Ethics* 82 (1972): 219–231.

8. Derek Parfit, "Energy Policy and the Further Future: The Identity Problem," in *Energy and the Future,* ed. D. MacLean and P. Brown (Rowman & Littlefield, 1983).

9. See Anthony Quinton, *Utilitarian Ethics* (Macmillan, 1973), pp. 49–50. Lewis and Quinton add a third type of consequence, namely, intended ones: An act is *subjectively* right if its agent intends or actually expects it to have the best consequences.

10. The famous nineteenth-century utilitarian Henry Sidgwick, in his *The Methods of Ethics* (Oxford, 1974), p. 483, argues that utilitarians should keep their views a secret for the good of society.

11. David Hume, *An Enquiry Concerning the Principles of Morals* (1751), Sec. 9, Pt. 1.

12. Arthur Koestler, *Darkness at Noon* (Macmillan, 1941), p. 80.

13. Bernard Williams, "A Critique of Utilitarianism," in *Utilitarianism: For and Against* (Smart & Williams), pp. 98–99.

14. Ibid.

15. This example and the trolley car example are found in Judith Jarvis Thomson, "The Trolley Problem," in *Rights, Restitution and Risk* (Cambridge: Harvard University Press, 1986), pp. 94–116.

16. Dietrich von Nieheim, Bishop of Verden, *De Schismate Libri*, A.D. 1311, quoted in Koestler, *Darkness at Noon*, p. 76.

FOR FURTHER REFLECTION

1. Consider the three purposes of morality mentioned in Chapter 1: (a) to promote human flourishing, (b) to lessen human suffering, and (c) to resolve conflicts of interest justly. Which of these does utilitarianism fulfill, and which does it fail to fulfill?

2. One criticism of utilitarianism is that it fails to protect people's rights. Try to develop this criticism and then explain whether or not you agree with it.

3. John Rawls maintains that utilitarianism errs in applying to society the principle of personal choice. For example, I have a right to go without a new suit so that I can save the money for my college education or for something else that I want. But utilitarianism demands that you forgo a new suit for someone else's college education or for the overall good of the community. Is this a fair criticism?

4. If slavery could be humane and yield great overall utility, would utilitarians accept it? Discuss.

5. Suppose you are an army officer who has just captured an enemy soldier who knows where a secret time bomb has been planted. Unless defused, the bomb will explode, killing thousands of people. Would it be morally permissible to torture the soldier to get him to reveal the bomb's location? Discuss this problem in the light of utilitarian and deontological theories.

6. Continuing the example in the previous question, suppose you have also captured the enemy soldier's children. According to utilitarianism would it be permissible to torture them to get him to reveal the bomb's location?

FOR FURTHER READING

Crisp, Roger. *Routledge Philosophy Guidebook to Mill on Utilitarianism*. London: Routledge, 1997.

Glover, Jonathan. *Utilitarianism and Its Critics*. New York: Macmillan, 1990.

Lyons, David. *Mill's Utilitarianism: Critical Essays*. Lanham, Md.: Rowman & Littlefield, 1997.

Scarre, Geoffrey. *Utilitarianism*. London: Routledge, 1996.

Scheffler, Samuel. *Consequentialism and Its Critics*. Oxford, Engl.: Oxford University Press, 1988.

Sen, Amartya Kumar, and Bernard Williams. *Utilitarianism and Beyond*. Cambridge, Engl.: Cambridge University Press, 1982.

Shaw, William H. *Contemporary Ethics: Taking Account of Utilitarianism*. Malden, Mass.: Blackwell, 1999.

Smart, J. J. C., and Bernard Williams. *Utilitarianism: For and Against*. Cambridge, Engl.: Cambridge University Press, 1987.

8

Kant and Deontological Theories

Kant's *Groundwork of the Metaphysics of Morals* is one of the small books which are truly great: it has exercised on human thought an influence almost ludicrously disproportionate to its size. In moral philosophy it ranks with the *Republic* of Plato and the *Ethics* of Aristotle; and perhaps it shows in some respects a deeper insight even than these. Its main topic—the supreme principle of morality—is of the utmost importance to all who are not indifferent to the struggle of good against evil. Its message was never more needed than it is at present, when a somewhat arid empiricism is the prevailing fashion in philosophy.

H. J. PATON, PREFACE TO KANT'S *GROUNDWORK OF THE METAPHYSIC OF MORALS*

Let's look again at our opening story in Chapter 7 on utilitarianism. A millionaire makes a dying request for you to donate $2 million to the Yankees. You agree but then are tempted to give the money to the World Hunger Relief Organization instead. What should you do? The utilitarian, who focuses on the consequences of actions, would tell you to act in a way that advances the greatest good for the greatest number. In essence, the end justifies the means. Accordingly, breaking your promise to the millionaire and donating to the World Hunger Relief Organization appears to be the way to go.

The deontological answer to this question, however, is quite the opposite. It is not the consequences that determine the rightness or wrongness of an act but certain features in the act itself or in the rule of which the act is a token or example. The end never justifies the means. For example, there is something right about truth telling and promise keeping even when such actions may bring

about some harm; and there is something wrong about lying and promise breaking even when such actions may bring about good consequences. Acting unjustly
is wrong even if it will maximize expected utility.

In this chapter, we explore deontological approaches of ethics, specifically
that by Immanuel Kant (1724–1804). The greatest philosopher of the German
Enlightenment and one of the most important philosophers of all time, Kant
was both an absolutist and a rationalist. He believed that we could use reason
to work out a consistent, nonoverridable set of moral principles.

KANT'S INFLUENCES

To understand Kant's moral philosophy, it is helpful to know a little about his
life. He was born in Königsberg, Germany, in 1724, and died there eighty
years later, never having left the surroundings of the city. He was a short,
quiet man and so methodical that, as tradition has it, the citizens of Königsberg
set their watches by his daily 3:00 p.m. walks. He never married. He devoted his
life to the study and teaching of philosophy at the University of Königsberg. His
greatest publication, *The Critique of Pure Reason* (1781), was heralded in his own
day as a monumental work, and his *Foundations of the Metaphysics of Morals* (1785)
is generally regarded as one of the two or three most important books in the history of ethics.

There were several strong influences on Kant's ethical thinking. The first was
Pietism, a sect within the Lutheran Church, which Kant's parents adhered to and
which set a tone of deep sincerity to his views. Pietists emphasized honesty, deep
feeling, and the moral life rather than theological doctrine or orthodox belief. It's
a religion of the heart, not the head, of the spirit rather than of ritual. However, as
an intellectual, Kant emphasized the head as much as the heart, but it was a head
concerned about the moral life, especially good will. It is not correct beliefs or
results that really matter but inner goodness. The idea is that, if we live within
our lights, we will be given more light and that God judges us not on how
lucky or successful we are in accomplishing our tasks but on how earnestly we
have lived according to our principles. This impacted Kant's notion of the
good will as the sole intrinsic good in life.

The second influence was the work of Jean-Jacques Rousseau (1712–1778)
on human freedom, especially his *Social Contract,* and it was said that the only
time Kant ever missed his afternoon walk was the day when he read that
book. Rousseau taught him the meaning and importance of human dignity,
the primacy of freedom and autonomy, and the intrinsic worth of human beings
apart from any functions they might perform.

The third influence was the philosophical debate of his time between **rationalism** and **empiricism.** The fourth influence was natural law intuitionist
theories that dominated moral philosophy at that time. Let's look at these latter
two influences in more detail.

Rationalism and Empiricism

The philosophical debate between rationalism and empiricism took place in the seventeenth and eighteenth centuries. Rationalists, such as René Descartes, Baruch Spinoza, Gottfried Leibniz, and Christian Wolff, claimed that pure reason could tell us how the world is, independent of experience. We can know metaphysical truth such as the existence of God, the immortality of the soul, freedom of the will, and the universality of causal relations apart from experience. Experience may be necessary to open our minds to these ideas, but essentially they are innate ideas that God implants in us from birth. Empiricists, led by John Locke and David Hume, on the other hand, denied that we have any innate ideas and argued that all knowledge comes from experience. Our minds are a *tabula rasa,* an empty slate, upon which experience writes her lessons.

The rationalists and empiricists carried their debate into the area of moral knowledge. The rationalists claimed that our knowledge of moral principles is a type of metaphysical knowledge, implanted in us by God, and discoverable by reason as it deduces general principles about human nature. On the other hand, empiricists, especially Francis Hutcheson, David Hume, and Adam Smith, argued that morality is founded entirely on the contingencies of human nature and based on desire. Morality concerns making people happy, fulfilling their reflected desires, and reason is just a practical means of helping them fulfill their desires. There is nothing of special importance in reason in its own right. It is mainly a rationalizer and servant of the passions. As Hume said, "Reason is and ought only to be a slave of the passions and can never pretend to any other office than to serve and obey them." Morality is founded on our feeling of sympathy with other people's sufferings, on fellow feeling. For such empiricists then, morality is contingent upon human nature:

Human nature → Feelings and Desires → Moral principles

If we had a different nature, then we would have different feelings and desires, and hence we would have different moral principles.

Kant rejected the ideas of Hutcheson, Hume, and Smith. He was outraged by the thought that morality should depend on human nature and be subject to the fortunes of change and the luck of empirical discovery. Morality is not contingent but necessary. It would be no less binding on us if our feelings were different from what they are. Kant writes,

> Every empirical element is not only quite incapable of being an aid to the principle of morality, but is even highly prejudicial to the purity of morals; for the proper and inestimable worth of an absolutely good will consists just in this, that the principle of action is free from all influence of contingent grounds, which alone experience can furnish. We cannot too much or too often repeat our warning against this lax and even mean habit of thought which seeks for its principle amongst empirical motives and laws; for human reason in its weariness is glad to rest on this pillow, and in a dream of sweet illusions it substitutes for morality a

bastard patched up from limbs of various derivation, which looks like anything one chooses to see in it; only not like virtue to one who has once beheld her in her true form.[1]

No, said Kant, it is not our desires that ground morality but our rational will. Reason is sufficient for establishing the moral law as something transcendent and universally binding on all rational creatures.

Act- and Rule-Intuitionism

Since the Middle Ages, one of the dominant versions of European moral philosophy was **natural law theory.** In a nutshell, this view maintained that, through rational intuitions embedded in human nature by God, we discover eternal and absolute moral principles. Medieval natural law philosopher Thomas Aquinas argued that we have a special mental process called *synderesis* that gives us general knowledge of moral goodness. From this knowledge, then, we derive a series of basic moral obligations. What's key here is the idea that humans have a natural faculty that gives us an intuitive awareness of morality. This general position is called **intuitionism.** During the seventeenth and eighteenth centuries, some sort of intuitionism was assumed in most ethical theories, and Kant was heavily influenced by some of them. Two basic forms emerged: act and rule intuitionism.

Act-intuitionism sees each act as a unique ethical occasion and holds that we must decide what is right or wrong in each situation by consulting our conscience or our intuitions or by making a choice apart from any rules. We must consult our conscience in every situation to *discover* the morally right (or wrong) thing to do. An expression of act-intuitionism is in the famous moral sermons of Joseph Butler (1692–1752), a bishop within the Church of England. He writes,

> [If] any plain honest man, before he engages in any course of action, ask himself, Is this I am going about right, or is it wrong? . . . I do not in the least doubt but that this question would be answered agreeably to truth and virtue, by almost any fair man in almost any circumstance.[2]

Butler believed that we each have a conscience that can discover what is right and wrong in virtually every instance. This is consistent with advice such as "Let your conscience be your guide." We do not need general rules to learn what is right and wrong; our intuition will inform us of those things. The judgment lies in the moral perception and not in some abstract, general rule.

Act-intuitionism, however, has some serious disadvantages. First, it is hard to see how any argument could take place with an intuitionist: Either you both have the same intuition about lying or you don't, and that's all there is to it. If I believe that a specific act of abortion is morally permissible and you believe it is morally wrong, then we may ask each other to look more deeply into our consciences, but we cannot argue about the subject. There *is* a place for deep intuitions in moral philosophy, but intuitions must still be scrutinized by reason and corrected by theory.

Second, it seems that rules are necessary to all reasoning, including moral reasoning, and act-intuitionists seem to ignore this. You may test this by thinking about how you learn to drive a car, to do long division, or to type. Even though you may eventually internalize the initial principles as habits so that you are unconscious of them, one could still cite a rule that covers your action. For example, you may no longer remember the rules for accelerating a car, but there was an original experience of learning the rule, which you continue unwittingly to follow. Moral rules such as "Keep your promises" and "Don't kill innocent people" seem to function in a similar way.

Third, different situations seem to share common features, so it would be inconsistent for us to prescribe different moral actions. Suppose you believe that it is morally wrong for John to cheat on his math exam. If you also believe that it is morally permissible for you to cheat on the same exam, don't you need to explain what makes your situation different from John's? If I say that it is wrong for John to cheat on exams, am I not implying that it is wrong for anyone relevantly similar to John (including all students) to cheat on exams? That is, morality seems to involve a universal aspect, or what is called the principle of universalizability: If one judges that X is right (or wrong) or good (or bad), then one is rationally committed to judging anything relevantly similar to X as right (wrong) or good (bad). If this principle is sound, then act-intuitionism is misguided.

The other intuitionist approach, **rule-intuitionism,** maintains that we must decide what is right or wrong in each situation by consulting moral rules that we receive through intuition. Rule-intuitionists accept the principle of universalizability as well as the notion that in making moral judgments we are appealing to principles or rules. Such rules as "We ought never to lie," "We ought always to keep our promises," and "We ought never to execute an innocent person" constitute a set of valid prescriptions regardless of the outcomes. The rule-intuitionist to have the greatest impact on Kant was German philosopher Samuel Pufendorf (1632–1694), the dominant natural law theorist of his time. Pufendorf describes the intuitive process by which we acquire moral knowledge:

> It is usually said that we have knowledge of this [moral] law from nature itself. However, this is not to be taken to mean that plain and distinct notions concerning what is to be done or avoided were implanted in the minds of newborn people. Instead, nature is said to teach us, partly because the knowledge of this law may be attained by the help of the light of reason. It is also partly because the general and most useful points of it are so plain and clear that, at first sight, they force assent.... Although we are not able to remember the precise time when they first took hold of our understandings and professed our minds, we can have no other opinion of our knowledge of this law except that it was native to our beings, or born together and at the same time with ourselves.[3]

The moral intuitions that we have, according to Pufendorf, fall into three groups: duties to God, to oneself, and to others. The duties in all these cases are moral rules that guide our actions. Within these three groupings, the main rules of duty that Pufendorf advocates are these:

- *To God.* Know the existence and nature of God; worship God.
- *To oneself.* Develop one's skills and talents; avoid harming our bodies, such as through gluttony or drunkenness, and not killing oneself.
- *To others.* Avoid wronging others; treat people as equals; promote the good of others; keep one's promises.

Kant was influenced by Pufendorf in two ways. First, Kant was a rule-intuitionist of a special sort: He believed that moral knowledge comes to us through *rational* intuition in the form of moral rules. As we'll see, Kant's moral psychology is rather complex, and his conception of intuition draws on a distinct notion of reason, which we don't find in Pufendorf. Second, Kant accepted Pufendorf's division of duties toward God, oneself, and others. Duties toward God, Kant argues, are actually religious duties, not moral ones. However, duties to oneself and others are genuine moral obligations.

THE CATEGORICAL IMPERATIVE

The principal moral rule in Kant's ethical theory is what he calls the categorical imperative—essentially meaning "absolute command." Before introducing us to the specific rule itself, he sets the stage with an account of intrinsic moral goodness.

Intrinsic Goodness and the Good Will

As we have noted, Kant wanted to remove moral truth from the zone of contingency and empirical observation and place it securely in the area of necessary, absolute, universal truth. Morality's value is not based on the fact that it has instrumental value, that it often secures nonmoral goods such as happiness; rather, morality is valuable in its own right:

> Nothing can possibly be conceived in the world, or even out of it, which can be called good without qualification, except the Good Will. Intelligence, wit, judgment, and the other *talents* of the mind, however they may be named, or courage, resolution, perseverance, as qualities of temperament, as undoubtedly good and desirable in many respects; but these gifts of nature also may become extremely bad and mischievous if the will which is to make use of them, and which, therefore constitutes what is called *character* is not good. . . . Even if it should happen that, owing to special disfavor of fortune, or the stingy provision of a stepmotherly nature, this Good Will should wholly lack power to accomplish its purpose, if with its greatest efforts it should yet achieve nothing, and there should remain only the Good Will, . . . then, like a jewel, it

would still shine by its own light, as a thing which has its whole value in itself. Its usefulness or fruitfulness can neither add to nor take away anything from this value.[4]

The only thing that is absolutely good, good in itself and without qualification, is the good will. All other intrinsic goods, both intellectual and moral, can serve the vicious will and thus contribute to evil. They are only *morally valuable* if accompanied by a good will. Even success and happiness are not good in themselves. Honor can lead to pride. Happiness without good will is undeserved luck, ill-gotten gain. Nor is utilitarianism plausible, for if we have a quantity of happiness to distribute, is it just to distribute it equally, regardless of virtue? Should we not distribute it discriminately, according to moral goodness? Happiness should be distributed in proportion to people's moral worth.

How successful is Kant's argument for the good will? Could we imagine a world where people always and necessarily put nonmoral virtues to good use, where it is simply impossible to use a virtue such as intelligence for evil? Is happiness any less good simply because one can distribute it incorrectly? Can't one put the good will itself to bad use as the misguided do-gooder might? As the aphorism goes, "The road to hell is paved with good intentions." Could Hitler have had good intentions in carrying out his dastardly programs? Can't the good will have bad effects?

Although we may agree that the good will is a great good, it is not obvious that Kant's account is correct, that it is the only inherently good thing. For even as intelligence, courage, and happiness can be put to bad uses or have bad effects, so can the good will; and even as it doesn't seem to count against the good will that it can be put to bad uses, so it shouldn't count against the other virtues that they can be put to bad uses. The good will may be a necessary element to any morally good action, but whether the good will is also a *sufficient* condition to moral goodness is another question.

Nonetheless, perhaps we can reinterpret Kant so as to preserve his central insight. There does seem to be something morally valuable about the good will, apart from any consequences. Consider the following illustration. Two soldiers volunteer to cross enemy lines to contact their allies on the other side. Both start off and do their best to get through the enemy area. One succeeds; the other doesn't and is captured. But, aren't they both morally praiseworthy? The success of one in no way detracts from the goodness of the other. Judged from a commonsense moral point of view, their actions are equally good; judged from a utilitarian or consequentialist view, the successful act is far more valuable than the unsuccessful one. Here, we can distinguish the agent's worth from the value of the consequences and make two separate, nonconflicting judgments.

Hypothetical versus Categorical Imperatives

For Kant, all mention of duties (or obligations) can be translated into the language of imperatives, or commands. As such, moral duties can be said to have imperative force. He distinguishes two kinds of imperatives: hypothetical and categorical.

The formula for a **hypothetical imperative** is "If you want A, then do B." For example, "If you want a good job, then get a good education," or "If you want to be happy, then stay sober and live a balanced life." The formula for a categorical imperative is simply: "Do B!" That is, do what reason discloses to be the intrinsically right thing to do, such as "Tell the truth!" Hypothetical, or means–ends, imperatives are not the kind of imperatives that characterize moral actions. Categorical, or unqualified, imperatives are the right kind of imperatives, because they show proper recognition of the imperial status of moral obligations. Such imperatives are intuitive, immediate, absolute injunctions that all rational agents understand by virtue of their rationality.

Kant argues that one must perform moral duty solely for its own sake ("duty for duty's sake"). Some people conform to the moral law because they deem it in their own enlightened self-interest to be moral. But they are not truly moral because they do not act for the sake of the moral law. For example, a businessman may believe that "honesty is the best policy"; that is, he may judge that it is conducive to good business to give his customers correct change and high-quality products. But, unless he performs these acts *because* they are his duty, he is not acting morally, even though his acts are the same ones they would be if he *were* acting morally.

The kind of imperative that fits Kant's scheme as a product of reason is one that universalizes principles of conduct. He names it the **categorical imperative** (CI): "Act only according to that maxim by which you can at the same time will that it would become a universal law." The categorical imperative, for Kant, is a procedure for determining the morality of *any* course of action. All specific moral duties, he writes, "can be derived from this single imperative." Thus, for example, duties to oneself such as developing one's talents and not killing oneself can be deduced from the categorical imperative. So too can duties to others, such as keeping promises and helping those in need.

The first step in the categorical imperative procedure is for us to consider the underlying maxim of our proposed action. By *maxim,* Kant means the general rule in accordance with which the agent intends to act. For example, if I am thinking about assisting someone in need, my underlying maxim might be this: "When I see someone in need, I should assist him or her when it does not cause an undue burden on me." The second step is to consider whether this maxim could be universalized to apply to everyone, such as "When anyone sees someone in need, that person should assist him or her when it does not cause an undue burden on the person." If it can be universalized, then we accept the maxim, and the action is moral. If it cannot be universalized, then we reject the maxim, and the action is immoral. The general scheme of the CI procedure, then, is this:

Maxim of action

↓

Universalize maxim

↓

Accept successfully universalized maxim (reject unsuccessful maxim)

According to Kant, there is only one categorical imperative, but he presents three formulations of it:

- *Principle of the law of nature.* "Act as though the maxim of your action were by your will to become a universal law of nature."
- *Principle of ends.* "So act as to treat humanity, whether in your own person or in that of any other, in every case as an end and never as merely a means."
- *Principle of autonomy.* "So act that your will can regard itself at the same time as making universal law through its maxims."

The theme that ties all of these formulations together is **universalizability:** Can a particular course of action be generalized so that it applies to any relevantly similar person in that kind of situation? For Kant, determining whether a maxim can successfully be universalized hinges on which of the three specific formulations of the categorical imperative that we follow. The bottom line for all three, though, is that we stand outside our personal maxims and estimate impartially and impersonally whether our maxims are suitable as principles for all of us to live by.

Let's look at each of these formulations, beginning with the first and most influential, the principle of the law of nature.

The Principle of the Law of Nature: Four Examples

Again, the CI principle of the law of nature is this: "Act as though the maxim of your action were by your will to become a universal law of nature." The emphasis here is that you must act analogous to the laws of physics, specifically insofar as such laws are not internally conflicting or self-defeating.[5] For example, nature could not subsist with a law of gravity that had an object fall both up and down at the same time. Similarly, a system of morality could not subsist when a universalized maxim has an internal conflict. If you could consistently will that everyone would act on a given maxim, then there is an application of the categorical imperative showing the moral permissibility of the action. If you could not consistently will that everyone would act on the maxim, then that type of action is morally wrong; the maxim must then be rejected as self-defeated.

Kant gives four examples of the application of this test: (1) making a lying promise, (2) committing suicide, (3) neglecting one's talent, and (4) refraining from helping others. The first and fourth of these are duties to others, whereas the second and third of these are duties to oneself. Kant illustrates how the CI principle of the law of nature works by applying it to each of these maxims.

Making a Lying Promise   Suppose I need some money and am considering whether it would be moral to borrow the money from you and promise to repay it without ever intending to do so. Could I say to myself that everyone should make a false promise when he is in difficulty from which he otherwise cannot escape? The maxim of my act is M:

M. Whenever I need money, I should make a lying promise while borrowing the money.

Can I universalize the maxim of my act? By applying the universalizability test to M, we get P:

P.   Whenever anyone needs money, that person should make a lying promise while borrowing the money.

But, something has gone wrong, for if I universalize this principle of making promises without intending to keep them, I would be involved in a contradiction:

> I immediately see that I could will the lie but not a universal law to lie. For with such a law [that is, with such a maxim universally acted on] there would be no promises at all. . . . Thus my maxim would necessarily destroy itself as soon as it was made a universal law.[6]

The resulting state of affairs would be self-defeating because no one in his or her right mind would take promises as promises unless there was the expectation of fulfillment. Thus, the maxim of the lying promise fails the universalizability criterion; hence, it is immoral. Now, I consider the opposite maxim, one based on keeping my promise:

M1.   Whenever I need money, I should make a sincere promise while borrowing it.

Can I successfully universalize this maxim?

P1.   Whenever anyone needs money, that person should make a sincere promise while borrowing it.

Yes, I can universalize M1 because there is nothing self-defeating or contradictory in this. So, it follows, making sincere promises is moral; we can make the maxim of promise keeping into a universal law.

Committing Suicide   Some of Kant's illustrations do not fare as well as the duty to keep promises. For instance, he argues that the categorical imperative would prohibit suicide because we could not successfully universalize the maxim of such an act. If we try to universalize it, we obtain the principle, "Whenever it looks like one will experience more pain than pleasure, one ought to kill oneself," which, according to Kant, is a self-contradiction because it would go against the very principle of survival upon which it is based. But whatever the merit of the form of this argument, we could modify the principle to read "Whenever the pain or suffering of existence erodes the quality of life in such a way as to make nonexistence a preference to suffering existence, one is permitted to commit suicide." Why couldn't this (or something close to it) be universalized? It would cover the rare instances in which no hope is in sight for terminally ill patients or for victims of torture or deep depression, but it would not cover the kinds of suffering and depression most of us experience in the normal course of life. Kant seems unduly absolutist in his prohibition of suicide.

Neglecting One's Talent   Kant's other two examples of the application of the CI principle of the law of nature are also questionable. In his third example, he claims that we cannot universalize a maxim to refrain from developing our talents. But again, could we not qualify this and stipulate that under certain circumstances it is permissible not to develop our talents? Perhaps Kant is correct in that, if everyone selfishly refrained from developing talents, society would soon degenerate into anarchy. But couldn't one universalize the following maxim M3?

M3. Whenever I am not inclined to develop a talent, and this refraining will not seriously undermine the social order, I may so refrain.

Refraining from Helping Others   Kant's last example of the way the CI principle of the law of nature functions regards the situation of not coming to the aid of others whenever I am secure and independent. He claims that I cannot universalize this maxim because I never know whether I will need the help of others at some future time. Is Kant correct about this? Why could I not universalize a maxim never to set myself a goal whose achievement appears to require the cooperation of others? I would have to give up any goal as soon as I realized that cooperation with others was required. In what way is this contradictory or self-defeating? Perhaps it would be selfish and cruel to make this into a universal law, but there seems nothing contradictory or self-defeating in the principle itself. The problems with universalizing selfishness are the same ones we encountered in analyzing egoism, but it is dubious whether Kant's categorical imperative captures what is wrong with egoism. Perhaps he has other weapons that do elucidate what is wrong with egoism (we return to this later).

COUNTEREXAMPLES TO THE PRINCIPLE OF THE LAW OF NATURE

Kant thought that he could generate an entire moral law from his categorical imperative. The above test of universalizability advocated by Kant's principle of the law of nature seems to work with such principles as promise keeping and truth telling and a few other maxims, but it doesn't seem to give us all that Kant wanted. It has been objected that Kant's categorical imperative is both too wide and too unqualified. The charge that it is too wide is based on the perception that it seems to justify some actions that we might consider trivial or even immoral.

Counterexample 1: Mandating Trivial Actions

For an example of a trivial action that might be mandated by the categorical imperative, consider the following maxim M:

M. I should always tie my right shoe before my left shoe.

This generates the following principle P:

P.   We should always tie our right shoe before our left shoe.

Can we universalize P without contradiction? It seems that we can. Just as we universalize that people should drive cars on the right side of the street rather than the left, we could make it a law that everyone should tie the right shoe before the left shoe. But it seems obvious that there would be no point to such a law—it would be trivial. But it is justified by the categorical imperative.

It may be objected that all this counterexample shows is that it may be *permissible* (not obligatory) to live by the principle of tying the right shoe before the left because we could also universalize the opposite maxim (tying the left before the right) without contradiction. That seems correct.

Counterexample 2: Endorsing Cheating

Another counterexample, offered by Fred Feldman,[7] appears to show that the categorical imperative endorses cheating. Maxim M states:

M.   Whenever I need a term paper for a course and don't feel like writing one, I will buy a term paper from Research Anonymous and submit it as my own work.

Now we universalize this maxim into a universal principle P:

P.   Whenever anyone needs a term paper for a course and doesn't feel like writing one, the person will buy one from a suitable source and submit it as his or her own.

This procedure seems to be self-defeating. It would undermine the whole process of academic work because teachers wouldn't believe that research papers really represented the people who turned them in. Learning would not occur; grades and transcripts would be meaningless, and the entire institution of education would break down; the whole purpose of cheating would be defeated.

But suppose we made a slight adjustment to M and P, inventing M1 and P1:

M1.   When I need a term paper for a course and don't feel like writing one, and no change in the system will occur if I submit a store-bought one, then I will buy a term paper and submit it as my own work.

P1.   Whenever anyone needs a term paper for a course and doesn't feel like writing it, and no change in the system will occur if one submits a store-bought paper, then one will buy the term paper and submit it as one's own work.

Does P1 pass as a legitimate expression of the categorical imperative? It might seem to satisfy the conditions, but Kantian students have pointed out that for a principle to be universalizable, or lawlike, one must ensure that it is public.

However, if P1 were public and everyone was encouraged to live by it, then it would be exceedingly difficult to prevent an erosion of the system. Teachers would take precautions against it. Would cheaters have to announce themselves publicly? In sum, the attempt to universalize even this qualified form of cheating would undermine the very institution that makes cheating possible. So, P1 may be a thinly veiled oxymoron: Do what will undermine the educational process in such a way that it doesn't undermine the educational process.

Counterexample 3: Prohibiting Permissible Actions

Another type of counterexample might be used to show that the categorical imperative refuses to allow us to do things that common sense permits. Suppose I need to flush the toilet, so I formulate my maxim M:

M. At time t_1, I will flush the toilet.

I universalize this maxim:

P. At time t_1, everyone should flush their toilet.

But I cannot will this if I realize that the pressure of millions of toilets flushing at the same time would destroy the nation's plumbing systems, and so I could not then flush the toilet.

The way out of this problem is to qualify the original maxim M to read M1:

M1. Whenever I need to flush the toilet and have no reason to believe that it will set off the impairment or destruction of the community's plumbing system, I may do so.

From this we can universalize to P1:

P1. Whenever anyone needs to flush the toilet and has no reason to believe that it will set off the destruction of the community's plumbing system, he or she may do so.

Thus, Kant seems to be able to respond to some of the objections to his theory.

Counterexample 4: Mandating Genocide

More serious is the fact that the categorical imperative appears to justify acts that we judge to be horrendously immoral. Suppose I hate people of a certain race, religion, or ethnic group. Suppose it is Americans that I hate and that I am not an American. My maxim is this:

M. Let me kill anyone who is American.

Universalizing M, we get P:

P. Always kill Americans.

Is there anything contradictory in this injunction? Could we make it into a universal law? Why not? Americans might not like it, but there is no logical contradiction involved in such a principle. Had I been an American when this command was in effect, I would not have been around to write this book, but the world would have survived my loss without too much inconvenience. If I suddenly discover that I am an American, I would have to commit suicide. But as long as I am willing to be consistent, there doesn't seem to be anything wrong with my principle, so far as its being based on the categorical imperative is concerned.

As with the shoe-tying example, it would be possible to universalize the opposite—that no one should kill innocent people. Nevertheless, we certainly wouldn't want to say that it is permissible to adopt the principle "Always kill Americans."

We conclude, then, that even though the first version of the categorical imperative is an important criterion for evaluating moral principles, it still needs supplementation. In itself, it is purely formal and leaves out any understanding about the content or material aspect of morality. The categorical imperative, with its universalizability test, constitutes a necessary condition for being a valid moral principle, but it does not provide us with a sufficiency criterion. That is, if any principle is to count as rational or moral, it must be universalizable; it must apply to everyone and to every case that is relevantly similar. If I believe that it's wrong for others to cheat on exams, then unless I can find a reason to believe that I am relevantly different from these others, it is also wrong for me to cheat on exams. If premarital heterosexual coitus is prohibited for women, then it must also be prohibited for men (otherwise, with whom would the men have sex—other men's wives?). This formal consistency, however, does not tell us whether cheating itself is right or wrong or whether premarital sex is right or wrong. That decision has to do with the material content of morality, and we must use other considerations to help us decide about that.

OTHER FORMULATIONS OF THE CATEGORICAL IMPERATIVE

We've discussed Kant's first formulation of the categorical imperative; now we will consider the two others: the principle of ends and the principle of autonomy.

The Principle of Ends

Again, the principle of ends is this: "So act as to treat humanity, whether in your own person or in that of any other, in every case as an end and never as merely a means." Each person as a rational being has dignity and profound worth, which entails that he or she must never be exploited or manipulated or merely used as a means to our idea of what is for the general good (or to any other end).

What is Kant's argument for viewing rational beings as having ultimate value? It goes like this: In valuing anything, I endow it with value; it can have no value apart from someone's valuing it. As a valued object, it has *conditional* worth, which is derived from my valuation. On the other hand, the person who values the object is the ultimate source of the object, and as such belongs to a different sphere of beings. We, as valuers, must conceive of ourselves as having *unconditioned* worth. We cannot think of our personhood as a mere thing because then we would have to judge it to be without any value except that given to it by the estimation of someone else. But then that person would be the source of value, and there is no reason to suppose that one person should have unconditional worth and not another who is relevantly similar. Therefore, we are not mere objects. We have unconditional worth and so must treat all such value-givers as valuable in themselves—as ends, not merely means. I leave it to you to evaluate the validity of this argument, but most of us do hold that there is something exceedingly valuable about human life.

Kant thought that this formulation, the principle of ends, was substantively identical with his first formulation of the categorical imperative, but most scholars disagree with him. It seems better to treat this principle as a supplement to the first, adding content to the purely formal CI principle of the law of nature. In this way, Kant would limit the kinds of maxims that could be universalized. Egoism and the principle regarding the killing of Americans would be ruled out at the very outset because they involve a violation of the dignity of rational persons. The process would be as follows:

1. Formulate the maxim (M).
2. Apply the ends test. (Does the maxim involve violating the dignity of rational beings?)
3. Apply the principle of the law of nature universalization test. (Can the maxim be universalized?)
4. Successful moral principles survive both tests.

In any event, we may ask whether the CI principle of ends fares better than the CI principle of the law of nature. Three problems soon emerge. The first has to do with Kant's setting such a high value on rationality. Why does reason and only reason have intrinsic worth? Who gives this value to rational beings, and how do we know that they have this value? What if we believe that reason has only instrumental value?

Kant's notion of the high inherent value of reason will be plausible to those who believe that humans are made in the image of God and who interpret that (as has the mainstream of the Judeo-Christian tradition) as entailing that our rational capabilities are the essence of being created in God's image: We have value because God created us with worth—that is, with reason. But, even nontheists may be persuaded that Kant is correct in seeing rationality as inherently good. It is one of the things rational beings value more than virtually anything else, and it is a necessary condition to whatever we judge to be a good life or an ideal life (a truly happy life).

Kant seems to be correct in valuing rationality. It does enable us to engage in deliberate and moral reasoning, and it lifts us above lower animals. Where he may have gone wrong is in neglecting other values or states of being that may have moral significance. For example, he believed that we have no obligations to animals because they are not rational. But surely the utilitarians are correct when they insist that the fact that animals can suffer should constrain our behavior toward them: We ought not cause unnecessary harm. Perhaps Kantians can supplement their system to accommodate this objection.

This brings us to our second problem with Kant's formulation. If we agree that reason is an intrinsic value, then does it not follow that those who have more of this quality should be respected and honored more than those who have less?

(1) Reason is an intrinsic good.

(2) The more we have of an intrinsically good thing, the better.

(3) Therefore, those who have more reason than others are intrinsically better.

Thus, by Kantian logic, people should be treated in exact proportion to their ability to reason, so geniuses and intellectuals should be given privileged status in society (as Plato and Aristotle might argue). Kant could deny the second premise and argue that rationality is a threshold quality, but the objector could come back and argue that there really are degrees in ability to use reason, ranging from gorillas and chimpanzees all the way to the upper limits of human genius. Should we treat gorillas and chimps as ends in themselves while still exploiting small babies and severely senile people because the former do not yet act rationally and the latter have lost what ability they had? If we accept the Kantian principle of ends, what should be our view on abortion, infanticide, and euthanasia?

Kant's principle of ends says all humans have dignity by virtue of their rationality, so they are permitted to exploit animals (who are intelligent but not rational). But suppose Galacticans who visited our planet were superrational, as superior to us as we are to other animals. Would we then be second-class citizens whom the Galacticans could justifiably exploit for their purposes? Suppose they thought we tasted good and were nutritious. Would morality permit them to eat us? Kantians would probably insist that minimal rationality gives one status—but then, wouldn't some animals who deliberate (chimps, bonobos, gorillas, and dolphins) gain status as persons? And don't sheep, dogs, cats, pigs, and cows exhibit minimally rational behavior? Should we eat them? (The Chinese think nothing is wrong with eating dogs and cats.)

There is a third problem with Kant's view of the dignity of rational beings. Even if we should respect them and treat them as ends, this does not tell us very much. It may tell us not to enslave them or not to act cruelly toward them without a good reason, but it doesn't tell us what to do in situations where our two or more moral duties conflict.

For example, what does it tell us to do about a terminally ill woman who wants us to help her die? What does it tell us to do in a war when we are about to aim our gun at an enemy soldier? What does it mean to treat such a rational being as an end? What does it tell us to do with regard to the innocent, potential victim and the gangsters who have just asked us the whereabouts of the victim? What does it tell us about whether we should steal from the pharmacy to procure medicine we can't afford in order to bring healing to a loved one?

It's hard to see how the notion of ends helps us much in these situations. In fairness to Kant, however, we must say that virtually every moral system has trouble with dilemmas and that it might be possible to supplement Kantianism to solve some of them.

The Principle of Autonomy

The final formulation of the categorical imperative is the principle of **autonomy:** "So act that your will can regard itself at the same time as making universal law through its maxims." That is, we do not need an external authority—be it God, the state, our culture, or anyone else—to determine the nature of the moral law. We can discover this for ourselves. And the Kantian faith proclaims, everyone who is ideally rational will legislate exactly the same universal moral principles.

The opposite of autonomy is **heteronomy:** The heteronomous person is one whose actions are motivated by the authority of others, whether it is religion, the state, his or her parents, or a peer group. The following illustration may serve as an example of the difference between these two states of being.

In the early 1960s, Stanley Milgram of Yale University conducted a series of social psychological experiments aimed at determining the degree to which the ordinary citizen was obedient to authority. Volunteers from all walks of life were recruited to participate in "a study of memory and learning." Two people at a time were taken into the laboratory. The experimenter explained that one was to play the role of the "teacher" and the other the role of the "learner." The teacher was put in a separate room from which he or she could see the learner through a window. The teacher was instructed to ask the learner to choose the correct correlate to a given word, and the learner was to choose from a set of options. If the learner got the correct word, they moved on to the next word. But, if the learner chose the wrong word, he or she was punished with an electric shock. The teacher was given a sample shock of 45 volts just to get the feeling of the game. Each time that the learner made a mistake, the shock was increased by 15 volts (starting at 15 volts and continuing to 450 volts). The meter was marked with verbal designations: slight shock, moderate shock, strong shock, very strong shock, intense shock, extreme-intensity shock, danger: severe shock, and XXX. As the experiment proceeded, the learner would generally be heard grunting at the 75-volt shock, crying out at 120 volts, begging for release at 150 volts, and screaming in agony at 270 volts. At around 300 volts, there was usually dead silence.

Now, unbeknown to the teacher, the learner was not actually experiencing any shocks; the learners were really trained actors simulating agony. The results of the experiment were astounding. Whereas Milgram and associates had expected that only a small proportion of citizens would comply with the instructions, 60 percent were completely obedient and carried out the experiment to the very end. Only a handful refused to participate in the experiment at all once they discovered what it involved. Some 35 percent left at various stages. Milgram's experiments were later replicated in Munich, Germany, where 85 percent of the subjects were found to be completely "obedient to authority."

There are two ways in which the problems of autonomy and heteronomy are illustrated by this example. In the first place, the experiment seems to show that the average citizen acts less autonomously than we might expect. People are basically heteronomous, herd followers. In the second place, there is the question about whether Milgram should have subjected people to these experiments. Was he violating their autonomy and treating them as means (rather than ends) in deceiving them in the way he did? Perhaps a utilitarian would have an easier time justifying these experiments than a Kantian.

In any case, for Kant, it is our ability to use reason in universalizing the maxims of our actions that sets rational beings apart from nonrational beings. As such, rational beings belong to a kingdom of ends. Kant thought that each of us—as a fully rational, autonomous legislator—would be able to reason through to exactly the same set of moral principles, the ideal moral law.

THE PROBLEM OF EXCEPTIONLESS RULES

One of the problems that plagues all formulations of Kant's categorical imperative is that it yields unqualified absolutes. The rules that the categorical imperative generates are universal and exceptionless. He illustrates this point with regard to truth telling: Suppose an innocent man, Mr. Y, comes to your door, begging for asylum, because a group of gangsters is hunting him down to kill him. You take the man in and hide him in your third-floor attic. Moments later the gangsters arrive and inquire after the innocent man: "Is Mr. Y in your house?" What should you do? Kant's advice is to tell them the truth: "Yes, he's in my house."[8]

What is Kant's reasoning here? It is simply that the moral law is exceptionless. It is your duty to obey its commands, not to reason about the likely consequences. You have done your duty: hidden an innocent man and told the truth when asked a straightforward question. You are absolved of any responsibility for the harm that comes to the innocent man. It's not your fault that there are gangsters in the world.

To many of us, this kind of absolutism seems counterintuitive. One way we might alter Kant here is simply to write in qualifications to the universal principles, changing the sweeping generalization "Never lie" to the more modest "Never lie, except to save an innocent person's life." The trouble with this way of solving the problem is that there seem to be no limits on the qualifications that would need to be attached to the original generalization—for example, "Never lie, except to save an innocent person's life (unless trying to save that person's life will undermine the entire social fabric)" or "Never lie, except to save an innocent person's life (unless this will undermine the social fabric)" or "Never lie, except to spare people great anguish (such as telling a cancer patient the truth about her condition)." And so on. The process seems infinite and time consuming and thus impractical.

However, another strategy is open for Kant—namely, following the prima facie duty approach advocated by twentieth-century moral philosopher William

D. Ross (1877–1971). Let's first look at the key features of Ross's theory and then adapt it to Kant's.

Ross and Prima Facie Duties

Today, Ross is perhaps the most important deontological theorist after Kant, and, like Pufendorf, Ross is a rule-intuitionist. There are three components of Ross's theory. The first of these is his notion of "moral intuition," internal perceptions that both discover the correct moral principles and applies them correctly. Although they cannot be proved, the moral principles are *self-evident* to any normal person upon reflection. Ross wrote,

> That an act, qua fulfilling a promise, or qua effecting a just distribution of good . . . is prima facie right, is self-evident; not in the sense that it is evident . . . as soon as we attend to the proposition for the first time, but in the sense that when we have reached sufficient mental maturity and have given sufficient attention to the proposition it is evident without any need of proof, or of evidence beyond itself. It is evident just as a mathematical axiom, or the validity of a form of inference, is evident. . . . In our confidence that these propositions are true there is involved the same confidence in our reason that is involved in our confidence in mathematics. . . . In both cases we are dealing with propositions that cannot be proved, but that just as certainly need no proof.[9]

Just as some people are better perceivers than others, so the moral intuitions of more reflective people count for more in evaluating our moral judgments. "The moral convictions of thoughtful and well-educated people are the data of ethics, just as sense-perceptions are the data of a natural science."[10]

The second component of his theory is that our intuitive duties constitute a plural set that cannot be unified under a single overarching principle (such as Kant's categorical imperative or the utilitarian highest principle of "the greatest good for the greatest number"). As such, Ross echoes the intuitionism of Pufendorf by presenting a list of several duties, specifically these seven:

1. Promise keeping
2. Fidelity
3. Gratitude for favors
4. Beneficence
5. Justice
6. Self-improvement
7. Nonmaleficence

The third component of Ross's theory is that our intuitive duties are not absolute; every principle can be overridden by another in a particular situation. He makes this point with the distinction between **prima facie duties** and **actual duties.** The term *prima facie* is Latin for "at first glance," and Ross's point is that all seven of the above listed moral duties are tentatively binding on us until one duty conflicts with another. When that happens, the weaker one disappears, and the stronger one emerges as our actual duty. Thus, although prima facie duties are not actual duties, they may become such, depending on the circumstances. For example, if we make a promise, we put ourselves in a situation in which the duty to keep promises is a moral consideration. It has presumptive force, and if no conflicting prima facie duty is relevant, then the duty to keep our promises automatically becomes an actual duty.

What, for Ross, happens when two duties conflict? For an absolutist, an adequate moral system can never produce moral conflict, nor can a basic moral principle be overridden by another moral principle. But Ross is no absolutist. He allows for the overridability of principles. For example, suppose you have promised your friend that you will help her with her homework at 3:00 p.m. While you are on your way to meet her, you encounter a lost, crying child. There is no one else around to help the little boy, so you help him find his way home. But, in doing so, you miss your appointment. Have you done the morally right thing? Have you broken your promise?

It is possible to construe this situation as constituting a conflict between two moral principles:

1. We ought always to keep our promises.
2. We ought always to help people in need when it is not unreasonably inconvenient to do so.

In helping the child get home, you have decided that the second principle overrides the first. This does not mean that the first is not a valid principle—only that the "ought" in it is not an absolute "ought." The principle has objective validity, but it is not always decisive, depending on which other principles may apply to the situation. Although some duties are weightier than others—for example, nonmaleficence "is apprehended as a duty of a more stringent character...than beneficence"—the intuition must decide each situation on its own merits.

Kant and the Prima Facie Solution

Many moral philosophers—egoists, utilitarians, and deontologists—have adopted the prima facie component of Ross's theory as a convenient way of resolving moral dilemmas. In doing so, they typically don't adopt Ross's account of moral intuitions or his specific set of seven duties (that is, the first two components of Ross's theory). Rather, they just incorporate Ross's concepts of prima facie duty and actual duty as a mechanism for explaining how one duty might override another.

How might this approach work with Kant? Consider again Kant's innocent-man example. First, we have the principle L: "Never lie." Next, we ask whether any other principle is relevant in this situation and discover that that is principle P: "Always protect innocent life." But we cannot obey both L and P (we assume for the moment that silence will be a giveaway). We have two general principles; neither of them is to be seen as absolute or nonoverridable but rather as prima facie. We have to decide which of the two overrides the other, which has greater moral force. This is left up to our considered judgment (or the considered judgment of the reflective moral community). Presumably, we will opt for P over L, meaning that lying to the gangsters becomes our actual duty.

Will this maneuver save the Kantian system? Well, it changes it in a way that Kant might not have liked, but it seems to make sense: It transforms Kant's absolutism into a *modest objectivist* system (as described in Chapter 3). But now we need to have a separate criterion to resolve the conflict between two competing prima facie principles. For Ross, moral intuitions performed that function. Since Kant is more of a *rational* intuitionist, it would be the job of reason to perform that function. Perhaps his second formulation of the categorical imperative—the principle of ends— might be of service here. For example, in the illustration of the inquiring killer, the agent is caught between two compelling prima facie duties: "Never lie" and "Always protect innocent life." When determining his actual duty, the agent might reflect on which of these two duties best promotes the treatment of people as ends—that is, beings with intrinsic value. This now becomes a contest between the dignity of the would-be killer who deserves to hear the truth and the dignity of the would-be victim who deserves to live. In this case, the dignity of the would-be victim is the more compelling value, and the agent's actual duty would be to always protect innocent life. Thus, the agent should lie to protect the life of the would-be victim.

THE PROBLEM OF POSTERITY

In the chapters on egoism (Chapter 6) and utilitarianism (Chapter 7), we explored the problem of posterity: What obligations do we owe to future generations? This question is especially relevant now as we wrestle with issues of environmental responsibility. People today can undermine the environment in ways that may not seriously impact us while we're alive but will have devastating consequences on the well-being of future generations. The issue concerns the moral obligations that we have toward people who do not yet exist. We've seen that egoists, with their emphasis on personal self-interest, gain nothing by preserving natural resources for future generations that do not yet exist and thus can give no benefit to the egoist. Utilitarians, we've seen, do better: We have a duty to maximize general happiness, and it does not matter that we cannot identify these future people.

What, though, do deontologists say about the problem of posterity? Intuitionists such as Butler or Ross might find it self-evident that we do or we don't have obligations to future generations; thus, they are not much help in offering a systematic account of our duty to posterity. The situation is not much better with Kant who, with his strong emphasis on particular rational people, would have a particularly difficult time generating principles that would require duties to future agents. Kant seems to require identifiable people as the objects of our duties.

Here, though, is one solution that might be extracted from Kant's moral philosophy. Like earlier deontologists of his time such as Pufendorf, Kant distinguishes between perfect and imperfect duties. *Perfect duties* are those that require precise behavior toward particular people. For example, my duty to tell the truth is a perfect duty because it mandates in each situation that I should be truthful to each person who I communicate with. *Imperfect duties,* by contrast, do not require precise behavior toward particular people. An example of this would be my duty to be charitable. Although I should help those in need, I am not obligated to help *everyone* in need or even any *particular person* in need. It is up to me to determine who the receivers of my charity should be.

Applying this distinction to the problem of posterity, we might recognize an imperfect duty to promote the well-being of people who will exist in the future— even if we don't know who they are. As long as we are reasonably sure that they will exist, we have a duty to see to it that their lives are reasonably good. Although this helps somewhat in addressing the problem of posterity, it is not the best solution. Because imperfect duties are so undefined, they may be overridden by perfect duties. Thus, my imperfect duty to preserve the environment for future generations may be overridden by my perfect duty of justice to allow existing people in developing countries to exploit the environment for their economic advancement. This dilemma regarding developing countries is in fact at the heart of much of the environmental debate today.

Here's another solution offered by some Kantians: We do have obligations to the future world in the persons of our children. We have an obligation to leave the environment in good shape for our children, and they in turn will have such an obligation for their children, and so on, so that the question of posterity is taken care of. The duty carries over to future generations. But this seems to commit a fallacy of transitivity:

If A has a duty X to B and if B has a duty X to C, then A has a duty X to C.

This formula is invalid. I may have a duty to keep my promise to you, and you have a duty to keep your promise to your neighbor, but I don't have a duty to keep my promise to you to your neighbor. Similarly, our generation may have a duty to provide the next generation (our children) with an adequate living, but we don't have an obligation to provide the next generation with one. In fact, given scarce resources, it may be that simply sharing our resources with the next generation will use up a considerable amount so that the next generation will be unable to pass down a sufficient amount to the next generation. Considering the importance of the problem of posterity in environmental ethics today, defenders of Kant will undoubtedly wish to explore other more successful solutions.

CONCLUSION: A RECONCILIATION PROJECT

Utilitarianism and deontological systems such as Kant's are radically different types of moral theories. Some people seem to gravitate to the one and some to the other, but many people find themselves dissatisfied with both positions. Although they see something valid in each type of theory, at the same time there is something deeply troubling about each. Utilitarianism seems to catch the spirit of the purpose of morality, such as human flourishing and the reduction of suffering, but undercuts justice in a way that is counterintuitive. Deontological systems seem right in their emphasis on the importance of rules and the principle of justice but tend to become rigid or to lose focus on the central purposes of morality.

One philosopher, William Frankena, has attempted to reduce this tension by reconciling the two types of theories in an interesting way. He calls his position "mixed deontological ethics" because it is basically rule centered but in such a way as to take account of the teleological aspect of utilitarianism.[11] Utilitarians are right about the purpose of morality: All moral action involves doing good or alleviating evil. However, utilitarians are wrong to think that they can measure these amounts or that they are always obligated to bring about the "greatest balance of good over evil," as articulated by the principle of utility.

In place of the principle of utility, Frankena puts forth a near relative, the *principle of beneficence,* that calls on us to strive to do good without demanding that we be able to measure or weigh good and evil. Under his principle of beneficence, he lists four hierarchically arranged subprinciples:

1. One ought not to inflict evil or harm.
2. One ought to prevent evil or harm.
3. One ought to remove evil.
4. One ought to do or promote good.

In some sense, subprinciple 1 takes precedence over 2, 2 over 3, and 3 over 4, other things being equal.

The *principle of justice* is the second principle in Frankena's system. It involves treating every person with equal respect because that is what each is due. To quote John Rawls, "Each person possesses an inviolability founded on justice that even the welfare of society as a whole cannot override.... The rights secured by justice are not subject to political bargaining or to the calculus of social interests."[12] There is always a presumption of equal treatment unless a strong case can be made for overriding this principle. So even though both the principle of beneficence and the principle of justice are prima facie principles, the principle of justice enjoys a certain priority. All other duties can be derived from these two fundamental principles.

Of course, the problem with this kind of two-principle system is that we have no clear method for deciding between them in cases of moral conflict. In such cases, Frankena opts for an intuitionist approach similar to Ross's: We need to use our intuition whenever the two rules conflict in such a way as to leave us undecided on whether beneficence should override justice. Perhaps we cannot decisively solve every moral problem, but we can solve most of our problems successfully and make progress toward refining our subprinciples in a way that will allow us to reduce progressively the undecidable areas. At least, we have improved on strict deontological ethics by outlining a system that takes into account our intuitions in deciding complex moral issues.

NOTES

1. Immanuel Kant, *Foundations of the Metaphysics of Morals,* Sec. 1, adapted from *Fundamental Principles of the Metaphysics of Ethics,* trans. T. K. Abbott (London: Longman's, 1965).

2. Joseph Butler, *Five Sermons* (Liberal Arts Press, 1949), p. 45.

3. Samuel Pufendorf, *The Duty of Man and Citizen* (1673), Ch. 3, adapted from *The Whole Duty of Man According to the Law of Nature* (London: Charles Harper, 1691).

4. Kant, *Foundations,* Sec. 1.

5. Kant's notion of self-defeating is ambiguous, and scholars differ as to whether it means "self-contradictory" or simply "resulting in an unstable state of affairs." My view is that Kant wanted to say it was self-contradictory, but analysis shows only that universalizing certain maxims, such as promise breaking, would result in unstable states of affairs.

6. Kant, *Foundations,* Sec. 2.

7. Fred Feldman, *Introductory Ethics* (Prentice Hall, 1978), pp. 114–115.

8. Immanuel Kant, "On a Supposed Right to Lie from Altruistic Motives" (1797), in *Immanuel Kant: Critique of Practical Reason and Other Writings in Moral Philosophy,* ed. Lewis Beck White (Garland Press, 1976).

9. William D. Ross, *The Right and the Good* (Oxford University Press, 1930), pp. 39–41.

10. Ibid., p. 21.

11. William Frankena, *Ethics,* 2nd ed. (Prentice Hall, 1973), pp. 43–53.

12. John Rawls, *A Theory of Justice* (Harvard University Press, 1971), p. 3.

FOR FURTHER REFLECTION

1. Why does Kant believe that the good will is the only thing that is good without qualification? Do you agree with him?

2. Do you think that the Kantian argument that combines the principle of natural law with the principle of ends is successful?

3. Critics of Kant charge that he is too rigid in his absolutism and rejection of happiness as a motive for morality. Critics suggest that many people use the idea of moral duty to keep themselves and others from enjoying life and showing mercy. Do you think that there is a basis for this criticism?

4. Oliver Wendell Holmes, Jr., opposed Kant's principle of the end on the grounds that it runs contrary to how we treat enemy soldiers: "The enemy we treat not even as a means but as an obstacle to be abolished, if so it may be. I feel no pangs of conscience over either step, and naturally am slow to accept a theory that seems to be contradicted by practices that I approve" [*Collected Legal Papers* (Harcourt, Brace & Jovanovich, 1920), p. 340]. Evaluate Holmes's argument.

5. Examine the Galactican superrational counterexample. Would superrational beings be justified in treating us as we treat animals, even eating us?

6. Would a Kantian condemn the Milgram experiments as treating individuals merely as means rather than as ends in themselves? Do you think that the information derived from the experiments justified the experiments?

7. Evaluate Frankena's reconciliation project. How plausible is his attempt to reduce morality to two fundamental intuitions? Can you exercise moral reasoning without appeal to intuitions at some point in your deliberations? Explain your answer.

FOR FURTHER READING

Acton, Harry. *Kant's Moral Philosophy*. London: Macmillan, 1970.

Guyer, Paul, ed. *Kant's Groundwork of the Metaphysics of Morals: Critical Essays*. New York: Rowman & Littlefield, 1998.

Guyer, Paul. *Kant's Groundwork for the Metaphysics of Morals: A Reader's Guide*. London: Continuum, 2007.

Pasternack, Lawrence. *Immanuel Kant: Groundwork of the Metaphysics of Morals in Focus*. London: Routledge, 2002.

Pufendorf, Samuel. *On the Duty of Man and Citizen According to Natural Law*, ed. James Tully. Cambridge, Engl.: Cambridge University Press, 1991.

Sullivan, Roger J. *Immanuel Kant's Moral Theory*. Cambridge, Engl.: Cambridge University Press, 1989.

Ward, Keith. *The Development of Kant's Views of Ethics*. Oxford, Engl.: Blackwell, 1972.

Wolff, Robert P. *The Autonomy of Reason: A Commentary on Kant's Groundwork of the Metaphysics of Morals*. New York: Harper & Row, 1973.

9

※

Virtue Theory

Suppose, however, that in articulating the problems of morality the ordering of evaluative concepts has been misconceived by the spokesman of modernity and more particularly of liberalism; suppose that we need to attend to virtues in the first place in order to understand the function and authority of rules.
ALASDAIR MACINTYRE, *AFTER VIRTUE*

Morality is internal. The moral law...has to be expressed in the form "be this," not in the form "do this."...[T]he true moral law says "hate not," instead of "kill not."...[T]he only mode of stating the moral law must be as a rule of character.
LESLIE STEPHENS, *THE SCIENCE OF ETHICS*

John hears that 100,000 people are starving in Ethiopia. He feels deep sorrow about this and sends $100 of his hard-earned money to a famine relief project in that country. Joan hears the same news but doesn't feel anything. However, out of a sense of duty, she sends $100 of her hard-earned money to the same famine relief project. Consider another example. Jack and Jill each have the opportunity to embezzle $1 million from the bank at which they work. Jill never even considers embezzling; the possibility is not an option for her. Jack wrestles valiantly with the temptation, almost succumbs to it, but through a grand effort of will finally succeeds in resisting the temptation.

Who, if anyone, in each of these cases is more moral? We'd most likely say that it's John and Jill for the simple reason that they've internalized their moral convictions and do the right thing spontaneously without having to reflect on and struggle over the situation. In a word, John and Jill have special moral qualities that we call **virtues:** trained behavioral dispositions that result in habitual acts of moral goodness. The opposite mental quality is that of a **vice:** trained behavioral dispositions that result in habitual acts of moral wrongness. An entire ethical system called **virtue theory,** or **virtue ethics,** is based on this notion, the central theme of which is that morality involves producing excellent persons, who act well out of spontaneous goodness and serve as examples to inspire others. John and Jill, for example, are the morally good persons because of their good character that enables them to spontaneously do the right thing. There is a teleological (that is, "goal-oriented") aspect in virtue ethics, but it differs from the kind usually found in utilitarianism, which asks what sort of action will maximize happiness or utility. The virtue-based concept of teleology focuses, rather, on the goal of *life:* living well and achieving excellence.

According to virtue theorists, the ideal moral person should accumulate a range of virtues; the Greek philosopher Plato offered a short list that has been dubbed **cardinal virtues**—simply meaning "main virtues." They are wisdom, temperance, courage, and justice. Another brief list, given in the New Testament by Paul, is faith, hope, and charity; these have been called the **theological virtues.** For centuries, the combined list of cardinal and theological virtues held a prominent place in Western civilization's moral theories. We also find a strong emphasis on virtues in the moral traditions of the East. Hinduism advocates the virtues of nonviolence, truth, purity, and self-control. Confucius stated that perfect virtue consists of the five qualities of courtesy, generosity, honesty, persistence, and kindness. Although these lists may differ somewhat in tone, they all stress fixing behavioral habits that restrain one's desires and express kindness toward others.

We examine virtue ethics in this chapter, beginning with a general account of the theory itself. Then we'll look at the battle that has recently emerged between virtue ethics and its rival theories.

THE NATURE OF VIRTUE ETHICS

Virtue ethics says that it is important not only to do the right thing but also to have the proper dispositions, motivations, and emotions in being good and doing right. It is important that normally we are not even tempted to steal, lie, or cheat and that normally we enjoy doing good because we are good. Virtue ethics is not only about action but about emotions, character, and moral habit. It calls us to aspire to be an ideal person.

Virtues are excellences of character, trained behavioral dispositions that result in habitual acts. Traditionally, they have been divided into two types: moral and nonmoral virtues:

- *Moral virtues:* honesty, benevolence, nonmalevolence, fairness, kindness, conscientiousness, gratitude

■ *Nonmoral virtues:* courage, optimism, rationality, self-control, patience, endurance, industry, musical talent, cleanliness, wit

The exact classification of various virtues is debatable. Courage sometimes falls into the moral category, and virtues such as kindness (as opposed to impartial benevolence) might fit into either category. The moral virtues are more closely associated with what has been deemed essential for the moral life and incompatible with the immoral life. But the distinction seems rough and inexact because many of the moral virtues could be used for bad purposes—for example, the benevolent person who has an inclination for making things worse. The nonmoral virtues, while generally seen as contributing to the moral life, are more easily expropriated for immoral purposes—for example, the courageous criminal who is more dangerous than the cowardly one.

Although most virtue systems recognize that there are principles of action that serve as action guides (at least as rules of thumb), these entities are not the essence of morality. Likewise, even though it is sometimes appropriate to reason about what to do, such reasoning or deliberating should also give significant attention to feelings such as sympathy and loyalty. The primary focus is not on abstract reason but on types of good persons. Discovering and imitating the proper moral example thus replaces meticulous reasoning as the most significant aspects of the moral life. Eventually, the apprentice-like training in virtue gained by imitating the ideal model results in a virtuous person who spontaneously does what is good. There are two different ways this comes into focus: either through an examination of ideal types of persons or through following someone who is an ideal type. Let's examine each of these in turn.

The Ideal Type: Aristotle's *Nicomachean Ethics*

In Aristotle's classic work on the virtues, *Nicomachean Ethics,* he identified the virtues as simply those characteristics that enable individuals to live well in communities. To achieve a state of well-being (from the Greek *eudaimonia,* meaning "happiness" or "human flourishing"), proper social institutions are necessary. Thus, the moral person cannot really exist apart from a flourishing political setting that enables him or her to develop the required virtues for the good life. For this reason, ethics is considered a branch of politics. The state is not neutral toward the good life but should actively encourage citizens to inculcate the virtues, which in turn are the best guarantee of a flourishing political order.

For Aristotle, humanity has an essence, or function. Just as it is the function of a doctor to cure the sick and restore health, the function of a ruler to govern society well, and the function of a knife to cut well, so it is the function of humans to use reason in pursuit of the good life (*eudaimonia*). The virtues indicate the kind of moral—political characteristics necessary for people to attain happiness.

After locating ethics as a part of politics, Aristotle explains that the moral virtues are different from the intellectual ones. Whereas the intellectual virtues may be taught directly, the moral ones must be lived to be learned. By living well, we acquire the right habits; these habits are in fact the virtues. The virtues are to be sought as the best guarantee to the happy life. But, again, happiness requires that we be lucky enough to live in a flourishing state. The morally virtuous life consists in living in moderation, according to the Golden Mean. By the Golden Mean, Aristotle means that the virtues are at a middle ground between excess and deficiency. For example, courage is the mean between cowardice and fool-hardiness; liberality is the mean between stinginess and unrestrained giving. He writes,

> We can experience fear, confidence, desire, anger, pity, and generally any kind of pleasure and pain either too much or too little, and in either case not properly. But to experience all this at the right time, toward the right objects, toward the right people, for the right reason, and in the right manner—that is the mean and the best course, the course that is the mark of virtue.[1]

Aristotle held a rather elitist view that people have unequal abilities to be virtuous: Some are endowed with great ability, but others lack it altogether; some people are worthless, natural slaves. External circumstances could prevent even those capable of developing moral dispositions from reaching the goal of happiness. The moral virtues are a necessary but not a sufficient condition for happiness. One must, in addition to being virtuous, be healthy, wealthy, wise, and have good fortune.

What seems so remarkable to contemporary ethicists is that Aristotle hardly mentions moral rules or principles. It wasn't that he thought them unnecessary; they are implied in what he says. For example, his condemnation of adultery may be read as a principle ("Do not commit adultery"). Aristotle seems to think that such activities are inherently and obviously bad so that it is laboring the point to speak of a rule against adultery or against killing innocent persons. What is emphasized in place of principles is the importance of a good upbringing, good habits, self-control, courage, and character, without which the ethical life is impossible. A person of moral excellence cannot help doing good—it is as natural as the change of seasons or the rotation of the planets.

The Ideal Individual

In 1941 Father Maximilian Kolbe, a Polish friar from Warsaw, was arrested for publishing anti-Nazi pamphlets and sentenced to Auschwitz. There he was beaten, kicked by shiny leather boots, and whipped by his prison guards. After one prisoner successfully escaped, the prescribed punishment was to select ten other prisoners who were to die by starvation. As ten prisoners were pulled out of line one by one, Fr. Kolbe broke out from the ranks, pleading with the commandant to be allowed to take the place of one of the prisoners, a Polish worker with a wife and children dependent upon him. "I'm an old man, sir, and good for nothing. My life will serve no purpose," the 45-year-old priest pleaded. He was taken, thrown down the stairs into a dank dark basement with the other nine prisoners, and left to starve. Usually, prisoners punished like this spent their last days howling, attacking each other, and clawing the walls in a frenzy of despair.

But this time, a seeming miracle was heard coming from the death chamber: "[T]hose outside heard the faint sounds of singing. For this time the prisoners had a shepherd to gently lead them through the shadows of the valley of death, pointing them to the Great Shepherd." The Nazi guards were utterly astounded to see the men they were killing by starvation, at peace with themselves, quietly singing hymns just before they died. To keep one's heart and head in love and courage, in the midst of horror and degradation—not letting oneself become degraded but answering hate with love—that is a miracle of moral heroism. A few weeks later, several SS troopers, along with a doctor and a prisoner who survived to report the incident, entered the basement to remove the bodies. In the light of their flashlight, they saw Fr. Kolbe, a living skeleton, propped against the wall. His head was inclined a bit to the left. He had a smile on his lips and his eyes were wide open with a faraway gaze, as if seeing something invisible to the SS troopers. The doctor injected a poison-filled needle into Fr. Kolbe's arm, and in a moment he was dead. He was starved to death by the Nazis—but not before he had aided the other starving prisoners in facing their own deaths.[2]

Most of us learn by watching others and imitating them; this is a characteristic of virtue ethics. Rules cut up moral reality in fragmented and unnatural ways, but lives exhibit appropriate attitudes and dispositions in a holistic fashion. The lives of Socrates, Gandhi, Mother Teresa, and Father Kolbe provide examples of possibilities of moral excellence and inspire us to become ideal types. To put it poetically, they are people who light up our moral landscape as jewels who shine in their own light. Albert Schweitzer, who with four PhDs and a promising medical and musical career in Europe, renounced fame and fortune to open up a medical clinic at his own expense in Lambarine French West Africa, and developed the concept of *reverence for life,* is one of the most important and neglected role models of our time, far more important and interesting than the Hollywood characters or athletes idolized by our culture.

Perhaps no figure has served as an example for more people in Western culture than Jesus. An example of how his image has helped form the moral conscience of individuals is related by Paul Levy:

> The habit of examining one's conscience by asking oneself "What would Jesus do?" is conducive to the frame of mind required to enable one to ask oneself "What is the right (or the good) thing to do?" And it is only a short step from asking oneself what Jesus would do, to the realization that one is not asking an historical question such as "What in fact did Jesus do?," but a question that means "What would Jesus have done in these circumstances?" In the end . . . he is appealing to the idea of Jesus as a perfectly moral human being to give him ethical standards.[3]

The saints and moral heroes are the salt by which the world is preserved.

In an influential article, "Moral Saints," philosopher Susan Wolf argues that moral saints are unattractive because they lack the "ability to enjoy the enjoyable in life" and are so "very, very nice" that they must be "dull-witted or humorless or bland." Their lives are "strangely barren."[4] But is this true? Are the lives of the above-listed people "dull-witted or humorless or bland"? One may doubt it.

There is nothing "strangely barren" about Jesus' embodying the spirit of love, putting high **altruism** to practice as never before seen, accepting the pariahs of society, and bringing out their innate dignity. So too with Gandhi's fearlessly confronting the British Empire in the name of justice, his "quiet and determined voice" saying to the Indian people, "Be not afraid," and giving them courage. Consider also Martin Luther King, Jr., standing quietly and courageously praying for his enemies while they are about to unleash police dogs on him and his followers. And then there are those incredible, often unnamed, prisoners of Auschwitz who shared their food and precious possessions and who refused to be dehumanized by Nazi barbarities. So too with Mother Teresa, who spent her days healing the wounds and saving the lives of the disease-ridden homeless in the stench-filled slums of Calcutta. These are people who have reached a deeper way of living, who embody the Good in ways that far surpass our ordinary expressions of morality, as the sun's light outshines that of a flickering candle.

Wolf says the saints are boring when compared to such "interesting" and "attractive" people as Hollywood's most fashionable stars. But perhaps what we find interesting or boring is more a function of our moral education and development or appreciation than it is attributable to any saints or moral heroes. Perhaps it is not their fault if we do not see their inherent beauty? As one of the most saintly heroes of the twentieth century, Albert Schweitzer seems to have possessed those aesthetic qualities that Wolf finds lacking in moral saints. And yet, even if they may on average lack aesthetic talents, these saints and moral heroes do more than merely inspire our admiration. In them, we have living proof that a higher way of life is available to each of us. They shame us for being satisfied with our moral mediocrity. They challenge us to aspire to moral heights. The lesson of the exemplars is "If these humans can overcome temptation and live a deeply moral life, then so can I."

There is a further reason for affirming the value of moral saints. If we compare the actions of moral saints with the behavior of the thirty-nine witnesses to Kitty Genovese's brutal murder in Queens in 1964 (see Chapter 1), we can see why it is good for society to have a proportionate number of highly virtuous people in it to enhance the quality of life. Moral agents who go beyond minimal morality are necessary for a society if it is to overcome evil and produce a high degree of flourishing. Shouldn't we all be more altruistic than we are?

CRITICISMS OF ACTION-BASED ETHICS

Historically, virtue theory was a dominant player in moral philosophy for 2000 years, and philosophers who followed Aristotle made virtues the centerpiece of their systems. But even non-Aristotelian philosophers gave virtue a prominent role, a good example being Thomas Hobbes. For Hobbes, morality emerges through a series of social agreements that we make with each other as we attempt to leave a state of war and enter one of peace. We agree to keep our contracts, show gratitude toward others, be sociable, avoid signs of hatred toward others, compromise on our differences, and several other rules that ensure peace. But the main job of moral philosophy, Hobbes argues, is to teach people the virtues that will enable us to spontaneously follow these specific rules, such as the virtues of justice, gratitude, and sociability. We should also shun vices that will prevent us from acting on these rules, such as the vices of injustice, pride, and arrogance. Virtues, for Hobbes, are essential for keeping the peace.

But attitudes toward virtue theory began to change in the eighteenth century with the coming of utilitarianism and Kantianism. Utilitarian philosophers, particularly Jeremy Bentham and John Stuart Mill, argued that what matters in morality are the pleasing or painful consequences of our actions; virtues play no role in making such assessments. Mill makes this point here:

> [N]o known ethical standard decides an action to be good or bad because it is done by a good or a band man, still less because done by an amiable, a brave, or a benevolent man, or the contrary. These considerations are relevant, not to the estimation of actions, but of persons.[5]

For Kant, the core of morality is one's duty to follow the moral law as we rationally discover it through the categorical imperative. Just because you have a virtue, Kant argues, doesn't mean that you'll follow the moral law. A successful villain, for example, has the virtue of being coolheaded, though he clearly is not doing his moral duty.

As utilitarianism and Kantian deontology emerged as the dominant ethical theories of the nineteenth and early twentieth centuries, many theorists simply ignored virtue theory as being irrelevant to the new science of ethics. In recent decades, though, virtue ethics has reemerged as a major ethical theory, largely because of dissatisfaction with both utilitarian and Kantian moral theories.

In essence, then, there are two general approaches to moral theories: an action-based approach advocated by utilitarian and deontological philosophers, and a virtue-based approach defended by virtue theorists. In their most extreme forms, here are their principal differences:

- **Virtue-based theory:** (1) We should acquire good character traits, not simply act according to moral rules; (2) morality involves being a virtuous person.

- **Action-based theory:** (1) We should act properly by following moral rules; (2) we judge people based on how they act, not on whether they are virtuous people.

Virtue-based ethics centers in the heart of the agent—in his or her character—and emphasizes *being* rather than merely *doing*. The crucial moral question for this approach is "What sort of person should I become?" Virtue-based systems are sometimes called *aretaic ethics* (from the Greek *arete,* which we translate as "excellence" or "virtue"). By contrast, action-based theories emphasize the need to act according to moral rules, such as the utilitarian principle or the categorical imperative, and the central moral question for this approach is "What should I do?" These theories are sometimes referred to as *rule-governed* because of their emphasis on acting according to rules, or *deontic* (a term that incorporates both utilitarian and deontological reliance on action-guiding rules).

Our next task is to examine the views of recent virtue theorists and what they think is lacking in the action-based moral theories of utilitarianism and Kantianism.

Action-Based Ethics Lack a Motivational Component

Contemporary virtue theorists claim that action-based ethics are uninspiring, even boring—and largely negative. They fail to motivate or inspire to action. Ethics becomes a sort of mental plumbing, moral quibbling, a set of hairsplitting distinctions that somehow loses track of the purpose of morality altogether. But what good are such rules without the dynamo of character that propels the rules to action?

That deontological systems may be uninspiring is illustrated by their largely negative nature. Most of the commandments and rules in such systems are inherently negative: "Thou shall not _____!" As Mill complained about the so-called Christian morality of the Victorian Age,

> Christian morality (so-called) has all the characters of a reaction; it is, in great part, a protest against Paganism. Its ideal is negative rather than positive, passive rather than active; Innocence rather than Nobleness; Abstinence from Evil, rather than energetic Pursuit of the Good; in its precepts "Thou shalt not" predominates unduly over "Thou shalt." Whatever exists of magnanimity, highmindedness, personal dignity, even the sense of honor, is derived from the purely human, not the religious part of our education, and never could have grown out of a standard of ethics in which the only worth, professedly recognized, is that of obedience.[6]

There is something unsatisfactory about a morality that is so disproportionately defined in terms of "Thou shall nots," stressing innocence rather than an "energetic Pursuit of the Good." Deontological systems focus on an egoistic, minimal morality whose basic principles seem to be more preventive than positive. The only sure principle is a reciprocal duty to do no harm. This sort of theory places a very low value on morality, judging it primarily as a necessary evil. The virtue theorist rejects this judgment, seeing morality as an intrinsically worthwhile activity.

Action-Based Ethics Are Founded on an Obsolete
Theological–Legal Model

In 1958 Cambridge University philosopher Elizabeth Anscombe published a watershed article, "Modern Moral Philosophy," in which she argued that "it is not profitable for us at present to do moral philosophy" until we have an adequate philosophical psychology, and that our concepts of *moral obligation* and *moral duty* are derived from a theological–legal tradition that is no longer the dominant worldview.[7] Let's elaborate Anscombe's argument.

Moral language in traditional schemes usually has a structure that resembles that of law. Typically, the notions of right and wrong occur within the structure of a legal context in which there is a clear authority. Traditional, natural law ethics used this model with integrity because it saw moral principles as analogous to law and God as analogous to the sovereign ruler. Now, however, ethics has been detached from its theological moorings. It has become an autonomous activity, leaving the legal model without an analogue so that it is now an incoherent metaphor. The virtue ethicist rejects this model. Rather than spend time on moral hairsplitting and puzzle solving, ethics should help us develop admirable characters that will generate the kinds of insights needed for the requirements of life.

In this regard, the legalistic approach in modern moral theory has the effect of undermining the spirit of morality: "Morality was made for man, not man for morality." Rules often get in the way of kindness and spontaneous generosity. An illustration of this is the following passage from Mark Twain's *Huckleberry Finn,* in which Huck sees that his duty is to obey the law and turn in his black friend, the runaway slave Jim. Huck's principles tell him to report Jim to the authorities:

> Conscience says to me: "What had poor Miss Watson done to you, that you could see her nigger go off right under your eyes and never say one single word? What did that poor old woman do to you, that you could treat her so mean?" I got to feeling so mean and miserable I most wished I was dead. . . . My conscience got to stirring me up hotter than ever, until at last I says to it: "Let up on me—it ain't too late, yet—I'll paddle ashore at first light and tell." (Ch. 16)

Huck intends to report Jim and soon has the opportunity when two slave hunters ask him whether the man on his raft is black. But something in his character prevents Huck from turning Jim in. Virtue ethicists point out that Huck does the right thing because of his character, not because of his principles, and that sometimes, at least, our moral principles actually conflict with a deeper moral action that arises out of character.

Action-Based Ethics Ignore the Spontaneous Dimension of Ethics

Virtue theorists also charge that action-based ethics reduce all moral assessments to judgments about actions. By doing so, action-based ethics neglect the spontaneous aspect of moral conduct that emerges from a person's ingrained qualities of gratitude, self-respect, sympathy, having one's emotions in proper order, and aspiring to become a certain kind of person.

Consider the case of Jack and Jill mentioned at the beginning of this chapter. Both have the opportunity to embezzle. For Jack, it is a strenuous effort of the will that enables him to resist the temptation to embezzle, whereas for Jill the temptation does not even arise. She automatically rejects the fleeting thought as out of the range of her character. Now, it might be said that Jack has the important virtue of considerable strength of will but lacks the virtue of deep integrity that Jill possesses. Whereas stringent action-based ethics (such as Kant's, which puts the emphasis on conscientiousness, or doing one's duty for duty's sake) would say that Jack is the only one of the two who is moral, virtue ethics would say that Jill is the superior moral being. She has something good about her character that Jack lacks.

Consider the case of John and Joan also mentioned at the chapter's opening. Both send money to charity, but John does it with a deep feeling of sorrow for the famine victims whereas Joan does it simply out of a sense of duty. The virtue ethicist would argue that John has the right moral feelings whereas Joan is merely a cold, calculating moral machine who lacks the appropriate warmth of judgment toward the starving.

Virtue ethicists often cite Kant's theory as a paradigm of an antivirtue ethic. They point out that an examination of Kant's extreme action-based approach highlights the need for a virtue alternative. For Kant, natural goodness is morally irrelevant. The fact that you actually want to help someone (because you like them or just like doing good deeds) is of no moral importance. In fact, because of the emphasis put on the good will (doing duty for duty's sake), it seems that Kant's logic would force him to conclude that you are actually moral in proportion to the amount of temptation that you have to resist in performing your duty: For little temptation, you receive little moral credit; if you experience great temptation, you receive great moral credit for overcoming it.

To virtue ethicists, this is preposterous. Taken to its logical conclusion, the homicidal maniac who always just barely succeeds in resisting his perpetual temptation to kill is actually the most glorious saint, surpassing the "natural saint" who does good just because of a good character. True goodness is to spontaneously, cheerfully, and enjoyably do what is good. As Aristotle said,

> We may even go so far as to state that the man who does not enjoy performing noble actions is not a good man at all. Nobody would call a man just who does not enjoy acting justly, nor generous who does not enjoy generous actions, and so on.[8]

It is not the hounded neurotic who barely manages to control himself before each passing temptation but the natural saint—the one who does good out of habit and from the inner resources of good character—who is the morally superior person.

Action-Based Ethics Are Minimalist and Neglect the Development of Character

David L. Norton has argued for a fundamental distinction between traditional action-based ethics and classical virtue ethics.[9] Traditional action-based ethics tends to be minimalist, calling on us to adhere to a core of necessary rules (for example, do not steal, harm, murder, or lie) for society to function. The accent is on *social control:* Morality is largely preventive, safeguarding rights and moral space where people may carry out their projects unhindered by the intrusions of others. Daniel Callahan characterizes such a *moral minimalist ethic* this way:

> It has been one that stressed the transcendence of the individual over the community, the need to tolerate all moral viewpoints, the autonomy of the self as the highest human good, the informed consent contract as the model of human relationships. We are obliged under the most generous reading of a minimalist ethic only to honor our voluntarily undertaken family obligations, to keep our promises, and to respect contracts freely entered into with other freely consenting adults. Beyond those minimal standards, we are free to do as we like, guided by nothing other than our private standards of good and evil.[10]

However, according to Norton, classical virtue ethics, going back to Socrates, Plato, and Aristotle, presupposes two theses that go well beyond minimalist ethics. First, there is no separate moral-free zone, and prudence cannot be separated from morality, at least not to the extent that minimalism separates it. The Good is good for you. Second, virtue ethics supposes a duty of moral development or growth so that, while not everyone is called on to be a saint or hero, if we develop properly we may all develop moral sensitivities and abilities in ways that approximate those of the saints and heroes. A hero is one who accomplishes good deeds when the average person would be prevented by fear, terror, or a drive of self-interest. A saint is one who acts for good when inclination, desire, or self-interest would prevent most people from so acting.

The crucial factor in virtue-based ethics is the *duty* to grow as a moral person so that one may be able to take on greater moral responsibility. With increased responsibility comes increased competence in making moral choices and increased exhilaration at scaling moral mountain peaks. Norton has identified a crucial problem in contemporary moral theory: It is not enough to get people to adhere to a minimal morality. We must come to realize that we have a duty to not only obey core moral injunctions but also a responsibility to develop our moral sensitivities and abilities to the point where we can live life on a higher moral plane, both enjoying the exhilaration of high and challenging places and bearing burdens unknown to fledglings in moral climbing.

If this argument is correct, moral learning never stops, and moral education from childhood onward is one of the most important things we can engage in, both for society's sake (for it is in our interest to have deeply moral citizens) and for our own sake (it is in our interest to be deeply moral people).

Action-Based Ethics Overemphasize Autonomy and Neglect Community

In his book *After Virtue* (1981), Alasdair MacIntyre argues that rule-governed ethics is a symptom of the Enlightenment, which exaggerated the *principle of autonomy*—that is, the ability of each person to arrive at a moral code by reason alone. However, MacIntyre maintains, all moral codes are rooted in practices that themselves are rooted in traditions or forms of life. We do not make moral decisions as rational atoms in a vacuum, and it is sheer ideological blindness that allows this distorted perception. MacIntyre does not want to embrace relativism. We can discover better ways of living, but they will probably be founded on an account of what the good life is and what a good community is.

It is in communities that such virtues as loyalty, natural affection, spontaneous sympathy, and shared concerns arise and sustain the group. It is out of this primary loyalty (to family, friends, and community) that the proper dispositions arise that flow out to the rest of humanity. Hence, moral psychology is more important than traditional ethics has usually recognized. Seeing how people actually learn to be moral and how they are inspired to act morally is vital to moral theory itself, and this, it seems, has everything to do with the virtues.

In sum, action-based systems are uninspiring and unmotivating, negative, improperly legalistic, neglectful of the spiritual dimension, overly rationalistic, and atomistic. Against this background of dissatisfaction with traditional moral theory, virtue ethics has reasserted itself as offering something that captures the essence of the moral point of view.

CONNECTIONS BETWEEN VIRTUE-BASED AND ACTION-BASED ETHICS

So far we've seen the tension that exists between virtue-based and action-based ethics. Which approach is right, if either? Can the two be reconciled with each other? There are three basic relationships that might exist between virtues and moral rules, and all of them are positions held today by various philosophers. In this section and the following, we examine these positions. Briefly, here are the three relationships:

1. *Pure virtue-based ethics.* The virtues are dominant and have intrinsic value. Moral rules or duties are derived from the virtues. For example, if we claim that we have a duty to be just or beneficent, we must discover the virtues of fairness and benevolence in the good person.

2. *The standard action-based view.* Action-guiding principles are the essence of morality. The virtues are derived from the principles and are instrumental in performing right actions. For each virtue, there is a corresponding principle that is the important aspect of the relationship.

3. *Complementarity (pluralistic) ethics.* Both action-based and virtue-based models are necessary for an adequate or complete system. Neither the virtues nor rules are primary; they complement each other, and both may have intrinsic value.

Let's look at each in more detail.

Pure Virtue-Based Ethics

The pure virtue-based view assigns the strongest moral weight to virtues; the moral rules that we have are just extracted from and reflect our virtues. But this approach faces serious challenges. Even though the formula for pure virtue-based ethics sometimes accurately describes how a moral act is generated (that is, we sometimes act spontaneously out of a good heart), it hardly seems to cover all ethical actions. Sometimes we do use rules and moral reasons to decide what to do. The question is whether these rules are really irrelevant to what morality is getting at. As of now, no one has worked out a complete, pure virtue-based account, so it is hard to know whether it can be done. It seems to suffer from two major types of problems: epistemological and practical.

The *epistemological problem* concerns how we know which habits and emotions constitute genuine virtues. Who is the virtuous person? Suppose you ask me, "What is the right thing to do?" I answer, "Do what the virtuous person would do!" But you counter, "Who is the virtuous person?" To which I reply, "The person who does the right thing." The reasoning is circular. Without principles, virtues lack direction; we need something to serve as a criterion for them.

Related to this epistemological problem is the problem of virtue relativism: What counts as a virtue changes over time and place. Whereas Aristotle valued pride as a special virtue, Christians see it as a master vice. An ancient caveman facing a herd of mastodons with a spear would be thought by his community to have "excessive" fear if he abandoned his fellow tribesmen and fled whereas contemporary society would make no such judgment. Capitalists view acquisitiveness as a virtue, whereas Marxists see it as a vice.

The *practical problem* with pure virtue-based ethics is it provides no guidance on how to resolve an ethical dilemma. In Aristotle's *Nicomachean Ethics,* precious little is said about what we are supposed to *do.* One would think that ethics should be, at least to some extent, action guiding. Aristotle's answer seems to be "Do what a good person would do." But, these questions arise: "who is the good person, and how will we recognize him or her?" Furthermore, even if we could answer those questions without reference to kinds of actions or principles addressed by nonvirtue-oriented ethicists, it is not always clear what ideal persons would do in our situations. Sometimes Aristotle writes as though the right action is that intermediate mean, or Golden Mean, between two extremes. The virtue of courage, for example, is at the mean between the more vices of rashness and cowardice. However, it is often hard, if not impossible, to determine how to apply this. As J. L. Mackie says,

> As guidance about what is the good life, what precisely one ought to do, or even by what standard one should try to decide what one ought to do, this is too circular to be very helpful. And though Aristotle's account is filled out with detailed descriptions of many of the virtues, moral as well as intellectual, the air of indeterminacy persists. We learn the names of the pairs of contrary vices that contrast with each of the virtues, but

very little about where or how to draw the dividing lines, where or how to fix the mean. As Sidgwick says, he "only indicates the whereabouts of virtue."[11]

In sum, virtue ethics has a problem of application: It doesn't tell us what to do in particular instances in which we most need direction.

Standard Action-Based Ethics: The Correspondence Thesis

The standard action-based view acknowledges moral virtues but gives them a secondary status. This view has three theses:[12]

1. *The action-nature of the rules thesis.* Moral rules require persons to perform or omit certain actions, and these actions can be performed by persons who lack the various virtues as well as by those who possess them. (For example, both the benevolent and those who lack benevolence can perform beneficent acts such as giving to charity.)

2. *The reductionist thesis.* The moral virtues are dispositions to obey the moral rules—that is, to perform or omit certain actions. (For example, the virtue of benevolence is a disposition to carry out the duty to perform beneficent acts.) According to the correspondence theory of virtues, each virtue corresponds to an appropriate moral principle.

3. *Instrumental value thesis.* The moral virtues have no intrinsic value but do have instrumental and derivative value. Agents who have the virtues are more likely to do the right acts (that is, obey the rules). The virtues are important only because they motivate right action.

By the standard view, it is important to make two different but related assessments within the scope of morality: We need to make separate evaluations of the agent and the act. Both are necessary to a full ethical assessment, but it is the act that is logically prior in the relationship. Why is this?

It has to do with the nature of morality. If we agree that the general point of morality is to promote human flourishing and to reduce suffering, then we may judge that it is good or right kinds of acts that are, in the end, of utmost importance. But if we agree that there is a general tendency in human affairs for social relations to run down because of natural inclinations toward self-interest, then we can see that special forces have to be put in motion to counteract natural selfishness. One of these forces is the external sanctions produced by the law and social pressure. But a deeper and more enduring force is the creation of dispositions in people to do what is morally commendable. As Geoffrey Warnock says,

> It is necessary that people should acquire, and should seek to ensure that others acquire, what may be called good dispositions, that is, some readiness on occasion voluntarily to do desirable things which not all human beings are just naturally disposed to do anyway, and similarly not to do damaging things.[13]

Warnock identifies four such virtues that are necessary for social well-being. Since in the competitive struggle for goods we have a natural tendency to inflict damage on others (especially those outside the circle of our sympathies), there is a need for the virtue of nonmaleficence (that is, nonharm). But we will all do better if we are not simply disposed to leave one another alone but are positively disposed to help one another whenever social cooperation is desirable. Thus, we should cultivate the virtue of beneficence. There is also a natural tendency to discriminate in favor of our loved ones or our own interests, so we must train ourselves to be just, impartial judges who give each person his or her due: We must acquire the virtue of fairness. Finally, there is a natural temptation to deceive in our own interest; we lie, cheat, and give false impressions when it is to our advantage. This deception, however, tends to harm society at large, generating suspicion, which in turn undermines trust and leads to the breakdown of social cooperation. So, we must cultivate the disposition to honesty or truthfulness, and we must value and praise those who have the right dispositions and safeguard ourselves against those who lack these virtues.

Duty-based ethical theorists who hold to the standard account recognize the importance of character, but they claim that the nature of the virtues can only be derived from right actions or good consequences. To quote William Frankena, "Traits without principles are blind."[14] Whenever there is a virtue, there must be some possible action to which the virtue corresponds and from which it derives its virtuousness. For example, the character trait of truthfulness is a virtue because telling the truth, in general, is a moral duty. Likewise, conscientiousness is a virtue because we have a general duty to be morally sensitive. There is a correspondence between principles and virtues, the latter being derived from the former, as the following suggests:

The Virtue (derived from)	The Principle (prima facie)
Nonmaleficence	Duty not to harm
Truthfulness	Duty to tell the truth
Conscientiousness	Duty to be sensitive to one's duty
Benevolence	Duty to be beneficent
Faithfulness	Duty to be loyal or faithful
Fairness	Duty to be just
Love	Duty to do what promotes another's good

Although derived from the right kind of actions, the virtues are nonetheless very important for the moral life: They provide the dispositions that generate right action. In a sense, they are motivationally indispensable. To extend the Frankena passage quoted earlier, "Traits without principles are blind, but principles without traits are impotent." Frankena modifies this position, distinguishing two types of virtues: (1) the standard moral virtues, which correspond to specific kinds of moral principles, and (2) nonmoral virtues, such as natural kindliness or gratefulness, industry, courage, and intelligence or rationality, which are "morality-supporting." They are sometimes called "enabling virtues" because they make it possible for us to carry out our moral duties. The relationship looks something like this:

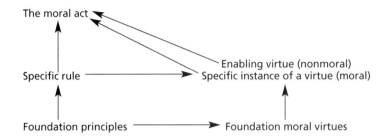

For example, consider the situation in which you have an obligation to save a drowning child despite some risk to your own life. The specific rule of "Always come to the aid of drowning people" is grounded in a foundational principle of general beneficence, which in turn generates the foundational virtue of benevolence. In this case, it gives rise to a tendency to try to save the drowning child. Whether or not you actually dive into the lake, however, may depend on the enabling (nonmoral) virtue of courage. Courage itself is not a moral virtue, as are benevolence and justice, because it is the kind of virtue that enhances and augments both virtues and vices (for example, think of the courageous murderer).

Standard Action-Based Ethicist's Responses
to Virtue-Based Criticisms

Can the correspondence theory answer the objections leveled against the action-based view earlier in this chapter? Let's consider the kinds of initial responses available to it.

First, to the charge that it lacks an adequate motivational component, philosophers such as Warnock would insist that we can bring up children to prize the correct principles and to embody them in their lives. Moral psychology will help us develop the necessary virtues in such a way as to promote human flourishing.

An action-based approach can honor the virtues and use them wisely without distorting their role in life. Sophisticated action-based theories can even insist that we have a duty to obtain the virtues as the best means to achieving success in carrying out our duties and that we have a special duty to inculcate in ourselves and others the virtue of conscientiousness (the disposition to do one's duty), which will help us achieve all our other duties. This kind of thinking shows that the story of Huck Finn's conscience (discussed earlier) is not really a good counterexample to action-based ethics. Sometimes our character is ahead of our principles, but that has nothing to do with the essential relationship between virtues and rules.

Second, to Anscombe's charge that action-based ethics is based on an improper theological–legal model, action-based ethicists respond that we can separate the rational decision-making procedures from the theological ones without violating those procedures. To the charge that this still leaves us with a skewed process of hairsplitting, they answer that it is important to come as close as possible to working out a consistent system because we want to have all the guidance for our actions that is possible. Appropriate modesty will inform us of our limits in this respect, but at least we have rules as guides—unlike the extreme virtue-based theorist, who only has dispositions.

Third, to the charge that action-based ethics neglects the spontaneous dimension of morality, the action-based ethicist responds that we can honor the virtues without restricting morality to them completely. It is better to have a virtue (such as benevolence) than not to have it because having the virtue gives us the best chance of acting rightly. However, there is no intrinsic value in the virtue. What really is important is *doing* the right act. This is not to deny that there may be aesthetic value in having correct attitudes or virtues besides their morally instrumental value, but we ought not to confuse ethical value with aesthetic value. In our opening example in this chapter, there is something satisfying about John's feeling sorrow over the starving Ethiopians, but it is an aesthetic satisfaction. Note the language describing deeply altruistic people: They are, to paraphrase Kant, "jewels who shine in their own light." The very metaphor should signal the fact that beyond their moral worth (in the actions they perform) we find something aesthetically attractive in their virtuous lives.

Fourth, regarding Norton's criticism that action-based ethics are minimalist and neglect the development of character, action-based ethicists point out that moral minimalism has the advantage that it appeals to minimal common sense and so can easily be universalized; its injunctions apply to all rational agents. Its claims are exceedingly modest because it permits most of life to go on without the scrutiny of morality. As Mill says, "Ninety-nine hundredths of all our actions are done from other [than moral] motives, and rightly so done if the rule of duty does not condemn them."[15] The major portion of life comes not under the domain of moral obligation but under the domain of the permissible. We are given a generous portion of morally free space in which to develop our personality and talents as we see fit—just as long as we do not break out of the broad confines of moral constraints. The morally free zone is sometimes identified with what is prudent or what pertains to our self-interest.

Fifth and finally, to MacIntyre's criticism that morality emerges in communities and cultures, action-based ethicists respond that if this is taken as the whole story, it implies ethical relativism, in which case the virtues have no objective status either. On the other hand, if MacIntyre allows that we can discover the Good for man in the context of an Aristotelian naturalism, then we can derive a core set of principles as well as the right virtues.

Pluralistic (Complementarity) Ethics

The virtue-based ethicist will not be satisfied with the standard action-based view and its correspondence theory, because it is still reductionistic, treating the virtues like second-class citizens, like servants of the master rules. Even if virtue theorists agree that virtue-based ethics cannot stand alone, they will not accept this kind of reductionism. There must be true complementarity, a recognition of the importance of both rules and virtues in ways that do not exhaust either. Some instances of carrying out the rule may be done without a virtue, and some virtues will be prized for their own sake even without any correspondence to a moral duty. This is the view of **pluralistic ethics**—derived from the term *plural,* meaning "more than one."

To clarify, let's recall the three theses of the standard action-based view: (1) the action-nature of the rules thesis, (2) the reductionist thesis, and (3) the instrumental value thesis. Pluralistic ethicists, like virtue theorists, must reject all three in order to elevate virtues from their second-class status and put them on an equal level with moral rules. Let's begin with the first:

1. *The action-nature of the rules thesis.* Moral rules require persons to perform or omit certain actions, and these actions can be performed by persons who lack the various virtues as well as by those who possess them.

Pluralistic ethicists have two problems with this thesis. First, it neglects the close causal link between virtue and action. Doing right without the requisite disposition is like a person who has never before played baseball hitting a home run against a leading major-league pitcher: He may have luck this time, but he shouldn't count on it. Likewise, without the virtues, we shouldn't expect right conduct, even though we may occasionally be surprised both by the right act of the nonvirtuous and by the wrong act of the virtuous. Because of the close causal connection, it is statistically improbable that the good will do wrong and the bad or indifferent will do right.

Second, the thesis fails to point out that we have moral obligations to be certain kinds of people—that is, to have the requisite dispositions and attitudes for their own sake. It specifies only rules requiring action, but there are other types of moral rules as well—those requiring virtue.

The second thesis of the standard action-based view is this:

2. *The reductionist thesis.* The moral virtues are dispositions to obey the moral rules—that is, to perform or omit certain actions. According to the correspondence theory of virtues, each virtue corresponds to an appropriate moral principle.

What is at issue here is whether the virtues are more than just dispositions to act— whether they include attitudes that may not involve action. Kant pointed out that love (in the passional or emotional sense) could not be a moral duty because it could not be commanded, for we have no direct control over our emotions. While the moral law may require me to give a part of my income to feed the poor, I don't have to like them; I give my money because it is right to do so.

Pluralistic ethicists reject this kind of thinking. Although we don't have direct control over our emotions, we do have indirect control over them. We cannot turn our dispositions on and off like water faucets, but we can take steps to instill the right dispositions and attitudes. If we recognize the appropriateness of certain emotions in certain situations, we can use meditation, sympathetic imagination, and therapy (and, if one is religious, prayer) to obtain those attitudes in the right way. We are responsible for our character. We must not only *be* good, but we must love the good. As Aristotle said, "There must first be a disposition to excellence, to love what is fine and loathe what is base."

Consider two people, Joe and Jane, whose actions are equally correct. However, there is a difference between their attitudes. Joe tends to rejoice in the success of others and to feel sorrow over their mishaps. Jane, on the other hand, tends to feel glee at their mishaps and to envy their success. As long as their outward actions (and their will to do right) are similar, the action-based ethicist regards them as equally moral. But not the virtue ethicist: Joe has but Jane lacks the requisite moral attitude—and Jane has a moral duty to change that attitude.

Thomas Hill tells the story of a woman who always does what is morally right or permissible but does it out of a motive born of low self-esteem.[16] She doesn't respect herself but defers to her husband and children with an attitude of self-condemnation. Self-respect doesn't appear to be easily dissected into separate action types, yet it seems plausible to believe that it is a virtue, one we have a duty to instill (assuming that we are intrinsically worthy as rational beings). If this is correct, then the duty to respect oneself is yet another counterexample to the second thesis.

There are reactive attitudes or emotions—such as grief, gratitude, respect, and sensitivity—that in many situations seem appropriate for their own sake, regardless of whether they can be acted upon. The standard action-based view neglects this feature of morality; it reduces morality to actions.

Here is the third and final thesis of the standard action-based position:

3. *Instrumental value thesis.* The moral virtues have no intrinsic value but do have instrumental and derivative value. The virtues are important only because they motivate right action.

Again, pluralistic ethicists reject this instrumental view of the virtues: The virtues have intrinsic value and are not merely derivative but part of what constitutes the good life. The Good is not simply good for others but is good for you as well. The virtues are an inescapable part of what makes life worth living—having the right dispositions and attitudes to the right degree expressed in the right way. Joe is a better person for grieving with the suffering and rejoicing with the successful. He has an appropriate attitude whereas Jane doesn't, and this reflects on the quality of their happiness. It is not enough to do the right thing—even to do the right thing for the right reason; it is also important to do it with the right attitude and to have the right attitude and dispositions even when no action is possible.

The difference between the standard action-based view and the pluralistic view is this: Both recognize that the promotion of human flourishing is an essential goal of morality, but the action ethicist thinks that morality only has to do with the kinds of actions that produce this state of affairs, whereas the pluralistic ethicist believes that the virtues are constitutive of what human flourishing is and, hence, partly define the state of affairs we ought to be trying to produce by our actions. For the virtue ethicist, the unvirtuous (virtue-indifferent or vicious) life is not worth living.

FEMINISM AND THE ETHICS OF CARE

In her groundbreaking book *In a Different Voice,*[17] Carol Gilligan presents evidence that, with regard to moral development, contrary to mainline thinking, girls develop differently from boys. Lawrence Kohlberg, the eminent Harvard professor, had set forth a theory of moral development that emphasized the ideals of justice, abstract principles universally applied as the highest form of moral thinking. A typical study asked 11-year-old boys to resolve the following moral dilemma: A man named Heinz has a very sick wife and cannot afford the costly drug necessary to save her life. Heinz has an opportunity to steal the drug from a pharmacy. *What should Heinz do?* A typical male response is that given by a boy called "Jack." Jack responds that Heinz should steal the drug. He reasons:

> For one thing, human life is worth more than money, and if the druggist only makes $1,000, he is still going to live, but if Heinz doesn't steal the drug, his wife is going to die.
> *Why is life worth more than money?*
> [Jack] Because the druggist can get a thousand dollars later from rich people with cancer, but Heinz can't get his wife again.
> *Why not?*
> [Jack] Because people are all different and so you couldn't get Heinz's wife again.
> *What if Heinz does not love his wife?*
> [Jack] He should still steal the drugs to save his wife's life, for there is "a difference between hating and killing."
> Jack places morality over the law, for "the laws have mistakes, and you can't go writing up a law for everything that you can imagine."[18]

Gilligan points out that Kohlberg's studies were entirely on males and contrasts this kind of (male) rational moral thinking with that of the average 11-year-old girl, whose moral reasons emphasize relationships. Typical of girls' responses to the Heinz dilemma is that of the girl called "Amy," who responds to the question of whether Heinz should steal the drugs:

> I don't think so. I think there might be other ways besides stealing it, like if he could borrow the money or make a loan or something, but he really shouldn't steal the drug—but his wife shouldn't die either.

Responding to the question "Why shouldn't Heinz steal the drug?" Amy points out the deleterious effect that stealing the drug could have on the couple's relationship:

> If he stole the drug, he might save his wife's life, but if he did, he might have to go to jail, and his wife might get weaker again, and he couldn't get more of the drug, and it might not be good. So, they should really just talk it out and find some other way to make the money.

Gilligan argues that, on average, a woman's moral point of view is different from a man's. Whereas men typically emphasize rights and principles of justice (moral justice even trumps the law in the Heinz dilemma), women typically focus on particular relationships, on care, in which principles are less important, and they place more importance on the process ("they should talk it out and find some other way to make the money").

Gilligan's view has inspired a large body of work on women's values, feminist ethics, and female moral development (which has generated much light and considerable heat), much of which goes beyond the scope of this book. But the contribution that is relevant with regard to virtue ethics is the development of **care-ethics,** the thesis that attitudes like caring and sensitivity to context is an important aspect of the moral life. Sometimes when reading feminist ethics, one gets the impression that there are two different ethical systems: one focusing on care and more suitable to females and one focusing on principles and more suitable to males, implying a treacherous relativism.[19]

I don't get this impression from Gilligan's work. As I read Gilligan, her point is not that female values are better than male values or that there are two moralities, one for males and one for females, but that we should recognize that we each develop differently. After all, Gilligan is only describing the average girl or boy. Some girls are deeply concerned with justice and rationality, and some boys are deeply sensitive to others. My interpretation of her studies is that we need to correct for a one-sided emphasis on principles and incorporate a virtue dimension into moral thinking. In particular, we need to see the ethics of caring, of being attentive to personal relationships, such as child rearing, family, and friendship, as more important than rule-governed ethics has sometimes supposed.

Care-ethics is similar to the Christian ethical theory of **agapeism,** which taken from the Greek word for "love," *agapē*. The inspiration for agapeism is the New Testament passage in 1 John 4: 7–8, "Beloved let us love one another, for love is of God, and he who loves is born of God and knows God. He who does not love does not know God, for God is love." In essence, agapeism is care-ethics applied universally, to include all humanity, and care-ethics is agapeism more narrowly focused on special relationships, the parent—child relationship, marriage partners, friends, and loved ones. Both systems are subject to the same problem: Love without the guidance of rules seems blind. When my child commits a heinous crime, although I may love my child, I still have a moral duty to society at large, as well as to my child, to report my child to the authorities. Both love and justice seem necessary for a full moral system and a full moral life.

Care and Particularism

Some philosophers go even further with this relational feature of our moral repertoire and argue that it is precisely these particular relations, not the abstract universal principles, that generate our ethics.[20] These philosophers reject classic universalist ethics, the idea that ethics consists in universal moral principles, applicable to all people at all times. Instead, they argue that universalism is too abstract to justify our special obligations to family, community, and nation. Morality flourishes in concrete relationships that give meaning and purpose to our lives; we misconstrue the subject when we transform it into the abstract, bloodless universal principles of the core morality. This larger theory (of which care-ethics is a part) is called **moral particularism.** It states that morality always involves particular relations with particular people, not lifeless abstractions.

What are we to make of their argument? Should particularism replace universalism? The particularist may be confusing the discovery of moral obligation with the justification of moral obligation. It is no doubt true that we discover what morality is about through the intimacy of family and communal interaction, but it is difficult to see how this undermines universalism. The universalist agrees that we have special obligations to family, friends, and community, but this obligation is not just particular to us but to all people in all communities everywhere. For example, Kantians argue that we have special relations to our families because we are more deeply responsible for them, and rule-utilitarians argue that we will maximize utility if we each concentrate on helping those close to us, our family and community, rather than trying to give equal attention to people in other countries because we understand our close relations better than we do strangers and foreigners and are more likely to maximize welfare if we concentrate on their needs. Of course, we have obligations to people in other countries, but they seldom override our primary obligations to our family or fellow countrymen.

We may compare a nation to a team. Consider a football team. The members cooperate with one another for a common purpose, to play well and win the game. Each member is concerned to help the other members in a way that they are not concerned with the good of members of rival teams. They may respect and admire rival team members and refrain from fouls and unnecessary harm, but they aim to win the game, to be the best team in the league, and this requires giving special attention to the needs of teammates consistent with the good of the whole. If a teammate forgets a play or runs a wrong pattern, other members have a duty to correct him or her; they do not have a duty to correct an opposing player's mistake. Indeed, they hope members of the opposing team will forget more plays and run more wrong patterns. Vice versa, members of other teams have special obligations to their teammates that they do not have to our team.

Thus, classical moral theory can incorporate the concerns of particularist, care-ethics and grant special obligations to family, friends, and nation, without denying the universal duties to strangers, and future and distant people, which classic ethics emphasizes. We can believe in love and justice. We can recognize the truth of the care-ethicists without surrendering our commitment to reason and universal principles.

CONCLUSION

Virtue-based ethics, including the feminist ethics of care, poses a significant challenge to standard action-based ethical theories. It is doubtful whether the standard action-based ethicist will be satisfied with the pluralistic thesis of virtues as set forth in this chapter, but we must leave the matter here—exactly where it is in the contemporary debate. Whether the correspondence or the pluralistic thesis is the correct thesis may not be the most important question. What is important is that we recognize that principles without character are impotent and that the virtues enliven the principles and empower the moral life in general. If nothing else, virtue ethicists have been successful in drawing attention to the importance of the virtues. There is a consensus in moral philosophy that the virtues have been neglected and that it is important to work them into one's moral perspective. On the other hand, a pure virtue ethic cannot stand alone without a strong action-based component. Principles of action are important largely in the way deontological and utilitarian accounts have said they were. The question is not whether these accounts were wrong in what they said but whether they were adequate to the complete moral life.

NOTES

1. Aristotle, *Nicomachean Ethics,* trans. Martin Ostwald (Indianapolis: Bobbs-Merrill, 1962), 1099a.

2. C. Colson, "The Volunteer at Auschwitz," in *The Moral Life,* ed. L. Pojman (Oxford University Press, 2000).

3. Paul Levy, *Moore* (Oxford University Press, 1979), p. 41.

4. Susan Wolf, "Moral Saints," *Journal of Philosophy* 79, no. 8 (1982): 419–439.

5. John Stuart Mill, *Utilitarianism* (Indianapolis: Bobbs-Merrill, 1957), Ch. 2.

6. John Stuart Mill, *Essay on Liberty* (Penguin Books, 1974), p. 112.

7. G. E. M. Anscombe, "Modern Moral Philosophy," *Philosophy* 33 (1958).

8. Aristotle, *Nicomachean Ethics,* 1099a.

9. David L. Norton, "Moral Minimalism and the Development of Moral Character," in *Midwest Studies in Philosophy,* Vol. 13, ed. Peter A. French et al. (University of Minnesota Press, 1988), pp. 180–195.

10. Daniel Callahan, "Minimal Ethics: On the Pacification of Morality," *Hastings Center Report* 11 (October 1981): 19–25.

11. J. L. Mackie, *Ethics: Inventing Right and Wrong* (Penguin Books, 1977), p. 186.

12. Adapted from Walter Schaller, "Are Virtues No More Than Dispositions to Obey Moral Rules?" *Philosophia* 20 (July 1990): 559–573.

13. Geoffrey Warnock, *The Object of Morality* (Methuen, 1971), p. 76.

14. William Frankena, *Ethics,* 2nd ed. (Prentice Hall, 1973).

15. John Stuart Mill, *Considerations on Representative Government* (Parker, 1861), p. 25.

16. Thomas Hill, "Servility and Self-Respect," *The Monist* (1973): 87–104.

17. Carol Gilligan, *In a Different Voice* (Harvard University Press, 1982).

18. Quoted in Gilligan, p. 26.

19. See C. MacKinnon, *Feminism Unmodified* (Harvard University Press, 1987); and Nell Noddings, *Care: A Feminist Approach to Ethics and Moral Education* (University of California Press, 1986).

20. David Miller, *On Nationality* (Oxford University Press, 1995); K. Addelson, "Moral Revolution," in *Women and Value,* ed. M. Pearsall (Wadsworth, 1986); Noddings, *Care: A Feminist Approach.*

FOR FURTHER REFLECTION

1. Compare the action of Father Kolbe with the thirty-nine witnesses to the beating and murder of Kitty Genovese, described at the beginning of Chapter 1. What conclusions do you draw about the importance of character or the virtues by such a comparison?

2. Examine the four criticisms of action-based ethics discussed near the outset of this chapter. How valid are they?

3. Some virtue ethicists maintain that it is not enough to habitually do the right act to be considered a virtuous person; one must also have the proper emotions. Is it morally significant not simply to do good but also to take pleasure in doing good—to enjoy it? And, conversely, is a lack of proper emotions in the right amount at the right time a sign of weak character? Explain your answers.

4. Both the correspondence theory of virtues and complementarity ethics embrace virtues and rules. Which if either of these two views is the best? Explain your answer.

5. How different are male and female moral development? Are there two different moral systems, one for women and one for men? Explain your answer.

6. What is the difference between care-ethics and Agapeism? Which do you think is more cogent and correct? Explain your answer.

7. Describe the difference between moral particularism and moral universalism. Does moral particularism collapse into relativism? Explain your answer.

FOR FURTHER READING

Adams, Robert Merrihew. *A Theory of Virtue.* New York: Oxford University Press, 2006.

Crisp, Roger, and Michael Slote, eds. *Virtue Ethics.* New York: Oxford University Press, 1997.

Darwall, Stephen, ed. *Virtue Ethics.* Malden, Mass.: Blackwell, 2003.

Hursthouse, Rosalind. *On Virtue Ethics.* New York: Oxford University Press, 1999.

Lindemann, Hilde. *An Invitation to Feminist Ethics.* New York: McGraw-Hill, 2006.

MacIntyre, Alasdair. *After Virtue,* 2nd ed. Notre Dame, Ind.: University of Notre Dame Press, 1984.

Sherman, Nancy. *The Fabric of Character: Aristotle's Theory of Virtue.* New York: Oxford University Press, 1989.

Taylor, Richard. *Virtue Ethics: An Introduction.* Amherst, N.Y.: Prometheus Books, 2002.

10

✳

Religion and Ethics

Does God love goodness because it is good, or is it good because God loves it?

PARAPHRASE OF SOCRATES' QUESTION IN PLATO'S *EUTHYPHRO*

The first half of human history has been the evolution from the ape to the man-god. The second half of human history will be the devolution from the man-god to the ape.

FYODOR DOSTOEVSKY, *THE POSSESSED*

A prominent bishop in the Church of England publicly stated that recent floods that destroyed large sections of the country were God's judgment on modern society for their moral corruption and environmental irresponsibility. Pro-gay laws, he argued, were responsible in part for the floods. He stated,

> This is a strong and definite judgment because the world has been arrogant in going its own way. We are reaping the consequences of our moral degradation, as well as the environmental damage that we have caused. We are in serious moral trouble because every type of lifestyle is now regarded as legitimate.... Our government has been playing the role of God in saying that people are free to act as they want. The sexual orientation regulations [which give greater rights to gays] are part of a general scene of permissiveness.[1]

The recent floods, he argued, were God's way of getting our attention and calling us to repentance.

Since the beginning of written history, morality has persistently been linked with religion. Morality has been identified with adherence to godliness, immorality with sin, and the moral law with the command of God so that the moral life

170

is seen as a personal relationship with a heavenly parent. To act immorally is essentially to disobey God. Whether it is the poor Calcutta untouchable accepting his degradation as his religious karma, the Shiite Muslim fighting a holy war in the name of Allah, the Jew circumspectly striving to keep kosher, or the Christian giving to charity in the name of Christ, religion has so dominated the moral land-scape as to be virtually indistinguishable from it. There have been exceptions: Confucianism in China is essentially a secular system, there are nontheist versions of Buddhism, and the philosophers of Greece contemplated morality independent of religion. But throughout most of our history, most people have identified mor-ality with religion, with the commands of God.

The question remains whether the equation is a valid one. Is morality essen-tially tied to religion so that the term *secular ethic* is a contradiction in terms? Can morality survive without religion? Tolstoy declared that to separate morality from religion is like cutting a flower from its roots and transplanting it rootless into the ground. In Dostoevsky's *Brother's Karamazov,* one of the characters proclaims, "If God doesn't exist, everything is permissible?" Are these views correct?

In this chapter, we address the connection between religion and morality by focusing on three questions: (1) Does morality depend on religion? (2) Is religion irrelevant or even contrary to morality? (3) Does religion enhance the moral life?

DOES MORALITY DEPEND ON RELIGION?

The first question is whether moral standards themselves depend on God for their validity or whether there is an independence of ethics so that even God is subject to the moral order. This question first arises in Plato's dialogue the *Euthyphro,* in which Socrates asks a religiously devout young man named Euthyphro, "Do the gods love holiness because it is holy, or is it holy because the gods love it?"[2] Changing the terms but still preserving the meaning, we want to know whether God commands what is good because it is good or whether the good is good because God commands it.

The Divine Command Theory

According to one view, called the **divine command theory** (DCT), ethical principles are simply the commands of God. They derive their validity from God's commanding them, and they mean "commanded by God." Without God, there would be no universally valid morality. Here is how theologian Carl F. H. Henry states this view:

> Biblical ethics discredits an autonomous morality. It gives theonomous ethics its classic form—the identification of the moral law with the Divine will. In Hebrew–Christian revelation, distinctions in ethics reduce to what

is good or what is pleasing, and to what is wicked or displeasing to the Creator-God alone. The biblical view maintains always a dynamic statement of values, refusing to sever the elements of morality from the will of God. . . . The good is what the Creator-Lord does and commands. He is the creator of the moral law, and defines its very nature.[3]

We can analyze the DCT into three separate theses:

1. Morality (that is, rightness and wrongness) originates with God.

2. *Moral rightness* simply means "willed by God," and *moral wrongness* means "being against the will of God."

3. Because morality essentially is based on divine will, not on independently existing reasons for action, no further reasons for action are necessary.

There are modified versions of the DCT that drop or qualify one or more of these three theses, but the strongest form includes all three assertions. We can characterize that position thusly:

> Necessarily, for any person S and for all acts A, if A is forbidden (required) of S, then God commands that not-A (A) for S. Likewise, if A is permitted for S, then God has commanded neither A nor not-A for S.

Bringing out the implications of this, we may list four propositions:

1. Act A is wrong if and only if it is contrary to the command of God.

2. Act A is right (required) if and only if it is commanded by God.

3. Act A is morally permissible if and only if it is permitted by the command of God.

4. If there is no God, then nothing is ethically wrong, required, or permitted.

We can summarize the DCT this way: Morality not only originates with God, but *moral rightness* simply means "willed by God" and *moral wrongness* means "being against the will of God." That is, an act is right *in virtue* of being permitted by the will of God, and an act is wrong *in virtue* of being against the will of God. Because morality essentially is based on divine will, not on independently existing reasons for action, no further reasons for action are necessary. So we may ask, "If God doesn't exist, everything is permissible?" If so, nothing is forbidden or required. Without God, we have moral nihilism. If there is no God, then nothing is ethically wrong, required, or permitted.

The opposing viewpoint, call it the *independence thesis,* denies the theses of the DCT, asserting, to the contrary, the following:

1. Morality does not originate with God (although the way God created us may affect the specific nature of morality).

2. Rightness and wrongness are not based simply on God's will.

3. Essentially, there are reasons for acting one way or the other, which may be known independent of God's will.

In sum, ethics exists independent of God, and even God must obey the moral law—as the laws of mathematics and logic do. Just as even God cannot make a three-sided square or make it the case that he never existed, so even God cannot make what is intrinsically evil good or make what is good evil.

Theists who espouse the independence thesis may well admit some episte-mological advantage to God: God knows what is right—better than we do. And because he is good, we can always learn from consulting him. But, in principle, we act morally for the same reasons that God does: We both follow moral reasons that are independent of God. We are against torturing the innocent because it is cruel and unjust, just as God is against torturing the innocent because it is cruel and unjust. By this account, if there is no God, then nothing is changed; morality is left intact, and both theists and nontheists have the very same moral duties.

The attractiveness of the DCT lies in its seeming to do justice to the omnip-otence or sovereignty of God. God somehow is thought to be less sovereign or necessary to our lives if he is not the source of morality. It seems inconceivable to many believers that anything having to do with goodness or duty could be "higher" than or independent of God because he is the supreme Lord of the believer's life, and what the believer means by *morally right* is that "the Lord com-mands it—even if I don't fully understand it." When the believer asks what the will of God is, it is a direct appeal to a personal will, not to an independently existing rule.

Problems with the Divine Command Theory

There are two problems with the DCT that need to be faced by those who hold it. One problem is that the DCT would seem to make the attribution of "goodness" to God redundant. When we say "God is good," we think we are ascribing a property to God; but if *good* simply means "what God commands or wills," then we are not attributing any property to God. Our statement "God is good" merely means "God does whatever he wills to do" or "God prac-tices what he preaches," and the statement "God commands us to do what is good" merely is the logically empty statement "God commands us to do what God commands us to do."

A second problem with the DCT is that it seems to make morality into some-thing arbitrary. If God's decree is the sole arbiter of right and wrong, it would seem to be logically possible for such heinous acts as rape, killing of the innocent for the fun of it, and gratuitous cruelty to become morally good actions—if God suddenly decided to command us to do these things. The radicality of the DCT is set forth by a classic statement of William of Ockham:

> The hatred of God, theft, adultery, and actions similar to these actions according to common law, may have an evil quality annexed, in so far as they are done by a divine command to perform the opposite act. But as far as the sheer being in the actions is concerned, they can be performed by God without any evil condition annexed; and they can even be

performed meritoriously by an earthly pilgrim if they should come under divine precepts, just as now the opposite of these in fact fall under the divine command.[4]

The implications of this sort of reasoning seem far reaching. If there are no constraints on what God can command, no independent measure or reason for moral action, then anything can become a moral duty, and our moral duties can change from moment to moment. Could there be any moral stability? The proponent of the DCT may object that God has revealed what is his will in his word, the sacred Scriptures. But the fitting response is "How do you know that God isn't lying?" If there is no independent criterion of right and wrong except what God happens to will, how do we know God isn't willing to make lying into a duty (in which case believers have no reason to believe the Bible)?

When I was a teenager, I read in the newspaper of a missionary in Africa who put a knife through the hearts of his wife and five children. Upon his arrest for murder, he claimed God commanded him to kill his family and he was only obeying God. The missionary might further argue, "Didn't God command Abraham to kill his son Isaac in Genesis 22?" How do we know that God didn't command him to do this horrible deed? He would only be sending his family to heaven a bit sooner than normal. Insane asylums are filled with people who heard the voice of God commanding them to do what we normally regard as immoral: rape, steal, embezzle, and kill. If the DCT is correct, we could be treating these people as insane simply for obeying God.

If God could make what seems morally heinous morally good simply by willing it, wouldn't morality be reduced to the right of the powerful—Nietzsche's position that "Might makes right"? Indeed, what would be the difference between the devil and God if morality were simply an arbitrary command? Suppose we had two sets of commands, one from the devil and one from God. How would we know which set was which? Could they be identical? What would make them different? If there is no independent criterion by which to judge right and wrong, then it's difficult to see how we could know which was which; the only basis for comparison would be who won. God would be simply the biggest bully on the block (granted it is a pretty big block—covering the entire universe).

Furthermore, the Scriptures speak of God being love: "Beloved, let us love one another, for love is of God, and he who loves is born of God and knows God. He who does not love does not know God; for God is love" (1 John 4: 7–8). Could you truly love people and at the same time rape, kill, or torture them? Could a loving God command you to torture them? If so, then I suppose Auschwitz could be considered God's loving act to the Jews.

The opponent of the DCT (that is, the proponent of the independence thesis) denies that God's omnipotence includes his being able to make evil actions good. Even as God's power does not include being able to override the laws of logic (for example, he cannot make a contradiction true or $2 + 2 = 5$), so likewise God cannot make rape, injustice, cruelty, and the torturing or killing of innocents good deeds. The objective moral law, which may be internal to God's nature, is a law that even God must follow if he is to be a good God.

Some philosophers and theologians acknowledge that God cannot change the moral law any more than he can change the laws of logic but claim that he is nevertheless the source of the moral law. For example, Christian philosopher William Lane Craig sets forth the following argument:[5]

(1) If there is no God, no moral absolute values exist.

(2) Evil exists (which is a negative absolute value and implies that the Good exists as an absolute positive value).

(3) Therefore, God exists.

Craig assumes that unless God is the ultimate source and authority of morality, it cannot have absolute or objective status. But if the independence thesis is correct, objective moral principles exist whether or not God exists. They are the principles that enable human beings to flourish, to make life more nearly a heaven than a hell. Rational beings can discover these principles independently of God or revelation—using reason and experience alone.

Kant: God Makes Morality Possible

Even if we don't accept the DCT view that morality is created by God, we can still ask if morality depends on God in other ways. German philosopher Immanuel Kant (1724–1804) argues that it does and that the mere possibility of meaningful ethics depends on religion. But Kant was no divine command theorist, and he held firmly to the independence thesis. There can be no difference between valid religious ethics and valid philosophical ethics, he argues, because God and humanity both have to obey the same rational principles and reason is sufficient to guide us to these principles:

> [Christianity] has enriched philosophy with far more definite and purer concepts than it had been able to furnish before; but which, once they are there, are freely assented to by Reason and are assumed as concepts to which it could well have come of itself and which it could and should have introduced.... Even the Holy One of the Gospels must first be compared with our ideal of moral perfection, before we can recognize him as such.[6]

However, Kant maintains, religion completes morality by directly linking morality with the immortality of the soul and God's existence. Immortality, he argues, is a necessary postulate for morality in this way: We are commanded by the moral law to be morally perfect. Because "ought" implies "can," we must be *able* to reach moral perfection. But we cannot attain perfection in this life because the task is an infinite one. Thus, there must be an afterlife in which we continue to make progress toward this ideal.

Similarly, God is a necessary postulate because there must be someone to enforce the moral law. That is, to be completely justified, the moral law must end in a just recompense of happiness in accordance to virtue—what Kant refers to as the "complete good." From the standpoint of eternity, the complete good requires that happiness should be proportioned to virtue in such a way that those who deserve happiness receive it in proportion to their moral merit. Likewise, evil people must be punished with unhappiness in proportion to their vice. This harmonious correlation of virtue and happiness does not happen in this life, so it must happen in the next life. Thus, there must be a God, acting as judge and enforcer of the moral law without which the moral law would be unjustified.

Kant is not saying that we can *prove* that God exists or that we ought to be moral *in order* to be happy. Rather, the idea of God serves as a completion of our ordinary ideas of ethics. Is Kant right about this? Critics point out that we can use Kant's argument against him. In its simplest form, here is Kant's argument:

(1) If morality is meaningful, then God exists.

(2) Morality is meaningful.

(3) Therefore, God exists.

For the sake of argument, let's grant his principal point in premise 1 that the justification of morality depends on the existence of God. Suppose, though, we find no convincing evidence for God's existence. Building on premise 1, then, we can then construct this argument to reject morality:

(1) If morality is meaningful, then God exists.

(2) It is not the case that God exists.

(3) Therefore, it is not the case that morality is meaningful.

The same kind of counterargument can be constructed regarding the immortality of the soul. The critic's point is that, on Kant's view, morality and God rise and fall together, and it may not be good to saddle morality with an issue as debatable as God's existence.

IS RELIGION IRRELEVANT OR EVEN CONTRARY TO MORALITY?

We now turn to the views of secularists who want to disentangle the relationship between religion and morality. Many secularists have argued against both the stronger claim of the DCT (that religion is the basis of ethics) and the weaker Kantian claim (that religion makes ethics possible). Secularists often take two approaches: Some argue that religion is irrelevant to morality, and others espouse that religion is actually contrary to true morality. We begin with the first of these.

Russell: Religion Irrelevant to Morality

British philosopher Bertrand Russell (1872–1970) was one of the twentieth century's most vocal critics of religion. In a famous essay, he stated that religion as a whole has made virtually no useful contributions to civilization and in fact has been the cause of incalculable suffering:

> My own view on religion is that of Lucretius. I regard it as a disease born of fear and as a source of untold misery to the human race. I cannot, however, deny that it has made some contributions to civilization. It helped in early days to fix the calendar, and it caused Egyptian priests to chronicle eclipses with such care that in time they became able to predict them. These two services I am prepared to acknowledge, but I do not know of any others.[7]

On the subject of the relation between religion and ethics, he argued that morality has no need of God: One can be moral and, within the limits of thoughtful stoic resignation, even happy. The world may well be a product of blind evolutionary striving, ultimately absurd, but this doesn't remove our duty to fill our lives with meaning and goodness. He writes,

> Nature, omnipotent but blind, in the revolutions of her secular hurryings through the abysses of space, has brought forth at last a child, subject still to her power, but gifted with sight, with knowledge of good and evil, with the capacity of judging all the works of his unthinking Mother.[8]

It is this conscious power of moral evaluation that makes the child superior to his all-powerful Mother. He is free to think, to evaluate, to create, and to live committed to ideals. So, despite suffering, despair, and death, humans are free. Life has the meaning that we give it, and morality will be part of any meaningful life.

Theists may, however, counter that secularists like Russell are "whistling in the dark." George Mavrodes has criticized Russell's secular view, calling it puzzling. If there is no God, then doesn't secular ethics suffer from a certain inadequacy? Mavrodes argues that the Russellian world of secular morality can't satisfactorily answer the question "Why should I be moral?" because, on its account, the common goods, at which morality in general aims, are often just those that we sacrifice in carrying out our moral obligations. Why should we sacrifice our welfare or self-interest for our moral duty?

The second oddity about secular ethics, according to Mavrodes, is that it is superficial and not deeply rooted. It seems to lack the necessary metaphysical basis afforded by a Platonic worldview (that is, reality and value essentially exist in a transcendent realm) or a Judeo-Christian worldview:

> Values and obligations cannot be deep in such a [secular] world. What is deep in a Russellian world must be such things as matter and energy, or perhaps natural law, chance, or chaos. If it really were a fact that one had obligations in a Russellian world, then something would be laid upon man that might cost a man everything but that went no further than man. And that difference from a Platonic world seems to make all the difference.[9]

Of course, the secularist will continue the debate. If what morality seeks is the good, as I have argued, then secular morality based on a notion of the good life is inspiring in itself because it promotes human flourishing and can be shown to be in all of our interests, whether or not a God exists. A religious or Platonic metaphysical orientation may not be necessary for a rational, secular, commonsense morality. To be sure, there will be differences in the exact nature of the ethical codes—religious ethics will be more likely to advocate strong altruism whereas secular codes will emphasize reciprocal altruism—but the core morality will be the same.

Hume: The Immorality of God and Religion

Some secularists go even further than Russell, claiming that not only are religious and secular morality dissimilar but also religious morality is an inferior brand of morality that actually prevents deep moral development.

Skeptical philosopher David Hume (1711–1776) is a case in point. He wrote at a time when it was just beginning to be politically safe in Europe to publish antireligious ideas; as such, he's one of the first purely secular ethicists since ancient Greece. Hume pointed out several problems with the traditional view that connected religion and morality. One problem, Hume argues, is that the very conception of God as popularly depicted in religions is that of an immoral tyrant who acts out with vengeance, severity, cruelty, and malice. He writes, "No idea of perverse wickedness can be framed, which those terrified devotees [that is, religious believers] do not readily, without scruple, apply to their deity."[10] This is true even of the most sophisticated conceptions of God: "as men farther exalt their idea of their divinity, it is their notion of his power and knowledge only, not of his goodness, which is improved."

A second problem with the traditional connection between religion and ethics, Hume argues, is that religious practices themselves are typically contrary to morality. The reason is that, as believers attempt to please God, they do so by performing absurd religious rituals and not through moral behavior:

> It is certain, that, in every religion, however sublime the verbal definition which it gives of its divinity, many of the votaries [that is, religious believers], perhaps the greatest number, will still seek the divine favor, not by virtue and good morals, which alone can be acceptable to a perfect being, but either by frivolous observances, by intemperate zeal, by rapturous ecstasies, or by the belief of mysterious and absurd opinions.

True morality, according to Hume, is a very natural and agreeable part of human life; by contrast, bizarre superstitious practices are difficult and tedious. Thus, when attempting to appease their finicky God, believers latch onto the more difficult approach, rather than the more natural one. The more extreme their superstition, the more they abandon morality. In his personal life, Hume was so distrustful of the conduct of religious believers that, as one of Hume's friends reported, "When he heard a man was religious, he concluded he was a rascal."

What should we think of Hume's arguments? Right off we should recognize that his views rest on some very broad generalizations: the average person's conception of God's morality and the average person's religious rituals. Nevertheless, many religious believers themselves agree with Hume's generalizations and maintain that people typically do have distorted views of God's nature and religious observance. Indeed, a common theme in most world religions is to expose moral flaws in the views and actions of dissenters, heretics, or rival religions. However, the believer's assumption is that there is a true and morally pure conception of God and religion. Hume goes a step further, though, and charges that the moral flaws within religion are so universally widespread that there is almost nothing morally salvageable in religion. To be truly moral, from Hume's perspective, I may not need to be an atheist, but I'd need to substantially reduce my religious superstition and fanaticism, perhaps to the point that religion is just a minor hobby in my life's routine. This is the part of Hume's theory that seems too extreme. Devout believers can keep a close watch on their conceptions of God and religious observance to avoid declining into moral madness. Hume is skeptical about whether the average person can actually do this, but we're not forced to accept Hume's level of skepticism here.

Nowell-Smith and Rachels: Religion Conflicts with Moral Autonomy

Like Hume, many contemporary secular philosophers have also argued that religion gives rise to an inferior morality. Two notable examples are P. H. Nowell-Smith and James Rachels, both of whom base their contention on the notion of autonomy. Nowell-Smith's argument is founded on child psychologist Jean Piaget's research in child development: Very small children have to be taught to value rules. When they do, they tend to hold tenaciously to those rules, even when games or activities would seem to call for a suspension of the rules. For example, suppose ten children are to play baseball on a rectangular lot that lacks a right field. Some children might object to playing with only five on a side and no right field, because that violates the official rules. Religious morality, in being rule governed, is analogous to the children who have not understood the wider purposes of the rules of games; it is an infantile morality.[11]

Rachels's argument alleges that believers relinquish their autonomy in worship and so are immoral. Using Kant's dictum that "kneeling down or groveling on the ground, even to express your reverence for heavenly things, is contrary to human dignity," he argues that since we have inherent dignity, no one deserves our worship. But, since the notion of *God* implies "being worthy of worship," God cannot exist. Rachels writes,

(1) If any being is God, he must be a fitting object of worship.

(2) No being could possibly be a fitting object of worship, since worship requires the abandonment of one's role as an autonomous moral agent.

(3) Therefore, there cannot be any being who is God.[12]

Are Nowell-Smith's and Rachels's arguments sound? They seem to have problems. Consider Nowell-Smith's contention that religious morality is infantile: Perhaps some religious people and some secularists as well are rigidly and unreasonably rule bound, but not all religious people are. Indeed, Jesus himself broke the rule regarding not working on the Sabbath day, to heal and do good, reprimanding his critics the Pharisees, saying, "The Sabbath was made for man, not man for the Sabbath." Does not the strong love motif in New Testament religious morality indicate that the rules are seen as serving a purpose—the human good?

With regard to Rachels's argument, premise 2 seems false. In worshipping God, you need not give up your reason, your essential autonomy. Doesn't a rational believer need to use reason to distinguish the good from the bad, the holy from what is not holy? A mature believer does not (or need not) sacrifice his or her reason or autonomy in worship; rather, these traits are part and parcel of what worship entails. The command to love God is for one to love him with one's whole *mind* as well as one's heart and strength. If there is a God, he must surely want us to be intelligent and discriminating and sensitive in all of our deliberations. Being a religious worshipper in no way entails or condones intellectual suicide.

Of course, a believer may submit his or her judgment to God's when there is good evidence that God has given a judgment. If this is sacrificing one's autonomy, then it only shows that autonomy is not an absolute value but rather a significant prima facie value. If I am working in the physics laboratory with Albert Einstein, whom I have learned to trust as a competent authority, and he advises me to do something different from what my amateur calculations dictate, I am likely to defer to his authority. But I don't thereby give up my autonomy. I freely and rationally judge that in this particular matter I ought to defer to Einstein's judgment on the grounds that it is more likely to be correct. Functioning autonomously is not to be equated with deciding each case from scratch; nor does it require self-sufficiency in decision making. Autonomy is a *higher-order* reflective control over one's life. A considered judgment that in certain kinds of cases someone else's opinion is more likely to be correct than one's own is an *exercise* of autonomy rather than an abdication of it.[13] Similarly, the believer may submit to God whenever he or she judges God's authority to override his or her own finite judgment. It seems eminently rational to give up that kind of autonomy. To do otherwise would be to make autonomy a foolhardy fetish.

DOES RELIGION ENHANCE THE MORAL LIFE?

So far we've seen that the case for morality's dependence on religion is weak, as also is the secularist's case for the view that true morality is incompatible with religion. Both of these claims are rather extreme, and it is no surprise that they defy conclusive proof. Let's now raise a more modest question: Does religion at least enhance the moral life?

The Case for Religion

Theists argue that there are at least six ways in which morality may be enriched by religion.

First, *if there is a God, good will win out over evil.* We're not fighting alone—God is on our side in the battle. Neither are we fighting in vain—we'll win eventually. As William James (1842–1910) said,

> If religion be true and the evidence for it be still insufficient, I do not wish, by putting your extinguisher upon my nature, to forfeit my sole chance in life of getting upon the winning side—that chance depending, of course, on my willingness to run the risk of acting as if my passional need of taking the world religiously might be prophetic and right.[14]

This thought of the ultimate Victory of Goodness gives us confidence to go on in the fight against injustice and cruelty when others calculate that the odds against righteousness are too great to oppose. While the secularist may embrace a noble stoicism, resigned to fate, as Russell asserts, the believer lives in faith, confident of the final triumph of the kingdom of God on earth.

Second, *if God exists, then cosmic justice reigns in the universe.* The scales are perfectly balanced so that everyone will eventually get what he or she deserves, according to their moral merit. It is true that in most religious traditions God forgives the repentant sinner his or her sins—in which case divine grace goes beyond what is strictly deserved. It's as though a merciful God will never give us *less* reward than we deserve, but if we have a good will, God will give us more than we deserve.

Nonetheless, the idea that "whatsoever a man sows, that will he also reap" (Galatians 6: 7) is emphasized in Judaism, Islam, Christianity, and most other world religions. In Hinduism, it is carried out with a rigorous logic of karma (that is, what you are now is a direct result of what you did in a previous life, and what you do with your life now will determine what kind of life you inherit in the next life).

The question that haunts secular ethics—"Why should I be moral, when I can get away with being immoral?" (for often it seems that we can profit by being immoral)—has a ready answer: I will not get away with immorality. God is the perfect judge who will bring my works to judgment so that my good works will be rewarded and my bad works punished. The good really is good for us.

Third, *if theism is true, moral reasons always override nonmoral reasons.* Let me illustrate this controversy: I once had an argument with my teacher Philippa Foot, of Oxford University, over the Gauguin case. Paul Gauguin abandoned his family and moved to Paris and then to Tahiti to fulfill his artistic dream. I argued that Gauguin did wrong, all things considered, to abandon his family. Foot, however, to my utter amazement, argued that although Gauguin did what was morally wrong, he did what was right, all things considered, for sometimes nonmoral reasons override moral ones. From a secular perspective, Foot's argument seems plausible: Why should moral reasons always override nonmoral ones? Here is the dilemma for secular ethics: *either* overridingness *or* objectivity, but not both. If you believe in **moral realism,** the idea that moral principles are universally valid whether or not anyone recognizes them, then the secularist is faced with the question "Why should I adhere to a given moral principle when I can get away with violating it?" If you hold to overridingness—that is, if you believe that moral reasons are always the highest motivating reasons, the best reasons all things considered—then it seems likely that you will adopt some sort of agent-relativity with regard to morals. From a religious perspective, however, the world is so ordered that the question "Why be moral?" can hardly be taken seriously: To be moral is to function properly, the way God intended us to live, and he will see that the good are ultimately rewarded and the wicked punished. God ensures the supremacy of morality. Moral reasons always override other reasons. We preserve both overridingness and objectivity.

Fourth, *if theism is true, then there is a God who loves and cares for us—his love inspires us.* If God exists, love really makes the world go round. You and I have a heavenly father who cares for us and is working for our good. A sense of gratitude pervades the life of the believer so that he or she is ready to make greater sacrifices for the good of others. That is, the believer has an *added reason* to be moral, beyond the ones a secular person already has, beyond even rewards and punishments: He or she wants to please a perfect God. Sayyid Qutb, the Egyptian founder of Islamic terror and the Al Qaeda movement, complained that the West, especially the United States, had become an immoral decadent, hedonistic, selfish civilization. Without a strong sense of God's love, we misuse our wealth and freedom for selfish, destructive purposes.

Fifth, *if there is a God who created us in his image, all persons are of equal worth.* Theism claims that God values us all equally. If we are all his children, then we are all brothers and sisters; we are family and ought to treat one another benevolently as we would family members of equal worth. Indeed, modern secular moral and political systems often assume the equal worth of the individual without justifying it. But without the parenthood of God, it makes no sense to say that all persons are innately of positive equal value. What gives us animals, the products of a process of the survival of the fittest, any value at all, let alone equal value? From a perspective of intelligence and utility, Aristotle and Nietzsche seem to be right; there are enormous inequalities, and why shouldn't the superior persons use the baser types to their advantage? In this regard, secularism, in rejecting inegalitarianism, seems to be living off the interest on a religious capital that it has relinquished.

If theism is false, then it may be doubtful whether all humans have equal worth or any worth at all, and it may be more difficult to provide an unequivocal response to the question "Why be moral even when it is not in my best interest?" If there is no sense of harmony and objective purpose in the universe, many of us will conclude that we are sadder and poorer because of it.

Sixth, *if God exists, we have a compelling solution to the posterity problem.* We have noted in previous chapters that it is difficult to give an adequate explanation of our intuition that we have obligations to future generations.

Suppose in forty or fifty or one hundred years from now people on earth collectively do a cost–benefit assessment and unanimously decide that life is not worth its inherent suffering and boredom. Perhaps people become tired of their technological toys and fail to find anything worth living for, so they decide to commit collective suicide. Would this be immoral? If you don't like the idea of suicide, suppose they all take a drug that will bring ecstatic happiness but has a side effect of rendering them permanently sterile—and they knowingly take it. The result in either case would be the end of humanity. Again, I ask, have these people done anything immoral? Have they violated anyone's rights?

The philosopher Joel Feinberg, in a pioneering article, responded to this question this way:

> "My inclination . . . is to conclude that the suicide of our species would be deplorable, lamentable, and a deeply moving tragedy, but that it would violate no one's rights. Indeed if, contrary to fact, all human beings could ever agree to such a thing, that very agreement would be a symptom of our species' biological unsuitability for survival anyway."[15]

Notice that this problem is not like normal cases of suicide. We can sometimes argue that suicide is immoral because the people contemplating self-slaughter have responsibilities to others who will be harmed by the suicide. For example, the parent who decides to end his or her life may have an overriding obligation to care for the children who will be orphaned or who will suffer the shock of dealing with the suicide of a parent. In this case, however, there are no children who will be left behind. As soon as they come of age, they too agree to die or not to procreate. And there's no one else whose identity needs to be taken into account—or so it seems. Future people can't be consulted, of course, because they don't exist and therefore can't be identified, which, as we noted in Chapter 7, is a serious problem for Kantian ethics because it holds that only actual persons have value and are ends in themselves.

Religion gives us two reasons to care for future generations: The first is because God commands us to continue the race. But religious believers have a second special reason to care for future people: God knows who will be born and loves these people as if they already existed. For God, the whole temporal span of the world's existence is good. In serving God as good stewards, we have a duty to him to be good to the earth, which includes leaving it healthy for future people who will be born and who are already loved by God. But all this, of course, supposes that God exists.

Add to these six theses the fact that theism doesn't deprive us of any of the autonomy that we have in nontheistic systems. If we are equally free to choose the good or the evil whether or not God exists (assuming that the notions of good and evil make sense in a nontheistic universe), then it seems plausible to assert that in some ways the world of the theist is better and more satisfying than one in which God does not exist. It could also be the case that through revelation the theist has access to deeper moral truths that are not available to the secularist.

The Case against Religion

The other side of the issue is that religion does not enhance morality but detracts from it and as a consequence religious morality makes the world a worse place than it would have been otherwise. We'll consider five arguments for this position.

First, *a lot of evil has been done by religious people in the name of religion.* We have only to look at our sordid history of heresy hunts, religious bigotry, and religious wars, some of which are still being fought. The terrorist attacks of September 11, 2001, on the World Trade Center and the Pentagon in which nearly 3,000 innocent people lost their lives and the subsequent suicide bombing attacks in Madrid and elsewhere were *faith initiatives,* revolting exhibitions of Muslim fanaticism. Osama bin Laden was videotaped giving thanks to Allah for his toppling the twin towers of the World Trade Center. Religion may be used as a powerful weapon for good as well as evil. In the hands of Mother Teresa or Father Kolbe, it can transform darkness into light, but in the hands of fanatics, like misguided suicide bombers or destroyers of abortion clinics, it can transform light into darkness.

Second, *we don't know for sure whether a benevolent God exists.* The arguments for the existence of God are not obviously compelling. Furthermore, even if a divine being exists, we don't have the kind of compelling evidence needed to prove that our interpretation of God's will and ways is the right one. Religion is based largely on faith rather than on hard evidence, so it behooves believers to be modest about their policies. It would seem that most of us are more certain about the core of our morality than about the central doctrines of theology. So, it is ill advised to require society to give up a morality based on reason for some injunctions based on revelation. Sometimes, a religious authority claims to put forth a command that conflicts with our best rational judgments, giving rise to the kind of confrontation that can rip society apart.

Third, *religious morality closes off dialogue.* Religious morality usually consists of more than just a theoretical conviction that God is behind moral standards. It also comes with specific moral stands that religious authorities take on a range of issues such as premarital sex, contraception, homosexuality, cloning, and capital punishment. The usual secular approach to debating these issues is to consider a range of question such as "What are the benefits of a particular moral policy? Who is harmed? Are rights violated?" With religious morality, though, the dialogue is quickly cut off with appeals to the doctrines of one's religious tradition that override all other considerations. The abortion debate today is a clear example of this, particularly when believers defend the special moral status of the fetus on purely religious grounds. There is no opportunity for real debate or compromise as there may be when nonreligious considerations are explored.

Fourth, *religious morality leads to group intolerance.* Organized religions are by their very nature exclusive groups, with members on the inside and nonmembers on the outside. Further, morality by its very nature is judgmental: We praise and condemn people for their moral and immoral behavior. Religious morality mixes these two factors, thus potentially creating a groupwide moral intolerance toward dissenting outsiders. Many groups and organizations have differences of opinion with their respective outsiders—including groups such as the Rotary Club or the YMCA. The difference here is that religious morality involves a *moral* condemnation by the in-group toward dissenters from the out-group. It in essence licenses them to express moral indignation against the dissenters in the name of that religion. History records countless examples of intolerance of one religious group toward another, including the Medieval Crusades and the Inquisition; the religious wars of the Reformation period; the present religious conflict in Northern Ireland between Roman Catholics and Protestants; the devastation of the former Yugoslavia, where Christians and Muslims killed each other; the Hindu–Muslim massacres in India; and the Ayatollah Khoumeni's order to kill author Salmon Rushdie for writing his allegedly blasphemous book *Satanic Verses*.

Fifth, *religious morality threatens church–state separation*. Related to the previous point, dogmatic and intolerant religion deeply and rightly worries the secularist, who sees religion as a threat to society and insists on a strong separation of church and state. Throughout most of the world's civilizations, an official state religion was the norm, and it is only in recent centuries that progressive countries have broken from that mold. Although a state religion might be a good thing for devoted believers of that faith, it's not so good for those outside the mainstream. Religious morality threatens church–state separation when the moral agendas of religious organizations transform into political efforts to transform society.

Our hope in solving such problems rests in working out an adequate morality on which theists and nontheists alike can agree. If there is an ethics of belief, then we can apply rational scrutiny to our religious beliefs as well as to all our other beliefs and work toward a better understanding of the status of our belief systems. It is a challenge that should inspire the best minds because it may turn out that it is not science or technology but rather deep, comprehensive ethical theory and moral living that will not only save our world but solve its perennial problems and produce a state of flourishing.

CONCLUSION

We asked whether morality depends on religion. We examined whether moral standards themselves depend on God for their validity or whether there is an independence of ethics so that even God is subject to the moral order. Does God command what is good because it is good, or is the good good because God commands it? We saw that the independence thesis was correct. God, if he exists, loves the good because of its intrinsic value. Morality has independent value so that moral truth exists whether or not God does. We argued that although religious ethics are not essentially different from secular ethics, religion can enhance the moral life by providing motivating reasons to be moral.

NOTES

1. Graham Dow, Bishop of Carlisle, quoted in Jonathan Wynne-Jones, "Floods Are Judgment on Society, Say Bishops," Telegraph.com.uk.

2. Plato, *Euthyphro,* trans. W. Jowett (Scribner, 1889).

3. Carl F. Henry, *Christian Personal Ethics* (Eerdmans, 1957), p. 210.

4. William of Occam, quoted in J. M. Idziak, ed., *Divine Command Morality* (Mellon, 1979).

5. William Lane Craig set forth this argument in a debate with Paul Draper at the U.S. Military Academy, Sept. 30, 1997.

6. Immanuel Kant, *Critique of Judgment,* trans. J. Bernard (Haefner, 1951), p. 410, and *Fundamental Principles of the Metaphysics of Ethics,* trans. T. K. Abbott (Longmans, Green, 1898), Sec. 2.

7. Bertrand Russell, "Has Religion Made Useful Contributions to Civilization?" in *Why I Am Not a Christian* (New York: Simon & Schuster, 1957).

8. Bertrand Russell, "A Free Man's Worship," in *Why I Am Not a Christian.*

9. George Mavrodes, "Religion and the Queerness of Morality," in *Ethical Theory: Classical and Contemporary Issues,* ed. L. Pojman (Wadsworth, 2007), p. 539.

10. David Hume, *The Natural History of Religion* (1757), Sec. 13 and 14.

11. Patrick H. Nowell-Smith, "Morality: Religious and Secular," in *Philosophy of Religion,* ed. L. Pojman (Wadsworth, 2003), pp. 550–560.

12. James Rachels, "God and Human Attitudes," in *Religious Studies* 7 (1971).

13. See Arthur Kuflik, "The Inalienability of Autonomy," *Philosophy & Public Affairs* (Fall 1984).

14. William James, *The Will to Believe* (Longmans, Green, 1897).

15. Joel Feinberg, "The Rights of Animals and Unborn Generations," in *Philosophy and Environmental Crisis,* ed. W. Blackstone (University of Georgia Press, 1974).

FOR FURTHER REFLECTION

1. Evaluate Leo Tolstoy's statement in his essay "Religion and Morality" (1893): "The attempts to found a morality apart from religion are like the attempts of children who, wishing to transplant a flower that pleases them, pluck it from the roots that seem to them unpleasing and superfluous, and stick it rootless into the ground. Without religion there can be no real, sincere morality, just as without roots there can be no real flower."

2. Evaluate the divine command theory (DCT). What are its strengths and weaknesses? What is the independence thesis, and how does it relate to the DCT?

3. How would a secularist respond to the six claims made in favor of religion's ability to give added meaning to morality? Do you think that religion really does enhance the moral life? Explain your answer.

4. Karl Marx said that religion was the opium of the people (today, the metaphor might better be changed to "cocaine" or "crack"): It deludes them into thinking that all will be well with the world, leading to passive acceptance of evil and injustice. Is there some truth in Marx's dictum? (Explain your answer.) How would a theist respond to this?

5. Imagine that a superior being appears to you and says, "I am God and I am good; therefore, obey me when I tell you to torture your mother." How would a proponent of the divine command theory deal with this problem?

6. Some religious people believe that abortion or homosexual behavior is morally wrong, based on religious authority. How should a secular ethicist who believes that these practices are not morally wrong argue with the believer? Can there be a rational dialogue? Explain your answer.

7. Examine the claim that theism provides a compelling solution to the posterity problem. Do you agree with this? Discuss your answer.

FOR FURTHER READING

Idziak, Janine Marie. *Divine Command Morality: Historical and Contemporary Readings*. New York: E. Mellen Press, 1979.

Meilaender, Gilbert, and William Werpehowski. *The Oxford Handbook of Theological Ethics*. New York: Oxford University Press, 2005.

Mitchell, Basil. *Morality: Religious and Secular*. Oxford, Engl.: Oxford University Press, 1980.

Mouw, Richard. *The God Who Commands*. Notre Dame, Ind.: University of Notre Dame Press, 1990.

Nielsen, Kai. *Ethics without God*. Buffalo, N.Y.: Prometheus Books, 1990.

Outka, Gene, and J. P. Reeder, eds. *Religion and Morality: A Collection of Essays*. Garden City, N.Y.: Anchor Books, 1973.

Quinn, Philip. *Divine Commands and Moral Requirements*. Oxford, Engl.: Clarendon Press, 1978.

11

✳

The Fact–Value Problem

> In every system of morality which I have hitherto met with, I have
> always remarked, that the author proceeds for some time in the ordinary
> way of reasoning, and establishes the being of a God, or makes
> observations concerning human affairs; when of a sudden I am surprised
> to find, that instead of the usual copulations of propositions, is, and is
> not, I meet with no proposition that is not connected with an ought, or
> an ought not.
>
> DAVID, HUME, *A TREATISE ON HUMAN NATURE*

Consider the following moral attack from an Internet Weblog:

> How could he hold such an immoral view?! It's outrageous, and the very
> idea fills me with disgust! This is the sort of thing that drags our whole
> society down into the deepest, stench-filled mire of debauchery! Such
> wickedness can only be described as repugnant, hideous and nauseating,
> and those who advocate it are mere living garbage! They are slime!
> There's a special place in the afterlife for this guy and his cohorts, and it's
> called hell!!! IMHO, of course;-)

The above quote does not mention the specific moral issue that ignited the
author's indignation, and in many ways it doesn't matter. Whether the issue is
abortion, euthanasia, sexual morality, or capital punishment, rants like this are
pervasive in discussions of moral issues in the media and in personal dialogue.

What's most interesting about the above quote is that the writer does not
appear to say anything factual. We see plenty of harsh judgment and emotion,
but the entire angry outburst reduces to the simple contention that "X is
immoral." Even when our rhetoric isn't as charged as this author's, our moral
assessments are frequently not really factual judgments. There certainly are a

188

number of factual elements that set the stage for our moral assessments: the fact that someone had an abortion, the fact that someone was executed, the fact that someone's behavior caused harm and suffering. But when it comes to the actual moral assessment itself, there appears to be a huge gap between the facts of the case and the value assessment that we make of it. When we claim that something is a fact, we imply that some object or state of affairs exists. When we make a value assessment, we are evaluating or appraising something in a way that differs from factual or logical judgment. Moral philosophers today call this the **fact– value problem**—the problem of determining whether values are essentially differ- ent from facts, whether moral assessments are derived from facts, and whether moral statements can be true or false like factual statements.

The method of inquiry used to address the fact–value problem is known as **metaethics**—philosophizing *about* the very terms of ethics and considering the structure of ethics as an object of inquiry. Whereas traditional philosophers mainly attempted to systematically describe the correct moral theory, many contempo- rary philosophers have been concerned with the metaethical functions of ethical terms, the status of moral judgments, and the relation of ethical judgments to nonethical factual statements. The central questions here are these: "What, if any- thing, is the meaning of the terms *good* and *right*?" and "How, if at all, can we justify our moral beliefs?" In this chapter, we explore the fact–value problem and the metaethical issues that it raises.

HUME AND MOORE: THE PROBLEM
CLASSICALLY STATED

While the fact–value problem is a centerpiece of debate today among philoso- phers, the issue was forecasted in earlier times by two British philosophers: David Hume and George Edward Moore. Let's look at each of their accounts and what they contributed to the ongoing discussion.

Hume: The Fallacy of Deriving Ought from Is

The story begins with David Hume (1711–1776) who while in his mid-twenties was finishing his monumental book, *A Treatise of Human Nature* (1739). In the last portion of this, he turned his eye toward standard ethical questions of his time, many of which we've already explored: moral objectivism, egoism, social contract theory, natural law theory, and religious morality. While examining these standard accounts of morality, he realized that they all make a fundamental mistake. Specif- ically, these theories begin by observing some specific facts about the world, and then they conclude from these some statements about our moral obligation. In his words, they move from statements about what *is* the case to statements about what *ought* to be the case. This is called the **fallacy of deriving ought from is.**

He describes this fallacy in the following famous passage, which we've already quoted at the outset of this chapter:

> In every system of morality which I have hitherto met with, I have always remarked, that the author proceeds for some time in the ordinary way of reasoning, and establishes the being of a God, or makes observations concerning human affairs; when of a sudden I am surprised to find, that instead of the usual copulations of propositions, is, and is not, I meet with no proposition that is not connected with an ought, or an ought not.[1]

According to Hume, we find this fallacy in both ordinary and sophisticated theories of morality. Here are examples of ordinary ones that he might have in mind:

- God exists; therefore, we should obey God's moral commands.
- God will punish and reward us in the afterlife; therefore, we should behave morally.
- People are sociable creatures; therefore, we should behave morally.
- Without rules society would fall into chaos; therefore, we should behave morally.

Here are examples of two sophisticated moral theories that he specifically mentions:

- Through reason we can detect eternal truths about fit behavior; therefore, we should behave morally as informed by our reason.
- There is a kind of sixth sense that detects inappropriate conduct; therefore, we should behave morally as informed by this sixth sense.

The problem with all of these is not necessarily with the facts at the beginning of each statement; it's with the transition to the moral component at each statement's end. Something new is added at the end of the sentence (an "ought") that is not contained in the beginning (an "is"). He makes this point here:

> This change is imperceptible; but is, however, of the last consequence. For as this ought, or ought not, expresses some new relation or affirmation, it is necessary that it should be observed and explained; and at the same time that a reason should be given, for what seems altogether inconceivable, how this new relation can be a deduction from others, which are entirely different from it. But as authors do not commonly use this precaution, I shall presume to recommend it to the readers; and am persuaded, that this small attention would subvert all the vulgar systems of morality, and let us see that the distinction of vice and virtue is not founded merely on the relations of objects, nor is perceived by reason.[2]

Thus, we cannot derive "ought" from "is" through any type of rational or factual inference. The mistake, according to Hume, is the assumption that moral judgments are rational deductions of the sort that we might use in math, logic, or science.

Hume's solution to the is—ought problem is that moral assessments are not rational inferences at all. Rather, they are emotional reactions—feelings of pleasure and pain that we experience in response to witnessing or hearing about some event. Suppose we witness some concrete "fact" such as a vengeful, cold-blooded killing. We don't then rationally infer that it is wrong; instead, we *feel* that it is wrong. The feeling is what introduces the new and distinctly moral element.

Hume's theory impacted contemporary moral theory in two ways. First, the fallacy of deriving ought from is illuminates a critical difference between *facts* that we know through rational observation and inference and *values* that come to us in a different way. This is the basic idea behind the fact—value problem as we discuss it today. Second, Hume's theory that moral assessments are *feelings* and not rational judgments has inspired several contemporary philosophers to equate moral utterances with emotional expressions. Today we call this position *emotivism*.

Moore: The Naturalistic Fallacy

In 1903 George Edward Moore published his *Principia Ethica,*[3] which inspired an ongoing inquiry among contemporary ethicists into such metaethical issues as the meaning of ethical terms and the relation of facts to values.

Moore begins his book by announcing that philosophers have been entangled in ethical problems largely because they have not clearly defined the territory of ethics and determined the kinds of questions that philosophers can properly ask about the subject. Ethics clearly involves the practical task of arriving at decision-making procedures for morally good behavior. But before doing this, Moore argues, we need to discover the meaning of the term *good* itself. In fact, the foundation of ethics is an understanding of the term *good:*

> That which is meant by "good" is, in fact, except its converse "bad," the only simple object of thought which is peculiar to Ethics.... Unless this first question be fully understood, and its true answer clearly recognized, the rest of Ethics is as good as useless from the point of view of systematic knowledge.

Philosophers in the past had also recognized the need to understand the meaning of the notion "good," and they attempted to define it in various ways. Utilitarians equated it with pleasure; Kant equated it with a person's rational will; evolutionary ethicists equated it with the notion of "being more evolved." According to Moore, though, all these theories are wrong for the basic reason that the notion "good" cannot be defined. In fact, Moore argues that it is a fallacy to identify "good" with any specific natural property such as "pleasure" or "being more evolved," and he calls this the **naturalistic fallacy.**

The reason why "good" is indefinable is because it is a *simple property*—that is, a property that has no parts and thus cannot be defined by constituent elements. For example, the color yellow is a simple property, which you can't explain to anyone who does not already know it what yellow is. Contrast this with a complex concept like "horse," which we can define in terms of constituent elements: It's a large mammalian animal, with an odd number of toes on its hooves. "Good" is like the simple notion of "yellow" (and not like the complex notion of "horse"). We intuitively recognize moral goodness when we see it, but it completely defies definition.

Moore offers a test to help us determine whether a moral theory commits the naturalistic fallacy, a test called the open-question argument. In its simplest form, the **open-question argument** is that for any property that we identify with "goodness," we can ask, "Is that property itself good?" For example, if I identify "goodness" as maximizing pleasure, the question can be asked, "Is maximizing pleasure itself good?" Because this question makes sense, it means that the maximizing pleasure and "goodness" are not truly identical. To illustrate, let's start with the following innocent statement:

S1. Charity is good.

Following utilitarians, let's now define *goodness* as "maximizing pleasure." Our innocent statement now becomes this:

S2. Charity maximizes pleasure.

Suppose we carry the investigation further and ask ourselves the following question:

Q1. Is it *good* to maximize pleasure through charity?

According to Moore, this shows "clearly that we have two different notions before our mind"—namely, the notion of "good" on the one hand and the property of "maximizing pleasure" on the other. The whole problem starts when we attempt to identify "goodness" with some natural property (such as "maximizing pleasure"), rather than just accepting the fact that goodness is a simple and indefinable quality.

Like Hume's fallacy of deriving ought from is, Moore's naturalistic fallacy is another way of articulating the fact–value problem. According to Moore, the *value* of "goodness" cannot be identified with *facts* like "maximizing pleasure" and "being more evolved." There is instead a gap between facts and values.

Moore's own solution to the problem was that we can intuitively recognize the presence of value (goodness) within facts (maximizing pleasure). Thus, charity may indeed maximize pleasure, and we can intuitively see goodness in it. However, it is one thing to recognize that goodness *accompanies* the maximizing of pleasure and quite another to *identify* goodness with the maximizing of pleasure. Regardless of how many things we intuitively recognize as being accompanied by moral goodness, there will always be a gap between the facts that we examine and the value that we find within them.

AYER AND EMOTIVISM

The next player in the story is Alfred Jules Ayer (1910–1989), who was influenced both by Hume's and Moore's presentation of the fact–value problem. Hume and Moore each showed two things. First, they explained why there is a fact–value problem; second, they offered solutions to the problem by showing what moral value really is. For Hume, the problem involves the fallacy of deriving ought from is, and his solution is that moral value rests on emotional reactions. For Moore, the problem involves the naturalistic fallacy, and his solution involves intuitively recognizing moral goodness within things.

Ayer also takes this two-pronged approach. First, he argues that the fact–value problem arises because moral statements cannot pass a critical test of meaning called the *verification principle*. Second, expanding on Hume, his solution is that moral utterances are only expressions of feelings, a position called emotivism. Let's look at each of these components.

Ayer's Theory

Regarding the verification principle, in the 1930s, Ayer went to Vienna to study with a group of philosophers called the "Logical Positivists," who believed that the meaning of a sentence is found in its method of verification. According to that test, all meaningful sentences must be either

(a) Tautologies (statements that are true by definition and of the form "A is A" or reducible to such statements) or

(b) Empirically verifiable (statements regarding observations about the world, such as "The book is red").

Based on this test, mathematical statements are meaningful, such as all triangles have three sides, because they are tautologies. The statement "The Empire State Building is in New York City" is meaningful because it is empirically verifiable.

What, though, about value statements such as "Charity is good"? According to the above test, they are meaningless because they are neither tautologies nor verifiable statements. That is, it is not true by definition that charity is good, and there is no way to empirically verify whether charity is good. Similarly, according to the above test, a theological statement such as "God is guiding your life" is meaningless because it is neither a tautology nor empirically verifiable. Ayer makes his point about the meaninglessness of value utterances here:

> [T]he fundamental ethical concepts are unanalyzable, inasmuch as there is no criterion by which one can test the validity of the judgments in which they occur. . . . The reason why they are unanalyzable is that they are mere pseudo-concepts. The presence of an ethical symbol in a proposition adds nothing to its factual content. Thus if I say to someone, "You acted wrongly in stealing that money," I am not stating anything more than if I had simply said, "You stole that money." In adding that the action is wrong, I am not making any further statement about it.[4]

His argument is essentially this:

(1) A sentence is meaningful if and only if it can be verified.

(2) Moral sentences cannot be verified.

(3) Therefore, moral sentences are not meaningful.

Thus, there is a fact—value problem insofar as moral utterances fail the verification test and are not factual statements.

Ayer's solution to the fact—value problem is to note that moral utterances function in a special nonfactual way. Although they are indeed factually meaningless, they are not just gibberish. For Ayer, utterances such as "Charity is good" express our positive feelings about charity in much the same way as if we shouted out "Charity—hooray!" Similarly, the utterance "Murder is wrong" expresses our negative feelings about murder just as if we shouted "Murder—boo!" The view that moral utterances merely express our feelings is called **emotivism.** Ayer is quick to point out that moral utterances don't even *report* our feelings; they just *express* our feelings. Here's the difference:

- *Reported feeling:* "Charity is good" means "I have positive feelings about charity."

- *Expressed feeling:* "Charity is good" means "Charity—hooray!"

Even reports of feelings are in some sense factual: It is either true or false that "I have positive feelings about charity," and I can empirically verify this with a psychological analysis of my mental state. However, the emotional expression "Charity—hooray!" is like a grunt or a sigh; there is nothing to factually report.

Philosophers have introduced two terms to distinguish between factual and nonfactual utterances: cognitive and noncognitive. When a statement has factual content, it is **cognitive:** We can know (or "cognize") its truth value—whether it is true or false. When a statement lacks factual content, it is **noncognitive:** It has no truth value. Traditional moral theories all claim to be cognitivist: They all purport that moral statements have truth value. Here is how four traditional theories would give a cognitivist interpretation of the moral utterance "Charity is good":

- *Egoism:* Charity maximizes self-interest.

- *Utilitarianism:* Charity maximizes general pleasure.

- *Kantianism:* Charity is a rational duty.

- *Virtue theory:* Charity promotes human flourishing.

Moore's emotivist solution to the fact—value problem is also cognitivist because for him "Charity is good" means "Charity has the indefinable property of moral goodness" (which, according to Moore, we know to be true through moral intuition). For Ayer, all these cognitivist theories are misguided. Because moral utterances like "Charity is good" do not pass the test for meaning by the verification principle, they cannot be cognitive. The content that they have is only noncognitive and takes the form of expressing our feelings.

Ayer's account of emotivism directly attacks many of our cherished assumptions about morality. We typically think that moral utterances are factually meaningful—not so according to Ayer. We typically think that morality involves some use of our reasoning ability—again, not so for Ayer. What's perhaps most unsettling about Ayer's theory is its implication that ethical disagreement is fundamentally a disagreement in attitude. Suppose you and I disagree about whether abortion is morally permissible and we debate the issue—in a civilized way without any emotional outbursts. On Ayer's view, this is still simply a matter of us having underlying emotional attitudes that conflict; it is not really a disagreement about facts of the matter.

Criticisms of Emotivism

Several objections against Ayer's emotivism were quickly forthcoming after the appearance of his book. A first criticism was that the verification theory of meaning, upon which Ayer's emotivism was founded, had serious problems. Specifically, it didn't pass its own test. Here in brief is the principle:

> **Verification principle:** A statement is meaningful if and only if it is either tautological or empirically verifiable.

We now ask the question, "Is the verification principle itself either tautological or empirically verifiable?" The answer is that it is not, which means that the verification principle is meaningless. If that's the case, then we are not obliged to use the verification principle as a test for moral utterances. The rest of Ayer's emotivist analysis of morality thus falls apart.

Second, there is a problem with the emotivist view that ethical disagreements are fundamentally disagreements in attitude. Specifically, this blurs an important distinction between having *reasons* for changing attitudes and having *causes* that change our attitudes. Suppose again that you and I are debating the abortion issue. Consider now two methods of resolving our dispute. Method 1 involves you giving me a series of reasons in support of your position, and I eventually agree with you. Method 2 involves a surgeon operating on my brain in a way that alters my emotional attitude about the abortion issue. Method 1 involves *reasons* behind my changed view, and Method 2 involves *causes* for my changed view. The emotivist theory cannot easily distinguish between these two methods of attitude change. One way or another, according to emotivism, changes in attitude will come only through some kind of causal manipulation with our emotions. This is a problem because virtually everyone would agree that there is a major difference between what is going on in method 1 and method 2, and it is only the former that is a legitimate way of resolving moral disagreements.

Third, morality seems deeper than mere emotions or acting on feelings or attitudes. Moral judgments are universalizable: If it is wrong for Jill to steal, then it is wrong for anyone relevantly similar to Jill to steal. Emotivism reduces morality to isolated emotive expressions or attitudes that don't apply universally. It makes more sense to see morality as a function of applying principles such as "It is wrong to steal," which has a universal element.

Ayer's version of emotivism is rather extreme, and it is no surprise that it creates so many problems. A more moderate version of emotivism was later proposed by Charles Leslie Stevenson (1908–1979) in his book *Ethics and Language* (1944).[5] Stevenson agrees that moral utterances have an emotive component that is noncognitive. However, he argues that moral utterances sometimes have cognitive elements too. Moral utterances are so complex, Stevenson says, that we cannot give a specific pattern that applies to all moral utterances all the time.

Nevertheless, a typical moral utterance like "Charity is good" might have these specific components:

- *Emotive expression (noncognitive):* "Charity—hooray!"
- *Report about feelings (cognitive):* "I approve of charity."
- *Description of other qualities (cognitive):* "Charity has qualities or relations X, Y, and Z" (for example, reduces suffering, reduces social inequality).

Stevenson's suggestion is quite reasonable. If we are unhappy with Ayer's extreme emotivism, we can still accept that there is *some* noncognitive emotive element to moral utterances. Indeed, considering how frequently emotion enters into our moral evaluations, such as the opening example from the Weblog, we will want to recognize at least a more limited role of emotive expressions.

HARE AND PRESCRIPTIVISM

Ayer is most famous for the emotivist theory that we've just examined. However, in *Language, Truth, and Logic,* he discusses a second noncognitivist element of moral utterances, namely, their **prescriptive** function: they recommend or command that others adopt our attitude. Ayer describes this here:

> It is worth mentioning that ethical terms do not serve only to express feeling. They are calculated also to arouse feeling, and so to stimulate action. Indeed some of them are used in such a way as to give the sentences in which they occur the effect of commands. Thus the sentence "It is your duty to tell the truth" may be regarded both as the expression of a certain sort of ethical feeling about truthfulness and as the expression of the command "Tell the truth."[6]

Like the emotive component of moral utterances, the prescriptive element is also nonfactual: It does not say anything true or false about the world but instead urges people to behave in certain ways. It is a bit like me gently poking you with a stick to get you to move along. Thus, according to Ayer, the moral utterance "Charity is good" has these two noncognitive elements:

- *Emotive:* "Charity—hooray!"
- *Prescriptive:* "Be charitable!"

The philosopher whose name is most associated with the prescriptive component of moral utterances is Richard Mervyn Hare (1919–2002), particularly in his book *The Language of Morals* (1952).[7] Hare acknowledges the fact–value gap brought out by Moore and Ayer. He also agrees with Ayer that we cannot ascribe truth or falsity to moral statements and that moral assessments are attitudinal. His focus, though, is more on the prescriptive element rather than the emotive one. According to Hare, there are four important features about moral judgments: (1) They are prescriptive, (2) they exhibit logical relations, (3) they are universalizable, and (4) they involve principles. Let's examine each of these.

Prescriptivity

According to Hare, moral judgments have both a descriptive (fact) and prescriptive (value) element. The descriptive element involves the facts about a particular action, such as "Charity maximizes pleasure." The prescriptive element is conduct guiding and recommends that others adopt our value attitude. For Hare, when making moral judgments, the prescriptive element is added onto the descriptive one; further, of the two elements, the prescriptive is more important than the descriptive. The reason is that our factual descriptions about things can change. One day we might describe charity as maximizing pleasure. The next we might describe it as exhibiting more evolved behavior or reflecting the will of God. However, the prescriptive element remains the same, regardless of how our descriptions change: We are recommending that others adopt our attitude toward X when we say that "X is good."

To illustrate this distinction between the descriptive and prescriptive elements, suppose I say of a particular automobile that it is a "good" car. I mean that it has certain characteristics: It doesn't often break down, it isn't rusted, it will go over 50 miles per hour, it gets at least 30 miles per gallon of gasoline, it serves its owner well for several years, and so forth. But I need not call all of this good. I could just as well describe my car item by item. Putting the adjective *good* next to the noun *car* simply means that I, like most people, would commend such an automobile. But Hot-Rod Harry, who has a passion for fast cars and is a skilled mechanic (so that he doesn't mind frequent breakdowns), might not agree with my evaluation. He might agree with my description of a given car and yet not agree that it was a good car. To me my 1990 Chevy is a good car, but to Harry it is a bad car and he wouldn't be seen dead in it. Here is the central distinction between a description and an evaluation of some thing:

- *Description:* Car C has features *a, b, c, . . . , n.*
- *Evaluation:* Good is always an attribution relative to some standard.

Hot-Rod Harry and I differ in calling car C *good* because we have different standards of reference. We can choose whatever standard of reference that we like; any such standard is not intrinsic to the nature of cars.

The point is that the descriptive component of *good* does not exhaust its meaning. There is something added—that is, the value factor. And this value aspect, the prescriptive nature of *good,* is a matter of guiding others' choices. Hare writes, "When we commend or condemn anything, it is always in order, at least indirectly, to guide choices, our own or other people's, now or in the future."[8]

Now, if I know that someone needs a car and has similar needs and values as mine, I can recommend a used Chevy sedan like mine to him. "It's a good car," I might say. Or, "If you want a good used car, get a Chevy sedan." Or, "You ought to buy an inexpensive secondhand Chevy like mine." All these statements have the same prescriptive force. The first sentence is an indicative value statement; the second is a hypothetical imperative (of the form, "If you want X, do A"); the third is an indicative sentence, containing the prescriptive verb *ought.*

It is important to note that moral judgments are not merely imperative commands, but through their prescriptive element they *contain* imperatives. "You ought not to cheat" is just another way of saying the imperative "Don't cheat, please!" When I accept the judgment that cheating is wrong—that people ought not to cheat—I am committing myself to live by that prescription myself. My moral judgment that you ought not to do X is meant to "guide" your action, not in the sense that it necessarily moves you to do X, but in the sense that your accepting my judgment commits you to doing X, and your not doing X implies that you have rejected my judgment.

The Logic of Moral Reasoning

A particular feature of Hare's theory that advances the program of noncognitivism is the idea that there is a logic to prescriptive judgments. Although moral judgments do not have truth value, they do have a logical form. We can argue about particular judgments and use arguments to reach particular prescriptions.

Hare holds two theses about the distinction between *is* and *ought*—between descriptive and prescriptive statements as they pertain to logical form:

1. No indicative conclusion can be validly drawn from a set of premises that cannot be validly drawn from the indicatives among them alone.

2. No imperative conclusion can be validly drawn from a set of premises that does not contain at least one imperative.

Let's focus on the second of these. A case of arguing from an indicative premise to an imperative would be

A1. This is a box.

A2. Therefore, take this box to the railroad station.

Something is clearly missing. We must add a major premise in the form of an imperative:

1. Take all the boxes to the railroad station.

As a result, the argument becomes

B1. Take all the boxes to the railroad station.

B2. This is a box.

B3. Therefore, take this to the railroad station.

When we recall that *ought* judgments are a type of imperative and then apply thesis 2 to moral judgments, we see that a valid moral argument must contain at least one *ought* (imperatival) premise to reach a moral conclusion:

C1. Students ought not to cheat on tests. (*Imperative form:* Never cheat, please!)

C2. Jill is taking a philosophy test. (*Indicative statement*)

C3. Therefore, Jill ought not to cheat on her test. (*Imperative form:* Therefore, don't cheat, Jill!)

Hare is in essence agreeing with Hume's fallacy of deriving ought from is. If our premises contain only factual *is* statements, then we cannot legitimately derive any *ought* statements of obligation from them. However, if at least one of the premises contains an *ought,* then we might legitimately carry this value element through to the conclusion.

Universalizability

Universalizability is the most important feature of Hare's moral theory because it gives the theory a formal structure. There is no special content to Hare's system, but there is a method. The method is essentially Kantian, similar to the categorical imperative: Act in such a way as to be able to will that the principle of your action could be a universal law. What distinguishes Kant's theory from Hare's is Kant's belief that the categorical imperative will generate substantive universal principles such as duties to develop one's talents; Hare rejects this idea.

The principle of universalizability is that in making a moral judgment one has to say that one would make the same judgment in all similar cases. A judgment is not moral unless the agent is prepared to universalize his or her principle. "To ask whether I ought to do A in these circumstances is to ask whether or not I will that doing A in such circumstances should become a universal law."[9] Universalizability is the recognition that "what is sauce for the goose is sauce for the gander." It constrains our choices to the extent that it warns us that by whatever judgment we judge we too will be judged. Hare argues that universalizability is both a necessary and sufficient condition of any moral judgment that one would impartially apply the same principle in any case of the same kind as the one in question. The distinction between "necessary" and "sufficient" condition is critical here and can be expressed as follows:

> *Universalizability as a necessary condition.* If a principle is a moral one, then it applies universally.
>
> *Universalizability as a sufficient condition.* If a principle applies universally, then it is a moral one.

Is Hare correct that universalizability is both a necessary and a sufficient condition for moral principles? A strong case can be made for viewing universalizability as a necessary condition. Generally speaking, if you say that object X has a certain property F and point out that object Y is exactly similar to X, then we would expect that Y would also have property F. If this cube of sugar is sweet and the one next to it is exactly similar in every relevant way, we should have to conclude that it is also sweet. Likewise with morality: If Bob does something that we judge to be immoral and Joe does something exactly similar in every relevant way, then we must judge that Joe's actual is also immoral.

However, the case is more difficult to make regarding universalizability as a sufficient condition. That is, not every universalizable principle that is prescriptive is a moral one such as this: "Do not immerse your hands in battery acid because this will burn your skin." This principle is prescriptive because it is urging a specific type of behavior. It is also universal because the directive applies to everyone—just as the harmful effects of battery acid on one's skin applies to everyone. And although immersing one's hands in battery acid may be a stupid thing to purposefully do, it is not necessarily an immoral act.

Principles

One of the most insightful aspects of Hare's work is his recognition of the centrality of principles in moral reasoning. To get a better look at this feature, let's contrast principle-centered systems with a nonprincipled system. One such type of ethics is situational ethics, especially as advocated by Joseph Fletcher in his book *Situation Ethics*. Fletcher relates the following story to illustrate his thesis that principles are unnecessary for moral living. During the 1964 election campaign, a friend of Fletcher's was riding in a taxi and happened to ask the taxi driver about his political views. The driver said, "I and my father and grandfather . . . and their fathers, have always been straight-ticket Republicans." "Ah," said the friend, who is himself a Republican, "I take it that means you will vote for Senator Goldwater." "No," said the driver, "there are times when a man has to push his principles aside and do the right thing."[10] The taxi driver is the hero of Fletcher's book, and his attitude is that we can jolly well do without principles.

But Hare would point out that, in Fletcher's mind, there is confusion between viewing principles as rigid absolutes and as reasons that are necessary to inform our deliberations. If Fletcher's friend had pressed the taxi driver a bit further, he no doubt would have gotten him to give some reasons for switching his vote. For example, he might have argued that Senator Goldwater wanted to escalate the war in Vietnam and such an escalation would both be unjust and lead to terrible consequences.

Indeed, Hare argues that all moral reasoning involves principles and that without principles most teaching would be impossible because we usually teach not particular items but a set of action-guiding principles; that is, we don't learn isolated individual acts but classes of acts within classes of situations:

> In learning to drive, I learn, not to change gear *now*, but to change gear when the engine makes a certain kind of noise. If this were not so, instruction would be of no use at all; for if all an instructor could do were to tell us to change gear now, he would have to sit beside us most of the rest of our lives in order to tell us just when, on each occasion, to change gear.[11]

After we have basic principles, we next learn when to use them and when to subordinate them to suit a complex situation. In driving, we first learn to draw to the side of the road before stopping. Later, we learn that this does not apply when stopping before making a left-hand turn onto a side road because then we must stop near the middle of the road until it is possible to turn. Still later, we learn that in this maneuver it is not necessary to stop at all if it is an uncontrolled junction, and we can see that there is no traffic that we will obstruct by turning. And so, the process of modifying our driving principles goes on.

> The good driver is one whose actions are so exactly governed by principles which have become a habit with him, that he normally does not have to think just what to do. But road conditions are exceedingly various, and therefore it is unwise to let all one's driving become a matter of habit. . . . The good driver constantly attends to his habits, to see whether they might not be improved; he never stops learning.[12]

Granted, then, we need principles in morality that will serve to habitually guide our conduct. But which moral principles should we follow? His answer is that there is no complete list of principles that we can list:

> [A]complete justification of a decision would consist of a complete account of its effects, together with a complete account of the principles which it observed, and the effects of observing those principles. . . . If pressed to justify a decision completely, we have to give a complete specification of the way of life of which it is a part. This complete specification it is impossible in practice to give; the nearest attempts are those given by the great religions. . . . If the inquirer still goes on asking "But why should I live like that?" then there is no further answer to give him, because we have already, *ex hypothesi,* said everything that could be included in this further answer. We can only ask him to make up his own mind which way he ought to live; for in the end everything rests upon such a decision of principle.[13]

Hare argues that we are free to choose our own principles, but having chosen, we must commit ourselves to those principles, thus universalizing them. He believes, though, that by using the imagination and putting oneself "in the shoes" of other people, we will be able to arrive at a group of common principles; if all normal people use this approach, he argues, they will in fact end up with a common normative moral theory—some form of utilitarianism.

Criticisms of Prescriptivism

Hare has been the target of attack by many ethicists over the decades; four specific criticisms leveled at his prescriptivism are these: (1) It is too broad and allows for conduct that we typically deem immoral, (2) it permits trivial judgments to count as moral ones, (3) it allows the moral substance in life to slip away from ethical theory, and (4) there are no constraints on altering one's principles.

First, prescriptivism is too broad: It allows terribly immoral people and acts to count as moral. Hare himself was the first to point this out in Chapter 6 of *Freedom and Reason* (1962). He admitted that the fanatic who prescribed that all people of a certain race should be exterminated could, on his account, be considered as moral judged by his theory. A convinced Nazi could validly use argument A:

A1. All Jews ought to be exterminated.

A2. David is a Jew.

A3. Therefore, David should be exterminated.

And a right-wing fanatic could reason

B1. No socialist should be allowed to teach in an American university.

B2. John is a socialist.

B3. Therefore, John should not be allowed to teach in an American university.

The only constraint on choosing moral principles is that one should use one's sympathetic imagination and put oneself "into the other person's shoes" before making the judgment. But this doesn't hinder the fanatic, who reasons, "If I were ever to become a socialist (or found to be a Jew), I would deserve the same treatment as I am prescribing." Many of us would argue that there is no way to justify these principles. Perhaps, the fanatic has been misinformed on the dangers of Jews or socialists, but there is no reason to accept his or her principles as legitimate. There must be something wrong with a theory that is so broad as to allow heinous acts to count as moral. Such a theory seems subject to the same criticisms as subjective relativism (see Chapter 2).

Second, prescriptivism allows the most trivial considerations to count as moral judgments. It would seem that any noncontradictory principle whatsoever could become a moral principle as long as it was prescriptively universalized by someone. Consider the following arguments:

C1. Everyone ought to rub his or her tummy on Tuesday mornings.

C2. Today is Tuesday, and it is morning.

C3. Therefore, you and I ought to rub our tummies.

D1. Everyone ought to tie one's right shoe before one's left.

D2. You are about to tie your shoes.

D3. Therefore, you have a moral duty to tie your right shoe before your left shoe.

Both of these arguments contain the four central features of Hare's theory: The moral judgment in the conclusion is a universalized prescriptive principle that follows the proper logical form. Morality for Hare has no special subject matter, no core content. This is the penalty that his theory pays for being so open ended.

Third, prescriptivism misses the point of morality: Not only does it allow too much to be counted as moral, it allows too much to slip through the moral net. We generally think that we have some moral obligations whether we are fully aware of them or not and whether we like it or not. We think it wrong in general to lie or cheat or kill innocent people or harm others without good reason, and any moral theory worth its salt would have to recognize these minimal principles as part of its theory. But there is no necessity to recognize these principles in Hare's theory; the principle "Killing innocent people is wrong" (or "One ought not to kill innocent people") is not a necessary principle in prescriptivism. One may choose the very opposite of that principle if one so wishes: "One ought to kill innocent people." So, when mass murderer Mike comes before the judge after being accused of killing forty-seven children, he may rightly say, "Your Honor, I protest your sentencing me to life imprisonment. Yes, I broke the law, but morality is higher than the law, and I was only doing what was morally right—killing innocent people. Mine were acts of civil disobedience."

A judge who was a prescriptivist would have to agree and reply, "Yes, I can see that you have a different set of moral principles from most of us and that there is no objectively valid way of deciding the issue. But one of my moral principles (indeed, I make my living by it) is to carry out the mandate of the law, so I am sentencing you to life imprisonment."

Perhaps we could imagine that a conversation like this might actually occur, but there is something counterintuitive about it. We think that morality is (or should be) about important aspects of human existence. Its principles are not something we invent but something we discover by reflection.

A fourth criticism is that Hare's theory allows us to switch our moral principles as we see fit. Hare admits that our moral principles are revisable, but he doesn't seem to notice how damaging this is for a stable moral system. Suppose when you are rich and I am poor, I universalize the principle that "The rich ought to help the poor in every way possible," and suppose also that I convince you to act on this principle. But suppose now that our situations have reversed—I am rich and you are poor; you notice that I am no longer acting on this principle, and you accuse me of hypocrisy. I can reply that I am not at all a hypocrite (which implies not living by one's principles); on the contrary, I am living by my principles—only they are altered principles! I have decided to live by the principle that "No one has a duty to help the poor." Of course, if I should become poor again, I might very well change my principles again. You may object that this is insincere. But why should I universalize the principle of universal consistency over time? I am sincere about living by my current principles, and that is all that Hare's moral theory requires. Perhaps this shows a lack of character, but then Hare's theory doesn't give us any objective standards for character. Perhaps I choose to universalize the principle that one may change one's character to suit one's principles. The point here is that there are no nonarbitrary constraints on when and why I may change my moral principles.

NATURALISM AND THE FACT–VALUE PROBLEM

All the noncognitivist solutions to the fact–value problem are troubling: Reducing moral utterances to emotional outbursts or mere universal prescriptions destroys many of the key elements that we find essential to morality. Still, the fact–value problem is a very serious one and demands some answer—hopefully one that matches our conceptions of what morality should do.

One answer, called **naturalism,** is to link moral terms with some kind of natural property. This is precisely the approach taken by traditional philosophers: Utilitarians link moral terms with the natural property of pleasure; egoists, with self-interest; virtue theories, with human flourishing. All these properties are *natural* ones insofar as they are found in the natural world, specifically the natural realms of human psychology and human society. Hume and Moore each argue that this commits a fallacy—the fallacy of deriving ought from is and the naturalistic fallacy. Contemporary moral naturalists disagree and try to show how moral terms and natural properties can be linked in a nonfallacious way.

Geoffrey Warnock, for example, argues that morality is linked with "the betterment—or nondeterioration of the human predicament."[14] According to Warnock, society has a natural tendency to get worse, an *entropy of social relations.* Because of limitations in resources, intelligence, knowledge, rationality, and sympathy, the social fabric tends to come apart, which as a result threatens to produce a Hobbesian state of nature in which chaos reigns. Morality is antientropic. It opposes these limitations, especially by concentrating on expanding our sympathies.

Naturalism and the Open-Ended Argument

Hume, Moore, and Ayer would accuse Warnock of making a serious fact—value blunder. Moore, for example, would charge that Warnock commits the naturalist fallacy by defining *good* in terms of the natural property of "bettering the human predicament." Applying the open-question argument, let's again start with the following statement:

S1. Charity is good.

For Warnock, *goodness* means "bettering the human predicament," which transforms S1 into this:

S2. Charity betters the human predicament.

Carrying the investigation further, Moore would have us ask,

Q1. Is it *good* to better the human predicament through charity?

Again, for Moore, this shows "clearly that we have different notions before our mind."

The best way to defend Warnock and other naturalists is to go on the offensive and show the inadequacies of Moore's naturalistic fallacy and open-ended argument. One serious problem with Moore's theory is that it regards the idea of goodness as though it were a thing. This error is sometimes called the *fallacy of hypostatization:* treating an idea as a distinct substance or reality. Consider this conversation in Lewis Carroll's *Through the Looking Glass:*

> "Just look along the road, and tell me if you can see either of the messengers," said the King.
> "I can see nobody on the road," said Alice.
> "I only wish I had such eyes," the King remarked in a fretful tone.

"To be able to see Nobody! And at that distance too! Why, it's as much as I can do to see real people, by this light."

[The messenger arrives] "Who did you pass on the road?" The King went on, holding out his hand to the Messenger for some more hay.

"Nobody," said the Messenger.

"Quite right," said the King; "this young lady saw him too. So of course Nobody walks slower than you."

"I do my best," the Messenger said in a sullen tone. "I'm sure nobody walks much faster than I do!"

"He can't do that," said the King, "or else he'd have been here first."[15]

The King makes the ludicrous mistake of treating an indefinite, functional pronoun ("nobody") as a proper noun. In like manner, Moore treats functional the common noun *goodness* as a proper noun; he treats the functional term *good* as though it were a thing, just as gold and water are things. This seems wrong.

Consider the way we use *good* in sentences.

- "The weather is good today."
- "That was a good catch that the football player made."
- "It's good to increase the gross national product."
- "Telling the truth is a good thing to do although sometimes it's the wrong thing to do."

It's difficult to give a satisfactory definition of *good*. Perhaps the closest ones are "the most general term of commendation" and "satisfying some requirement." When the weather suits our aesthetic or prudential desires, we call it "good"—although it is relative to the speaker because the sunbather and the farmer have different frames of reference. When the football player behaves in a manner befitting his function, we commend his execution. When a nation's productivity is increased, giving promise of a higher standard of living, we express our approval with the adjective *good*. Attributing goodness to an activity or artifact represents our approval of that activity or artifact—our judgment that it meets an appropriate standard.

Likewise in ethical discussions, *good* serves as a term of commendation, expressing the perception that such and such a behavior meets our standards of fitting behavior or contributes to goals we deem positive. When we say that telling the truth is a good thing to do, we do not mean that there is an independently existing form of the Good that truth telling somehow represents or is "plugged into." If we are reflective, we generally mean that there is something proper or valuable (either intrinsically or extrinsically) about truth telling. Furthermore, we generally do not judge that the goodness attached to truth telling is absolute because it can be overridden in some cases by other considerations. For example, we judge it to be a bad thing to tell the truth to criminals who will use the information given to murder an innocent person.

We have a notion of good ends that morality serves. Even if we are deontologists, we still think that there is a point to morality, and that point generally has to do with producing better outcomes—truth telling generally produces better outcomes than lying. These ends can be put into nonmoral natural language in terms of happiness, flourishing, welfare, equality, and the like; that is, at least part of our notion of moral goodness is predicated on a notion of nonmoral goodness. A certain logic pertains in what can be called morally good, depending on these nonmoral values.

If this analysis is correct, then it doesn't make much sense to treat the notion of "good" like a thing (for example, gold or water) and define it in the realist language, any more than it makes sense to treat "tallness" and "spectacularity" and "equality" as things. It's a category mistake to treat a functional term as though it were a thing.

CONCLUSION

In this chapter, we've examined the problem of how facts connect with values. We've seen three specific arguments that radically divide descriptive facts from value judgments about them: Hume's fallacy of deriving ought from is, Moore's naturalistic fallacy, and Ayer's verification principle. We've also explored attempts by these philosophers to solve the fact–value problem. For Hume, value judgments are emotional reactions that we have to specific facts, such as our reaction when seeing someone donate to charity. For Moore, value judgments involve intuitively recognizing value (goodness) within facts (maximizing pleasure through charity). For Ayer, value statements are merely expressions of feelings that we make in response to facts such as Smith donating to charity, a position called emotivism. We find in Ayer's solution an important distinction between the cognitive and noncognitive meaning of statements—that is, statements that have a truth value versus those that have no truth value. According to Ayer, emotive expressions of feelings in moral utterances are noncognitive. The central problem with Ayer's emotivism is that it goes too far by maintaining that moral statements are *only* expressions of feeling. Although there may indeed be a noncognitive emotive element to moral statements, they seem to have at least some cognitive component as well.

We've also examined Hare's theory of prescriptivism and how it relates to the fact–value problem. For Hare, moral statements of the sort "Charity is good" have both a descriptive (fact) element, such as "Charity maximizes pleasure," and a prescriptive (value) element that recommends that others adopt our attitude, such as "You should approve of charity!" Moral judgments, for Hare, involve four features: prescriptions, a proper logical form, universality, and principles. Critics argue that his theory does not have enough constraints on the sort of universal prescriptive principles that we adopt. We may either leave out important ones or include heinous ones. The inadequacies of emotivism and prescriptivism have inspired some recent philosophers to reject noncognitivism and adopt a cognitivist approach called naturalism that links moral terms with some kind of natural property. Warnock, for example, connects morality with the improvement of the human predicament.

NOTES

1. David Hume, *A Treatise of Human Nature* (1739–1740), 3.1.1.
2. Ibid.
3. George Edward Moore, *Principia Ethica* (Cambridge, Engl.: Cambridge University Press, 1903).
4. A. J. Ayer, *Language, Truth, and Logic,* 2nd ed. (Dover, 1946), p. 107.
5. See C. L. Stevenson, *Ethics and Language* (New Haven, Conn.: Yale University Press, 1944), and "The Emotive Meaning of Ethical Terms," *Mind* 46 (1937): 14–31.
6. Ayer, *Language, Truth, and Logic.*
7. R. M. Hare, *The Language of Morals* (Oxford University Press, 1952).
8. R. M. Hare, *Freedom and Reason* (Oxford University Press, 1963), p. 127.
9. Ibid., p. 70.
10. Joseph Fletcher, *Situation Ethics* (Westminster Press, 1966).
11. Hare, *The Language of Morals,* pp. 60–61.
12. Ibid., p. 63.
13. Ibid., p. 69.
14. Geoffrey Warnock, *The Object of Morality* (Methuen, 1971), p. 26.
15. Lewis Carroll, *Through the Looking Glass* (Pan Books, 1947), pp. 232–233. Compare this passage with the hypostatization of time in *Carroll's Alice's Adventures in Wonderland* (Pan Books, 1947), p. 54.

FOR FURTHER REFLECTION

1. Describe Hume's *fallacy of deriving ought from is* and how it applies to theories discussed earlier in this book, such as utilitarianism or Kantianism.
2. Many writers on ethics maintain that Hume's fallacy of deriving ought from is and Moore's naturalistic fallacy say basically the same thing. Compare and contrast these two fallacies and indicate whether you agree with that assessment.
3. Discuss the problems with Ayer's extreme version of emotivism and whether Stevenson's version satisfactory addresses those shortcomings.
4. Ayer appeared to think that the emotive element is more prominent in ethics than the prescriptive; Hare seems to think it's the reverse. Is one of these elements indeed more central to moral judgments than the other? Explain.
5. Does Moore's open-question argument commit the *fallacy of hypostatization* as suggested at the close of this chapter? Explain.
6. Philosopher John L. Mackie argues that metaethical questions such as those discussed in this chapter are completely irrelevant to whether a person holds traditional moral values. Are the metaethical and practical issues of morality as distinct as Mackie suggests?

FOR FURTHER READING

Frankena, William K. *The Naturalistic Fallacy*. New York: Macmillan, 1939.

Horgan, Terry, and Mark Timmons. *Metaethics after Moore*. Oxford, Engl.: Clarendon Press, 2006.

Hudson, W. D. *The Is—Ought Question*. London, Macmillan, 1969.

Miller, Alexander. *An Introduction to Contemporary Metaethics*. Cambridge, Engl.: Polity Press, 2003.

Putnam, Hilary. *The Collapse of the Fact/Value Dichotomy and Other Essays*. Cambridge, Mass.: Harvard University Press, 2002.

Schroeder, Mark. *Noncognitivism in Ethics*. London: Routledge, 2009.

Urmson, J. O. *The Emotive Theory of Ethics*. London: Hutchinson, 1968.

12

✳

Moral Realism and the Challenge of Skepticism

> Take any action allowed to be vicious; willful murder, for instance.
> Examine it in all lights and see if you can find that matter of fact, or real
> existence, which you call vice. . . . You can never find it till you turn
> your reflection into your own breast, and find a sentiment of
> disapprobation, which arises in you, towards that action.
> DAVID HUME, *A TREATISE OF HUMAN NATURE*

A man and women in Iran were recently sentenced to death for committing adultery; while that alone is rather shocking, what makes this judgment especially extreme is that the method of execution was to be death by stoning. The plan was to escort the convicted criminals to a graveyard, wrap them in sheets, partially bury them, and throw stones on them until dead. However, because of worldwide opposition, the Iranian government commuted the sentence to imprisonment.

One of the organizations responsible for putting pressure on the Iranian government was Amnesty International, a group that for decades has actively opposed human rights abuses throughout the world. Their stated mission is to "undertake research and action focused on preventing and ending grave abuses of the rights to physical and mental integrity, freedom of conscience and expression, and freedom from discrimination, within the context of its work to promote all human rights." The organization also states as its core values that it constitutes "a global community of human rights defenders with the principles of international solidarity, effective action for the individual victim, global coverage, the universality and indivisibility of human rights, impartiality and independence, and democracy and mutual respect."[1]

209

Within their mission statement, we find the familiar ethical notions of human rights, freedom, universality, impartiality, and respect. But there also appears to be an underlying assumption about the factual nature of morality: There are clear standards of proper treatment of human beings, and through "research" we can uncover abuses. Morality is not just a gut feeling that changes according to whims of people or society. It is grounded in objective moral facts that we can recognize and apply to concrete cases like the couple in Iran. The ethical position implied here is that of **moral realism:** Moral facts exist and are part of the fabric of the universe; they exist independently of our thoughts about them.

Moral realism has three main elements, the first two of which we have already explored in earlier chapters. First, there is an *objectivist element* regarding moral principles: They have objective validity and do not depend on social approval. Second, there is a *cognitivist element* regarding moral judgments: They involve assertions that can be evaluated as either true or false. Third, there is a *metaphysical element* regarding the existence of moral facts: They do in reality exist. Although moral realism involves all three of these components, the heart of the theory—and much of the debate surrounding it—concerns the metaphysical claim that moral facts exist.

Most traditional moral theories espouse some kind of moral realism and the notion of "moral facts." For example, *theistic moral realists* hold that moral values exist within God. On this view, morality depends on God's will or reason, which, according to the theist, are objective facts within the universe. *Naturalistic moral realists* maintain that moral values exist within the natural world and are connected with specific properties such as pleasure or satisfaction. Pleasure and satisfaction, in turn, are objective facts within the world. Egoism and utilitarianism are clear examples of this approach insofar as morality is directly linked with the pleasure or satisfaction that people experience as a result of their actions. Aristotle's virtue theory also espouses naturalistic realism because moral value is linked directly with human capacities for happiness and successful human activity, which are facts about the world.

And then there is **nonnaturalism,** a theory held by *nonnaturalistic moral realists* who ground moral values in nonnatural facts about the world—facts that can't be detected through scientific means. Morality is still rooted in facts, but they are facts of a very unique and sometimes other-worldly kind. Plato's account of morality, one of the most influential ethical theories ever, is the premier example of nonnaturalistic moral realism. According to Plato, the universe is divided into two radically different realms. The lower realm is the physical world of appearances, which is ever changing. The upper one, which exists in "a very central part of the universe," is spiritlike in nature and contains unchanging entities called *forms,* which are perfect ideal models—universal patterns—of imperfect things in the physical realm. With morality, there are forms of perfect Goodness, Justice, and Charity, and these are the standards by which we judge human conduct in the lower physical realm. A good human being like Socrates is good only because he participates in the universal form Goodness. Thus, for Plato, morality depends on real and objective facts of a very nonnatural sort—namely, universal forms that exist in a higher spirit-realm.

In this chapter, we examine two influential attacks on moral realism, one by J. L. Mackie and another by Gilbert Harman. Philosophers like these two who oppose moral realism are most generally called *antirealists,* although their specific strategies differ. Mackie, for example, defends a position called **moral skepticism,** which is a denial that moral values are objectively factual. Harman defends a position called **moral nihilism,** which for him means "that there are no moral facts, no moral truths, and no moral knowledge." We begin with Mackie.

MACKIE'S MORAL SKEPTICISM

In 1977 the Oxford philosopher J. L. Mackie in his *Ethics: Inventing Right and Wrong* set forth a radical interpretation of morality. He opens his book with the sentence "There are no objective values." He elaborates:

> The claim that values are not objective, are not part of the fabric of the world, is meant to include not only moral goodness, which might be most naturally equated with moral value, but also other things that could be more loosely called moral values or disvalues—rightness and wrongness, duty, obligation, an action's being rotten and contemptible, and so on. It also includes non-moral values, notably aesthetic ones, beauty and various kinds of artistic merit.[2]

He calls his position moral skepticism. His view is not about the *meaning* of moral statements but about objective *facts,* about whether there are any factually right or good actions. His answer is a skeptical one: We have no good reason to believe that objective moral facts exist. Certainly, we feel as though specific actions are objectively right or wrong and that happiness is better than misery, but these are just our subjective preferences—even if others agree, intersubjective agreement is still subjective. When we apply a philosophical microscope to our judgments, we are forced to conclude that moral objectivity is simply false. However nice it would be to have an objective moral authority, there is no reason to believe it exists. There are no objective moral truths.

Mackie acknowledges that the notion of objective moral values is ingrained in our language and thought; we presuppose the existence of objective moral facts in our very moral utterances. Nevertheless, there are no such objective values, despite our common assumptions. He calls this an **error theory** and describes it here:

> The denial of objective values will have to be put forward . . . as an "error theory," a theory that although most people in making moral judgments implicitly claim, among other things, to be pointing to something objectively prescriptive, these claims are all false.[3]

It is much like when people talk about ghosts living in haunted houses; although this presupposes that such ghosts actually exist, the reality is that they do not exist. For Mackie, "The claim to [moral] objectivity, however ingrained in our language and thought, is not self-validating."

Arguments from Relativity, Queerness, and Projection

Mackie offers three arguments for his skeptical position that moral values do not exist as objective facts about the world: from relativity, queerness, and projection.

The *argument from relativity* points out that there is no universal moral code that all people everywhere adhere to, which seems to indicate that morality is culturally dependent. It is an anthropological truism that the content of moral codes varies enormously from culture to culture. Some cultures promote monogamy, whereas others promote polygamy. Some cultures practice euthanasia, and others proscribe it. Our moral beliefs seem largely a product of our cultural upbringing. We tend to internalize the customs of our group. The argument from relativity holds that the best explanation for actual moral diversity is the absence of universal moral truths, rather than the distorted perceptions of objective principles.

Is Mackie's argument successful? The fact of cultural diversity in and of itself doesn't constitute a very strong argument against an objective core morality any more than disagreement about economics is good evidence against the thesis that some theories are better than others. Disagreement about morals could be the result of ignorance, immaturity, moral insensitivity, superstition, or irrational authority. A criminal I once knew, whom I will call Sam, was accused of attempted rape. Asked to compare the significance of rape with other actions, he replied, "It's like choosing between chocolate and vanilla ice cream." Why should I allow Sam's perception to undermine my confidence in the principle "Rape is immoral"? Just as there can be physical blindness or partial blindness, can't there be gross moral blindness? Can't I conclude that something is wrong with Sam—rather than concluding, "Oh, well, different strokes for different folks" or "Different morals for different cultures"? Mackie himself acknowledges that his argument from relativity is indecisive, and that all cultures may indeed follow a very general principle of universalizability—namely, one ought to conform to specific rules of any way of life in which one takes part. However, he argues, the specific moral rules that we adopt will vary depending on the circumstances of the society. Ultimately his argument rests on a judgment call between whether (1) so-called objective moral standards inform our ever-changing cultural practices or (2) our ever-changing cultural practices inform our human-created moral standards.

The *argument from queerness* aims at showing the implausibility of supposing that such things as values have an independent existence. If there were objective values, then they would have to be "of a very strange sort, utterly different from anything else in the universe." Plato's theory of the moral forms is a good example of Mackie's point: What exactly is a moral form, what is it made of, and where does it exist? The whole theory is too bizarre to be believable. Further, Mackie argues, if such strange moral objects existed, they would require a strange faculty for us to perceive them. Mackie thinks that all types of moral realism boil down to a conviction that there is a special sort of intuition that enables us to detect these strange moral objects. Further, there is a longstanding philosophical principle of simplicity that says do not multiply kinds of objects beyond necessity. Accordingly, the burden of proof seems to rest with the intuitionist to justify why we should espouse this unexplained, extra mechanism—this strange "moral sense." What evidence there is suggests that no such strange faculty exists. The principle of simplicity thus has us reject the thesis that moral facts exist in favor of the simpler explanation that moral principles are merely subjective judgments.

In response to this argument, a moral realist might agree with Mackie specifically about Plato's notion of objective moral forms; they are indeed strange entities that require a strange mental faculty to perceive. However, other versions of moral realism may not require entities or faculties that are as strange. For example, theistic moral realists say that the morality exists as an objective fact in the mind of God, and God then gives us human instincts to recognize some general rules of morality, such as "Be sociable." The special moral faculty here does not have to be anything strange and may be no different than our awareness of other general human instincts, such as the ability to acquire language or to count. Thus, according to the realist, Mackie portrays moral realism in an unfairly negative way by focusing mainly on Plato's view of moral forms.

The *argument from projection* aims to show that belief in objective value is the result of psychological tendencies to project subjective beliefs to the outside world. Why do we erroneously give moral notions an objective and factual status? In explaining our tendency to objectify morality, Mackie draws on an argument by David Hume. Hume writes,

> Take any action allowed to be vicious; willful murder, for instance. Examine it in all lights and see if you can find that matter of fact, or real existence, which you call vice. In whichever way you take it, you only find certain passions, motives, volitions and thoughts.... The vice entirely escapes you, as long as you consider the object. You can never find it till you turn your reflection into your own breast, and find a sentiment of disapprobation, which arises in you, towards that action.[4]

Hume's point is that when we perceive a murder we do not perceive the factual immorality within the act itself. Rather, we impose the notion of immorality onto it from within our own feelings. Hume speaks of our mind's "propensity to spread itself on external objects." Mackie calls this the *pathetic fallacy,* "our tendency to read our feelings into their objects. If a fungus, say, fills us with disgust, we may be inclined to ascribe to the fungus itself a non-natural quality of foulness." Similarly, because we internally perceive the morality or immorality of an external action, we then impose that moral quality onto the object and thus wrongly think it exists as a fact.

The realist has a response to this: Projection is a normal and even necessary way for people to interact with the external world, and the fungus example illustrates this well. Our internal sense of disgust is an important survival mechanism that keeps us away from potentially hazardous things. It's the product of evolution, and without it we'd almost certainly die a quick death. While the experienced quality of "disgust" does not exist in the fungus itself, the "disgust" experience reflects a reality of how fungi pose a risk to human health. Rather than call this the pathetic fallacy, we should call it the pathetic survival mechanism. Moral judgments work the same way. As Hume correctly notes, the feature of "immoral" doesn't exist within an act of murder itself. Rather, the immorality that we see in it reflects how murderous acts pose a special threat to us. This special threat is an objective fact just as much as is the health risk posed by fungi.

Inventing Morality

Mackie's attack on moral realism is primarily directed toward the metaphysical claim that moral values exist in an objective factual realm, external to human beings. Nevertheless, he argues, this has no impact on the more practical task of morality that involves devising moral rules of conduct. He writes,

> A man could hold strong moral views, and indeed ones whose content was thoroughly conventional, while believing that they were simply attitudes and policies with regard to conduct that he and other people held. Conversely, a man could reject all established morality while believing it to be an objective truth that it was evil or corrupt.[5]

When we engage in the practical task of devising moral rules, we are in essence *inventing* the notions of right and wrong, not discovering them in some objective realm.

What could this mean to "invent" right and wrong? The Greek philosopher Xenophon (570–478 BCE) said that religion is an invention, the making of God in the image of one's own group:

> The Ethiopians make their gods black and snub-nosed; the Thracians say theirs have blue eyes and red hair. Yes, and if oxen and horses or lions had hands, and could paint with their hands, and produce works of art as men do, horses would paint the forms of the gods like horses, and oxen like oxen, and make their bodies in the image of their several kinds.

Is this how we create morality—in our own images and according to our own desires, giving it authority in the process? Does Mackie mean that we consciously invent morality, principles, and sanctions to achieve social control? It seems so, for he writes:

> We need morality to regulate interpersonal relations, to control some of the ways in which people behave towards one another, often in

opposition to contrary inclinations. We therefore want our moral judge-
ments to be authoritative for other agents as well as for ourselves: objective validity would give them the authority required.[6]

Suppose Mackie is correct and we do invent these practices and institutions.
We find ourselves cooperating, and then we notice the wonderful benefits it brings;
thus reinforced, the behavior tends to be repeated and promoted. We notice that
truth telling is indispensable for achieving our goals, so we invent sanctions to
encourage it. But, even if we did create all our moral practices from the beginning
in the way Mackie seems to suppose, still it would be an objective matter—a matter
of *discovery*—to determine whether they really work. Morality is a discovery of
what will serve human needs and interests. To use the analogy from the Preface,
it is an invention like the wheel, which is a phenomenal tool that obeys physical
laws and transforms energy more efficiently. Wheels can have diverse purposes.
The water wheel is different from the wheel barrow, which is different from the
wheel of a bicycle or a car. A wheel can be constructed out of diverse materials—
wood, steel, stone, or rubber—but there are constraints. You can't make a square
or triangular wheel or wheels disproportionately heavy, but different kinds of
wheels serve different purposes in different situations.

Similarly, morality is a discovery, a discovery of those principles and strategies
that best promote a good individual and communal life. Our most fundamental
moral principles are both a rational invention and a rational discovery. Suppose
we decide to invent the practice of respecting property. We then discover that it
really enhances the freedom and meaning of our lives. Just as the Ethiopian invention of black gods doesn't make it true that gods are black, our invention of moral
practices doesn't make these practices true or valid or successful in meeting the relevant conditions. We don't invent the fact that respect for property brings us freedom and meaning. Either it does or it doesn't. There is a fact of the matter.

HARMAN'S MORAL NIHILISM

A second attack on moral realism is by Gilbert Harman in his book *The Nature of
Morality* (1979) where he defends a version of moral nihilism. Again, moral nihilism for Harman is the view that there are no moral facts, no moral truths, and no
moral knowledge.

His central position is what we may call the *disanalogy thesis:* Moral principles
cannot be tested by observation in the same way that scientific theories can. Scientific theories are tested against the world. So, if a predicted observation occurs,
then it confirms our theory; but if it doesn't occur, then we feel strong pressure to
alter or reject our theory. With regard to moral theories, we do not identify
"rightness" or "wrongness" in acts in the same way:

> Scientific hypotheses can . . . be tested in real experiments, out in the
> world. Can moral principles be tested in the same way, out in the
> world? You can observe someone do something, but can you ever

perceive the rightness or wrongness of what he does? If you round a cor-
ner and see a group of young hoodlums pour gasoline on a cat and ignite
it, you do not need to *conclude* that what they are doing is wrong; you can
see that it is wrong. But is your reaction due to the actual wrongness of
what you see or is it simply a reflection of your moral "sense," a "sense"
that you have acquired perhaps as a result of your moral upbringing?[7]

Illustrating his point, Harman asks us to compare cases of scientific and moral
observation. Consider first a scientific observation. A physicist makes an observation to test a scientific theory. Seeing a vapor trail in a cloud chamber, she thinks,
"There goes a proton." If the observation is relevant to the theory, then the observation confirms the existence of the proton. The best explanation of the vapor
trail is the scientific fact—a proton. On the other hand, consider a moral observation. You see some children pouring gasoline on a cat and setting the cat on fire.
You don't see "moral wrongness," nor do you infer it as the best explanation of
the event. The wrongness is something you impose on the observation. General-
izing from this comparison, Harman argues that there is a disanalogy between scientific observation of something (which leads us to posit scientific entities as the
best explanation) and so-called moral observation (which does not lead us to posit
special *moral facts* as the best explanation). The explanation of a scientific observation is in the world (external to the observer) whereas the explanation of a
moral observation is in the observer's psychological state (internal to the
observer). Moral insights occur because of our upbringing, not because of the
way the world is.

Because moral facts do not exist in the way that scientific facts do, Harman
concludes that moral nihilism is true. He describes his notion of moral nihilism
here:

> Nihilism is the doctrine that there are no moral facts, no moral truths,
> and no moral knowledge. This doctrine can account for why reference
> to moral facts does not seem to help explain observations, on the grounds
> that what does not exist cannot explain anything.
>
> An extreme version of nihilism holds that morality is simply an illu-
> sion: nothing is ever right or wrong, just or unjust, good or bad. In this
> version, we should abandon morality, just as an atheist abandons religion
> after he has decided that religious facts cannot help explain observations.
> Some extreme nihilists have even suggested that morality is merely a
> superstitious remnant of religion.[8]

Extreme nihilism as he describes is hard to swallow. It would say there is
nothing wrong with murdering your mother or exterminating 12 million people in Nazi concentration camps. Moderate nihilism holds that, although no
moral truths exist, moral discourse is expressive—roughly emotivist (see Chapter 11). Morality allows us to express our feelings and attempt to get others to
feel the way we do, but, at bottom, it is no more objective than extreme nihilism. Morality is merely a functionally useful way of projecting our feelings onto
the world.

Criticism: Scientific and Moral Observation Are Analogous

Richard Werner has opposed Harman on the grounds that scientific and moral observations are more similar than Harman maintains.[9] Even if we accept Harman's observation requirement, we should conclude that moral facts exist. There is no strong disanalogy between scientific and moral observation. The most reasonable explanation for many scientific observations is a scientific entity (for example, the proton in a cloud chamber). Likewise, the most reasonable explanation for a moral observation is a moral entity (for example, the wrongness of causing unnecessary suffering). One may argue that, just as one needs background knowledge to recognize that vapor in a cloud chamber is evidence of a subatomic particle, one needs background evidence about animal sentience and the properties of fire to infer that burning a cat is torturous and hence causes unnecessary suffering. Even if the children were ignorant of that evidence and burned the cat out of curiosity, we would still judge the act to be wrong—although we would judge the children to be guiltless. We would instruct them, "Don't you realize that cats feel extreme pain in being burned?" If the children know of the pain caused by extreme heat, then they will realize that burning hurts the cat and will realize that it is a bad thing to do, inasmuch as causing pain is a bad thing to do.

However, according to Harman, this argument still entails a disanalogy between scientific and moral reasoning. Werner illustrates Harman's disanalogy thesis by comparative diagrams as shown in Figures 12.1 and 12.2.

In Figure 12.1, principle SP is derivable from ST whereas SO and RSO are derivable from SP together with some observation (the trail in the cloud chamber). SO tends to verify SP, which in turn verifies ST. Thus, the entities posited in ST and SP must exist to be observed in SO.

In Figure 12.2, principle MP is derivable from MT whereas MO and RMO are derivable from MP together with some observation (the wanton burning of the cat). MO does not tend to verify MT because the most reasonable explanation

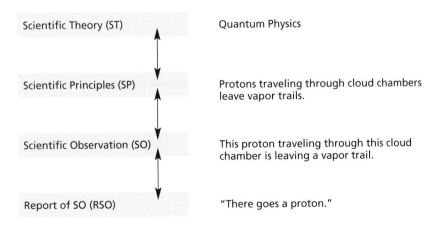

FIGURE 12.1 Scientific explanatory model

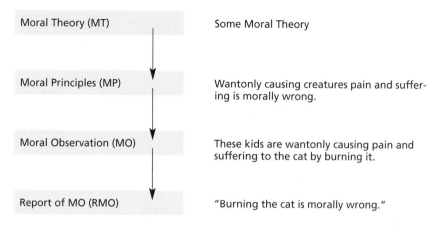

FIGURE 12.2 Moral explanatory model

of RMO depends on the observer's psychological set and does not require the positing of moral facts. Thus, there is a disanalogy between scientific and moral reasoning.

Werner thinks that the diagram in Figure 12.2 is incomplete. We could construct a set of upward-pointing arrows, saying that the best explanation for our moral observations is the truth of our moral principles and theory. Suppose our moral theory includes the principle that it is wrong to inflict unnecessary suffering on beings. The background conditions will include the fact that we socialize children to feel guilt about inflicting such cruelty on others. A second criterion will be that this socialization process must survive rational scrutiny (that is, we would have confidence in this process under conditions of impartiality and wide knowledge). We will appeal to the children's own experience of pain and suffering to confirm that pain is intrinsically bad. This would be hard to teach if, as rarely happens, the children cannot feel physical pain. But they could still comprehend psychological pain. Let's assume this connection between the idea that pain is intrinsically bad and the observation that we feel guilt if we cause cruelty or moral indignation at the sight of others causing cruelty—that is, unnecessary suffering. We can then say that our judging of the children as doing something wrong confirms the thesis that it is indeed wrong to cause unnecessary suffering. If this is correct, then Harman's disanalogy evaporates, and we can say that moral judgments are derivable from moral principles and theories and that they tend to confirm those principles and theories.

In the end, Harman is correct to point out that moral principles cannot be tested by observation in the same way that empirical theories can, but they can be tested. Cultures that fail to instantiate moral principles such as truth telling, promise keeping, cooperating, and not killing innocent members of the community will probably not survive, or if they do, their members will not be very happy or prosperous. Anthropological and sociological data confirm the need for morality as much as vapor trails in a cloud chamber confirm the existence of protons. So, in a way, our reflective moral judgments, those surviving critical scrutiny, do roughly confirm our moral theories. But, even as our scientific theories are open to revision and qualification, so our moral theories are open to revision in the light of better evidence and reflection.

A DEFENSE OF MORAL REALISM

We've seen that both Mackie's and Harman's arguments have serious obstacles and do not constitute decisive refutations of moral realism. Our next task is to defend moral realism by identifying possible candidates for moral facts.

Moral Facts about Happiness and Suffering

One possible set of facts that might count as "moral" relates to happiness and suffering. Let's return to Harman's contention that we cannot know by observation (or by any other way) that setting a cat on fire is immoral. How would we counter this contention? Perhaps we could set up the following argument:

(1) It is wrong to cause unnecessary suffering.

(2) Burning a cat causes unnecessary suffering.

(3) Therefore, it is wrong to burn the cat.

The first premise here is the key one, and it constitutes an objective moral fact. Suppose we have to justify the truth—that is, the factual basis—of this first premise. Intuitionists might argue that this is self-evident—either immediately obvious or self-evident on reflection by any rational person. The wrongness of causing unnecessary suffering, they would hold, is as apparent upon reflection as the truth that $2 + 2 = 4$ or that other minds exist. Although added justification might help, it is not necessary because the justification would be no more certain (to a rational person upon adequate reflection) than the original judgment itself is. Anyone who doesn't see this is just morally blind—as blind as someone who doesn't see the redness of apples or the greenness of grass. This answer agrees with Harman's argument that scientific and moral principles are tested differently but says that the difference doesn't matter. Each principle is true in its own sphere. This argument may be correct, but it is unsatisfactory for distinguishing valid intuitions from invalid ones. Anyone can play the intuitionist game and claim that some activity X is wrong or right. For example, an American might say, "It's just obvious that the American way of life is superior," or a Nazi might say, "It's just obvious that Jews should be exterminated." A racist may think it's intuitively obvious that people of other races are subhuman, even evil. Superstitions are often justified in this way. How do we distinguish superstitions from valid moral principles? We seem to need something more than mere intuitions.

Similarly, religionists might appeal to the laws of God. We must refrain from harming sentient beings for the fun of it because God has so commanded us or because God informs us of the wrongness of such actions. Perhaps this is so, but how do we know that God exists or that this particular command is really authentic? The appeal to religion just shifts the discussion to an equally difficult topic—justifying religion.

More important, suppose we are naturalists like Harman. How can we justify the first premise? We can theorize about sentience, holding that sentient beings desire happiness or pleasure and avoid pain or suffering. Moral principles are guides to action that, among other things, promote happiness and reduce suffering.[10] If principle P promotes happiness or lessens suffering, then P qualifies as a moral principle. It follows from the nature of principles that it is right to do P and to refrain from acting against P—that is, refrain from anything that would diminish another's happiness or increase another's suffering. Perhaps we could link moral principles with promoting the interests of sentient beings. Or perhaps, for some reason, you are not sure about including animals in the circle of morally considerable beings. Then, instead of premise 2, we could use premise 2′:

2′. Burning Jews in gas ovens causes unnecessary suffering.

Or, instead of premise 2′, we could use premise 2″:

2″. Burning little children causes unnecessary suffering.

This argument assumes that morality is a functional institution that concerns promoting happiness and reducing suffering. I think this assumption is correct. Why can't we characterize morality as having these features? If someone objects that this is begging the question about the definition of morality, my reaction is to say, "OK. I'll give you the word *morality*. Call this feature *lorality* and say that it consists of practices that, among other things, promote (human) happiness and reduce suffering." But, I see no need to use "lorality" because we already have a well-established commonsense notion of "morality" with a long history in Eastern and Western thought connecting this notion with promoting happiness, reducing suffering, striving for justice, and ensuring the survival of society.

Universals and Supervenient Properties

There are other ways to make sense of the realist position that moral principles are grounded in objective moral facts that make up the fabric of the universe. One such approach draws on the metaphysical concept of *universals*. To explain, not all truths or facts about the universe are empirical ones. For example, the laws of logic are not empirical, yet the logical law of noncontradiction is true of all possible worlds. Similarly, it may well be that the world contains universals and not just particulars. There is a universal property red that all red things have in common, a universal horse aspect that all horses have in common, a universal idea of pain that all experiences of pain have in common, a universal concept of belief that all beliefs have in common. There is a universal property of being a prime number that empiricism does not even bear on. There are two-placed relations such as the relationship of being to the left of something (for example, aRb, where R stands for the relation and a and b stand for the objects) that characterize objects in space and relations in time (for example, a occurred before b). If universals are admitted as part of the fabric of the universe, then I see no reason to withhold moral properties from this class of entities. There seem to be moral properties, and if so, then there are moral truths, whether or not anyone acknowledges them and whether or not we discover them.

Another metaphysical approach to defending moral realism involves the notion of **supervenient properties:** Moral properties supervene on (depend upon, emerge out of) natural ones. Here's an example of the general concept of supervenience. Our perception of the color red is a supervenient effect of the reflection of certain light waves off surfaces as communicated to our retinas. The color red supervenes on the noncolored properties of these surfaces. What we have here is a higher-level set of properties, one (the color red) of which depends on a lower-level set of properties (light rays and psychological perceptions). The color is not in the objects themselves, but there is a causal relationship between the light rays and our perceptions. In a similar way, moral properties may supervene, or emerge out of, natural ones. For example, badness is a supervenient property of the natural property of pain, goodness is of happiness. Rightness is supervenient of truth telling and promise keeping, and wrongness is supervenient of doing unnecessary harm. The benefit of this approach is that it connects moral properties to natural ones but does not reduce the moral ones to the natural ones; that is, it does not equate "moral badness" with pain or "moral goodness" with happiness. They're intimately interrelated but not identical. Thus, a realist might maintain that objective moral facts are the higher-order ones (badness, goodness) that depend on the lower-level natural ones (pain, pleasure).

I hasten to add that the solution from neither universals nor superveniency is foolproof, and critics charge that they rest on metaphysical crutches that are as shaky as the notion of "objective moral fact" is itself. The suspicions that moral skeptics have about bizarre entities like "moral facts" apply equally to bizarre metaphysical entities like universals and supervenient properties. According to the skeptic, neither of these are features of the real world but fabrications of philosophers. Nevertheless, the larger point is that if we're willing to grant the existence of at least some metaphysical entities (universals, supervenient properties), then they may help provide an account of objective moral facts.

Noncognitivism and Moral Realism

In Chapter 11, we looked at noncognitivist moral theories and the challenges these pose to traditional conceptions of morality. Noncognitivist theories also introduce problems for moral realism, and we conclude our defense of moral realism by addressing these.

Briefly, noncognitivism is the position that moral utterances such as "Murder is wrong" are not factual statements (that is, true or false statements about the world). Rather, moral utterances function in an entirely different way. First, there is an *emotivist* function: Moral utterances merely express our feelings, such as if I shout out "Boo for murder!" Second, there is a *prescriptivist* function: Moral utterances guide our actions, such as if I say in a commanding voice to you "Do not murder!" According to noncognitivism, then, there are no moral propositions because propositions are *descriptions,* characterizations of the way the world is, whereas moral principles are emotive expressions or prescriptions that guide our actions. And if there are no moral propositions, then out the window go moral facts and moral realism.

The moral realist has a solution to this noncognitivist problem: Meaningful propositions can be embedded in our prescriptions, and these have truth value. For example, we can say of a medical prescription that "taking an aspirin a day is the correct prescription if you want to prevent a heart attack." Similarly, with a moral prescription we can also correctly say, "Promoting human flourishing by deeds of kindness and love is the way to make this a better world." Both statements are true (or if they aren't, then their opposites are true). Thus, moral principles do entail truth claims in this broad sort of way. If this is correct, then we can conclude that moral realism, with its thesis that there are moral facts, is correct.

Suppose, though, that we are unclear about the strength of the argument for moral realism and are inclined toward noncognitivism. We could still adhere to a type of moral objectivism that's not as strong as full-fledged moral realism. We could still hold that, from an ideal perspective, a specific set of principles (such as those described in Chapter 3 on objective morality) is necessary for human flourishing. We would speak of these prescriptive principles as being *valid* or *adequate to our purposes,* rather than *true,* but we would still preserve the universality and objectivity of morality. So, although cognitivism and realism seem surer paths to moral objectivism, noncognitivism is compatible with it.

CONCLUSION

In this chapter, we have examined the moral realist position that moral facts are features of the universe, independently of our thoughts about them. We've examined the positions of two influential antirealists: Mackie and Harman. Mackie argues that moral realism is undermined by three considerations: There is no universal moral code that all people everywhere adhere to, moral facts would seem to be very strange and counterintuitive entities, and objective value is the result of psychological tendencies to project subjective beliefs to the outside world. Each of these arguments, we've seen, has problems. Harman argues that moral principles cannot be tested by observation in the same way that scientific theories can. We've seen that the disanalogy between science and morality may not be as extreme as Harman supposes. Finally, we've looked at different ways in which moral facts might exist. None of these explanations of moral facts may stand out as being the clear choice, but there are at least some good reasons to hold to some version of moral realism, even if we reject Plato's realist account of the moral forms.

NOTES

1. "Statute of Amnesty International," http://www.amnesty.org.
2. J. L. Mackie, *Ethics: Inventing Right and Wrong* (Penguin, 1977), p. 15.
3. Ibid., p. 35.
4. David Hume, *A Treatise of Human Nature* (1739–1740), 3.1.

5. Mackie, *Ethics,* p. 16.
6. Ibid., p. 3.
7. Gilbert Harman, *The Nature of Morality* (Oxford, Engl.: Oxford University Press, 1979), p. 4.
8. Ibid., p. 11.
9. Richard Werner, "Ethical Realism," *Ethics* 93 (1983): 653–679; see also Nicholas Sturgeon, "Moral Explanations," in *Essays in Moral Realism,* ed. G. Sayre-McCord (Ithaca, N.Y.: Cornell University Press, 1990).
10. I distinguish between pain and suffering. *Pain* is typically physiological or at least phenomenological, as in "I'm pained by his betrayal of his family." *Suffering,* as I define it, is more objective and encompasses pain but is broader in scope. I may be suffering from incurable cancer but not be aware of it, let alone be in pain. Both indicate harm to the agent, but pain is consciously experienced whereas suffering need not be.

FOR FURTHER REFLECTION

1. Consider Plato's theory of the moral forms discussed at the outset of this chapter. Does Mackie's argument from queerness successfully refute it? Explain.

2. Examine Mackie's argument from projection and explain whether it is a successful refutation of objective moral facts.

3. Does Werner successfully respond to Harman's contention that moral theories differ radically from scientific ones? Explain.

4. How might an antirealist respond to the argument at the end of the chapter that links moral facts with happiness and suffering?

5. Examine the metaphysical defense of moral realism from either universals or superveniency and explain whether they are successful.

6. Can noncognitivism be made compatible with moral realism in the ways described at the close of the chapter? Explain.

FOR FURTHER READING

Brink, David O. *Moral Realism and the Foundations of Ethics.* Cambridge, Engl.: Cambridge University Press, 1989.

Butchvarov, Panayot. *Skepticism in Ethics.* Bloomington: University of Indiana Press, 1989.

Darwall, Stephen, Allan Gibbard, and Peter Railton, eds. *Moral Discourse and Practice.* Oxford, Engl.: Oxford University Press, 1997.

Fumerton, Richard. *Reason and Morality.* Ithaca, N.Y.: Cornell University Press, 1990.

Sayre-McCord, Geoffrey. *Essays on Moral Realism.* Ithaca, N.Y.: Cornell University Press, 1988.

Shafer-Landau, Russ. *Moral Realism: A Defence.* Oxford, Engl.: Oxford University Press, 2003.

Smith, Michael. *The Moral Problem.* Oxford, Engl.: Blackwell, 1994.

Appendix

✳

How to Read and Write a Philosophy Paper*

Nothing worthwhile was ever accomplished without great difficulty.
PLATO, *THE REPUBLIC*

Just about everyone who comes to philosophy—usually in college—feels a sinking sensation in their stomach when first encountering this very strange material, involving a different sort of style and method from anything else they have ever dealt with. It was certainly my first reaction as a student. Lured by questions such as, "Is there a God? What can I truly know? What is the meaning of life? How shall I live my life?" I began to read philosophy on my own. My first book was Bertrand Russell's *History of Western Philosophy,* which is much more than a history of the subject; it is also Russell's own analysis and evaluation of major themes in the history of Western philosophy. Although it is not a terribly difficult text, most of the ideas and arguments were new to me. Since he opposed many of the beliefs that I had been brought up with, I felt angry with him. But since he seemed to argue so persuasively, my anger gave way to confusion and then to a sense of defeat and despair. Yet, I felt compelled to go on with this "forbidden fruit," finishing Russell's long work and going on to read Plato's *Republic,* René Descartes' *Meditations,* David Hume's *Dialogues on Natural Religion,* selected writings of Immanuel Kant, William James's *Will to Believe,* and finally contemporary readings by Antony Flew, R. M. Hare, John Hick, and Ludwig Wittgenstein. Gradually, I became aware that on every issue on which I disagreed

*Adapted from Louis P. Pojman, ed., *Introduction to Philosophy: Classical and Contemporary Readings* (Wadsworth, 1991), pp. 617–620.

with Hume or Russell, Kant or Hick, someone else had a plausible counterargument. Eventually, I struggled to the place where I could see weaknesses in arguments (sometimes in the arguments of those figures with whom I had agreed), and finally I came to the point where I could write out arguments of my own. The pain of the process slowly gave way to joy—almost addictive joy, let me warn you—so that I decided to go to graduate school to get an advanced degree in philosophy.

This textbook is meant to suggest responses to stimulate you to work out your own position on the questions addressed herein. This text, offering arguments on alternative sides of each issue, along with a teacher to serve as a guide—and, I hope, some fellow students with whom to discuss the material—should challenge you to begin to work out your own moral philosophy.

However, neither the textbook nor the teacher will be sufficient to save you from a sense of disorientation and uncertainty in reading and writing about philosophy, so let me offer a few tips from my experience as a student and as a teacher of the subject.

SUGGESTIONS FOR READING A PHILOSOPHY TEXT

The styles and methods of philosophy are different from those of other subjects with which you have been acquainted since grammar school: English, history, psychology, and science. Of course, there are many methods among philosophers. And some writings—for example, those of the existentialists: Søren Kierkegaard, Friedrich Nietzsche, Albert Camus, and Jean-Paul Sartre—resemble more what we encounter in literature than they do more typical essays in philosophical analysis. In some ways, philosophy resembles mathematics, since it usually strives to develop a deductive argument much like a mathematical proof; only the premises of the argument are usually in need of a lot of discussion and objections need to be considered. Sometimes, I think of arguing about a philosophical problem as a kind of legal reasoning before a civil court: Each side presents its evidence and gives reasons for accepting its conclusion rather than the opponent's. For example, suppose you believe in freedom of the will and I believe in determinism. We each set forth the best reasons we have for accepting our respective conclusions. The difference between philosophical argument and the court case is that we are also the jury. We can change our minds on hearing the evidence and even change sides by hearing our opponent make a persuasive case.

SUGGESTIONS FOR WRITING A PHILOSOPHY PAPER

Talking about philosophy and writing philosophy are excellent ways to improve your understanding of the content and process of the subject as well as to improve your philosophical reasoning skill. Writing an essay on a philosophical issue focuses your mind and forces you to concentrate on the essential arguments connected with the issue. The process is hard, but it's amazing how much progress you can make—some of us faster than others, but in my experience some of those who have the hardest time at first end up doing the deepest, most thorough work.

First, identify a *problem* you want to shed light on or solve or a *thesis* you want to defend. Be sure that you have read at least a few good articles on different sides of the issue and can put the arguments in your own words—or minimally can explain them in your own words.

Now you are ready to begin to write. Here are some suggestions that may help you.

1. Identify the problem you want to analyze. For example, you might want to show that utilitarianism is a tenable (or untenable) theory.

2. As clearly as possible, state the problem and what you intend to show. For example: "I intend to analyze the arguments for and against act-utilitarianism and show how utilitarianism can meet the main objections to it."

3. Set forth your arguments in logical order, and support your premises with reasons. It helps to illustrate your points with examples or to point out counterexamples to opposing points of view.

4. Consider alternative points of view as well as objections to your own position. Try to meet these charges and show why your position is more plausible.

5. Apply the principle of charity to your opponent's reasoning—that is, give his or her case the strongest interpretation possible—for unless you can meet the strongest objections to your own position, you cannot be confident that your position is the best. I should add that applying the principle of charity is one of the hardest practices in philosophical discussion. Even otherwise very good philosophers have an inclination to caricature or settle for a weak version of their opponent's arguments.

6. End your paper with a summary and a conclusion. That is, succinctly review your arguments and state what you think you've demonstrated. In the conclusion, it is always helpful to show the implications of your conclusion for other issues. Answer the question, "Why does it matter?"

7. Be prepared to write at least two drafts before you have a working copy. It helps to have another philosophy student go over the preliminary draft before you write a final draft. Make sure that your arguments are well constructed and that your paper as a whole is coherent.

8. Regarding style: Write *clearly* and in an active voice. Avoid ambiguous expressions, double negatives, and jargon. Put other people's ideas in your own words as much as possible, and give credit in the text and in bibliographical notes whenever you have used someone else's idea or quoted someone. Knowing just when to credit another person is an exercise in

good judgment. While academics are rightly indignant with students who fail to refer to their sources, some students are fastidious to a fault, even documenting where they heard common knowledge. There is a middle way that common sense should be able to discover.

9. Include a bibliography at the end of your paper. In it, list all the sources you used in writing your paper.

10. Put the paper aside for a day, then read it afresh. Chances are you will find things to change.

When you have a serious problem, do not hesitate to contact your teacher. That is what he or she is there for: to help you progress in your philosophical reasoning. Your teacher should have reasonable office hours in which he or she is available to discuss the work of students.

Good luck! I hope you come to enjoy philosophical inquiry—and especially moral philosophy—as much as I have.

Glossary

Absolutism, moral The theory that there are nonoverridable moral principles that one ought never violate.

Act-intuitionism The theory that we must consult our moral intuition or conscience in every situation to discover the morally right thing to do (Butler).

Action-based theory The view that we should act properly by following moral rules, and we judge people based on how they act, not on whether they are virtuous people.

Actual duty The stronger of two conflicting duties that overrides a weaker one (Ross).

Act-utilitarianism The utilitarian view that an act is right if and only if it results in as much good as any available alternative.

Agapeism The theory that morality is grounded in love toward others and toward God.

Altruism An unselfish regard or concern for others; disinterested, other-regarding action; contrasted with egoism.

Antirealism, moral The theory that there are no moral facts; contrasted with realism.

Applied ethics The branch of ethics that deals with controversial moral problems—for example, abortion, premarital sex, capital punishment, euthanasia, and civil disobedience.

Autonomy From the Greek for "self-rule," self-directed freedom.

Cardinal virtues Four principal virtues advocated by Plato—namely, wisdom, temperance, courage, and justice.

Care-ethics The theory that attitudes like caring and sensitivity to context is an important aspect of the moral life.

Categorical imperative A moral imperative that is unqualified and does not depend on one's desires, the general statement of which is "Act only according to that maxim by which you can at the same time will that it would become a universal law" (Kant).

Cognitivism The view that an utterance has truth value.

Consequentialism (teleological ethics) The theory that the center of value is the outcome or consequences of the act; if the consequences are on balance positive, then the action is right; if negative, then wrong.

Conventional ethical relativism (conventionalism) The theory that all moral principles are justified by virtue of their cultural acceptance.

Deontology The view that certain features in the act itself have intrinsic value.

Descriptive morality The study of actual beliefs, customs, principles, and practices of people and cultures.

Divine command theory The view that ethical principles are the commands of God.

Egoism, ethical The theory that everyone ought always to do those acts that will best serve his or her own best self-interest.

Egoism, psychological The theory that we always do that act that we perceive to be in our own best self-interest.

Emotivism The noncognitive theory that moral utterances are (or include) factually meaningless expressions of feelings (Ayer, Stevenson).

Empiricism The theory that we have no innate ideas and that all knowledge comes from experience.

Error theory The view that moral statements claim to report facts but such claims are in error and no moral claims are actually true (Mackie).

Ethical theory (moral philosophy) The systematic effort to understand moral concepts and justify moral principles and theories.

Ethnocentrism The prejudicial view that interprets all of reality through the eyes of one's own cultural beliefs and values.

Eudaimonistic utilitarianism A type of utilitarian view maintaining that happiness consists of higher-order pleasures (for example, intellectual, aesthetic, and social enjoyments).

Euthyphro dilemma The puzzle set forth in Plato's dialogue *Euthyphro* about whether God loves the pious because it is pious or whether the pious is pious because God loves it.

Fact-value problem The metaethical problem regarding whether values are essentially different from facts, whether moral assessments are derived from facts, and whether moral statements can be true or false like factual statements.

Fallacy of deriving ought from is A problem pointed out by Hume about moving from statements about what is the case to statements about what ought to be the case.

Game theory Models of social interaction involving games in which players make decisions that will bring each of them the greatest benefit.

Hedonic calculus The utilitarian view that we should tally the consequences of actions according to seven aspects of a pleasurable or painful experience (Bentham).

Hedonism, ethical The theory that pleasure is the only intrinsic positive value and that pain is the only negative intrinsic value.

Hedonism, psychological The theory that motivation must be explained exclusively through desire for pleasure and aversion of pain.

Heteronomy The determination of the will on nonrational grounds; contrasted with autonomy of the will, in which the will is guided by reason (Kant).

Hypothetical imperative The nonmoral principle that takes the form "If you want A, then do B" (Kant).

Indeterminacy of translation The view that languages are often so fundamentally different from each other that we cannot accurately translate concepts from one to another

(Quine); this seems to imply that each society's moral principles depend on its unique linguistically grounded culture.

Instrumental good A thing that is worthy of desire because it is an effective means of attaining our intrinsic goods.

Intrinsic good A thing that is good because of its nature and is not derived from other goods.

Intuitionism The theory that humans have a natural faculty that gives us an intuitive awareness of morality.

Metaethics The branch of ethical theory that involves philosophizing about the very terms of ethics and considering the structure of ethics as an object of inquiry.

Moderate objectivism The theory that at least one objective moral principle exists and some core moral values are shared by all or most cultures.

Natural law theory The theory that morality is a function of human nature and reason can discover valid moral principles by looking at the nature of humanity and society.

Naturalism The theory that moral values are grounded in natural properties within the world, such as pleasure or satisfaction.

Naturalistic fallacy A problem about identifying "good" with any specific natural property such as "pleasure" or "being more evolved" (Moore).

Negative responsibility The view that we are responsible for the consequences of our nonactions that we fail to perform (not just the actions that we perform).

Nihilism, ethical *See* Nihilism, moral

Nihilism, moral The theory that there are no moral facts, moral truths, and moral knowledge (Harman).

Noncognitivism The theory that an utterance has no truth value.

Nonnaturalism The theory that moral values are grounded in nonnatural facts about the world (facts that can't be detected through scientific means), such as Plato's forms or Moore's indefinable "good."

Objectivism, moral The theory that there are universal moral principles, valid for all people and social environments.

Obligatory act An action that morality requires one to do, contrasted with an optional act.

Open-question argument An argument to show that for any property that we identify with "goodness," we can ask, "Is that property itself good?" (Moore).

Optional act An act that is neither obligatory nor wrong to do; includes neutral acts and supererogatory acts; contrasted with an obligatory act.

Overridingness The view that moral principles have predominant authority and override other kinds of principles.

Paradox of ethical egoism The problem that true friendship is central to egoistic happiness yet requires altruism.

Paradox of hedonism The problem that we all want to be happy, but we don't want happiness at any price or to the exclusion of certain other values.

Paradox of morality and advantage The problem that sometimes the requirements of morality are incompatible with the requirements of self-interest (Gauthier).

Particularism, moral The theory that morality always involves particular relations with particular people, not lifeless abstractions.

Pluralistic ethics The theory that both action-based and virtue-based models are necessary for an adequate or complete system.

Practicability The view that moral principles must be workable and its rules must not lay a heavy burden on us when we follow them.

Prescriptivism The noncognitive theory that moral utterances are (or include) factually meaningless recommends that others adopt one's attitude (Hare).

Prescriptivity The practical, or action-guiding, nature of morality; involves commands.

Prima facie duty A duty that is tentatively binding on us until one duty conflicts with another (Ross).

Problem of posterity The problem of determining what obligations we owe to future generations of people who do not yet exist.

Publicity The view that moral principles must be made public in order to guide our actions.

Rationalism The theory that reason can tell us how the world is, independent of experience.

Realism, moral The theory that moral facts exist and are part of the fabric of the universe; they exist independently of whether we believe them.

Relativism, ethical The theory that moral principles gain their validity only through approval by the culture or the individual.

Rule-intuitionism The intuitionist view that we must decide what is right or wrong in each situation by consulting moral rules that we receive through intuition (Pufendorf, Ross).

Rule-utilitarianism The utilitarian view that an act is right if and only if it is required by a rule that is itself a member of a set of rules whose acceptance would lead to greater utility for society than any available alternative.

Satisfactionism The view that identifies all pleasure with satisfaction or enjoyment, which may not involve sensuality.

Sensualism The view that identifies all pleasure with sensual enjoyment.

Situationalism, ethical The theory that objective moral principles are to be applied differently in different contexts.

Skepticism, moral The theory associated with Mackie that there are no objectively factual moral values.

Social contract theory The moral and political theory that people collectively agree to behave morally as a way to reduce social chaos and create peace.

Sociobiology The theory that social structures and behavioral patterns are biologically based and explained by evolutionary theory.

Solipsism, moral The theory that a person's view that only he or she is worthy of moral consideration; it is an extreme form of egoism.

State of nature A war of all against all where there are no common ways of life, no enforced laws or moral rules, and no justice or injustice (Hobbes).

Subjective ethical relativism (subjectivism) The relativist view that all moral principles are justified by virtue of their acceptance by an individual agent him- or herself.

Supererogatory act An act that exceeds what morality requires.

Supervenient property A higher-level property (for example, the color red) that nonreductively depends on a lower-level property (for example, light rays and psychological perceptions).

Teleological ethics (consequentialism) The theory that the center of value is the outcome or consequences of the act; if the consequences are on balance positive, then the action is right; if negative, then wrong.

Theological virtues Three principal virtues articulated by Paul in the New Testament—namely, faith, hope, and charity.

Universalizability The view that moral principles must apply to all people who are in a relevantly similar situation.

Verification principle The view that meaningful sentences must be either (1) tautologies (statements that are true by definition and of the form "A is A" or reducible to such statements) or (2) empirically verifiable (statements regarding observations about the world, such as "The book is red").

Vice A trained behavioral disposition that results in a habitual act of moral wrongness.

Virtue A trained behavioral dispositions that results in a habitual act of moral goodness.

Virtue-based theories The view that we should acquire good character traits, not simply act according to moral rules, and morality involves being a virtuous person.

Virtue theory (virtue ethics) The view that morality involves producing excellent persons who act well out of spontaneous goodness and serve as examples to inspire others.

Index

Abraham, 83, 174
absolutism, moral, 32, 37, 138, 141
act-intuitionism, 124–25
action-based theories, 152–55, 157, 159,
    161–64, 167–68, 231
actual duty, 140–41
act-utilitarianism, 105–6, 111, 113, 226
agapeism, 166
altruism, 87, 89–91, 95–97, 151, 178, 230
Amnesty International, 209
Anscombe, G. E. M., 153–54, 161
Antigone, 102
applied ethics, 2–3
Aquinas, Thomas, 32–34, 124
aretaic ethics, 152
Aristotle, 11, 33, 41, 57, 121, 136,
    148–49, 151, 155, 158, 164, 182, 210
autonomy, 20, 122, 137–38, 155–56,
    179–80, 183, 229
Ayer, Alfred J., 192–96, 204, 206, 229

Bambrough, Renford, 38
Beelzebub, 68
Benedict, Ruth, 15, 19–21, 24, 46
Bentham, Jeremy, 10, 52, 103–105,
    152, 229
bin Laden, Osama, 184
Brandt, Richard, 106
Brave New World, 50
Bridge over the River Kwai, 43
Buddha/Buddhism, 171

Bundy, Ted, 17, 23
Butler, Joseph, 124, 141, 228

Callahan, Daniel, 155
Callatians, 15
cardinal virtues, 147
care-ethics, 166–67
Carroll, Lewis, 204
categorical imperative, 126, 128–35,
    138–39, 152, 199
Christianity/Christian, 5, 14–15, 123,
    153, 166, 171, 175, 181
cognitivism, 222
complementarity, ethics, 163
Confucius/Confucianism, 147, 171
conscience, 4, 22, 33, 83, 100–1, 124,
    150, 154, 161, 209, 228
consequentialism, 232
conventional ethical relativism, 18–19,
    21–22, 24–25
core morality, 39–42, 44, 167, 178, 212
cosmopolitan, 32
Craig, William Lane, 175
Critique of Pure Reason, 122
cultural relativism, 19, 25

Darkness at Noon, 114
Darwinian/Darwinism, 38, 95
Dawkins, Richard, 95–96
deontic ethics, 153
deontology, 102, 152

dependency thesis, 19, 25–26
Descartes, René, 123–24
descriptive morality, 2
diversity thesis, 19, 25
divine command theory, 173–75
doctrine of double effect, 32–38
Donne, John, 18
Dostoevsky, F. M., 170–71

egoism, 82, 86–93, 95–97, 102, 131,
    189, 228, 231
egoism, ethical, 82, 87–95, 97,
    102–3, 108
egoism, psychological, 76, 82–89
emotivism, 191, 193–96, 206
empiricism, 121–23, 220
Epicurus, 51, 103
error theory, 212
ethnocentrism, 15, 27
eudaimonistic utilitarianism, 104
Euthyphro dilemma, 170–71, 229
evolution, 26, 38, 49, 95, 170, 214
existentialists, 49, 225

fact-value problem, 189, 191–96,
    203–206
fallacy of deriving ought from is,
    190–93, 199, 204, 206, 229
Feinberg, Joel, 85, 183
Feldman, Fred, 132
Fletcher, Joseph, 200
Foot, Phillipa, 36, 181
Frankena, William, 143, 160

game theory, 72–74
Gandhi, Mohandas, 17, 22, 39, 150–51
Gauguin, Paul, 7, 181
Gauthier, David, 74–75, 230
Genovese, Kitty, 1–2, 5, 8, 108, 151
Gilligan, Carol, 165–66
Golden Mean, 149
Golden Rule, 7, 10, 31, 40, 88, 101
Golding, William, 67–68

Hardin, Garrett, 94
Hare, R. M., 102, 196–203, 206, 224, 231
Harman, Gilbert, 211, 215–20, 222, 230
hedonic calculus, 103–4
hedonism/hedonists/hedon, 50–53
Hemingway, Ernest, 16–17

Henry, Carl F., 68, 171
Herodotus, 15
Herskovits, Melville, 21
heteronomy, 137–38
Hill, Thomas, 164
Hitler, Adolf, 17–18, 21, 39, 69, 101,
    110, 127
Hobbes, Thomas, 57, 66–67, 69–70, 78,
    88–89, 91, 151–52, 231
Hobbesian, 18, 24, 39, 67, 204
Huckleberry Finn, 154
Hume, David, 30, 103, 114, 123, 178–79,
    188–93, 199, 204, 206, 209, 213–14,
    224–25, 229
Hutcheson, Francis, 100, 103, 123
Huxley, Aldous, 50
hypothetical imperatives, 128, 197

Ibsen, Henrik, 22
indeterminacy of translation, 26
instrumental/instrumental goods,
    47–49, 52
intrinsic/intrinsic goods, 48–49, 51–52,
    61, 122, 127, 136, 230
intuitionism, 124, 139, 228, 231

James, William, 181, 224
Jesus, 44, 101, 150–51, 180
Judeo Christian, 57, 135, 177

Kalin, Jesse, 92
karma, 171, 181
Kavka, Gregory, 76
Kennedy, Joseph P., 101
Kierkegaard, Søren, 225
King, Martin Luther, 22, 151
Kluckhohn, Clyde, 26
Koestler, Arthur, 114, 117
Kolbe, Maximillian, 149–50, 184
Kraut, Richard, 59

Ladd, John, 14, 19
Leibniz, Gottfried Wilhelm, 123
Leviathan, 66
Levy, Paul, 150
Lincoln, Abraham, 83–84, 86
Locke, John, 123
logical positivism, 193
Lord of the Flies, 67–69
Luther, Martin, 22, 97, 151

MacIntyre, Alasdair, 156–57, 162
Mackie, John L., 158, 211–15, 219,
    222, 229, 231
Marxism, 158
Mavrodes, George, 177
Medlin, Brian, 92
metaethics, 189
Mill, John Stuart, 10, 53, 60–61, 85,
    103–6, 109, 152–53, 162
moderate objectivism, 32, 44, 60
Moore, George Edward, 53, 189, 191–94,
    196, 204–6, 230

natural law theory, 32–34, 37, 122,
    124–25, 154, 177, 189
naturalism, 162, 204, 206
naturalistic fallacy, 191–93, 204, 206
negative responsibility, 107, 116
Nicomachean Ethics, 148, 155, 158
Nielsen, Kai, 107
Nietzsche, Friedrich, 174, 182, 225
nihilism, moral, 216, 230
noncognitivism, 198, 206, 221–22
Norton, David L., 155–56, 162
Nowell-Smith, Patrick H., 179

objectivism, moral, 15, 27, 31–32, 38–39,
    42, 113, 189, 222, 230
obligatory act, 9, 87, 89, 230
Ockham, William of, 173
open-question argument, 192, 204
optional act, 9, 230
overridingness, 7, 182

paradox of hedonism, 85–86, 91
paradox of morality and advantage, 75
Parfit, Derek, 108
particularism, moral, 167
Perry, Ralph B., 54, 61
Piaget, Jean, 179
Plato, 1, 48, 51, 53, 57–58, 61, 71–72,
    121, 136, 147, 155, 170–71, 210–11,
    213, 222, 224, 228–30
pluralistic ethics, 163
posterity, problem of, 108, 118, 141–42
practicability, 7–8
prescriptivism, 201–3, 206
prescriptivity, 7
prima facie duties, 38, 42, 138–41, 143,
    160, 180

problem of posterity, 108, 118, 141–42
psychological egoism, 76, 82–83, 85–89
publicity, 7–8, 82, 92, 113
Pufendorf, Samuel, 125–26, 139, 141, 231

Quine, Willard V., 26, 230

Rachels, James, 179–80
Rand, Ayn, 44, 81, 90–92
rationalism, 122–23
Rawls, John, 8, 57–58, 64, 77, 143
realism, moral, 182, 210–11, 213–15, 219,
    221–22, 228
relativism, ethical, 14–27, 31, 39, 41, 43,
    113–14, 157–58, 162, 166, 202, 229
remainder rule, 106, 117
Rescher, Nicholas, 47
revelation, 4, 6, 12, 59, 171, 175,
    183–84
Ross, William D., 38, 114, 139–41, 143,
    228, 231
rule-intuitionism, 125
Russell, Bertrand, 176–78, 181, 224–25

Sartre, Jean-Paul, 49, 225
satisfactionism, 61
Scheper-Hughes, Nancy, 20–21
Schweitzer, Albert, 150–51
secular ethics, 4, 177, 181–82, 185
sensualism, 61
Sidgwick, Henry, 159
situationalism, ethical, 43
skepticism, moral, 179, 211
Smith, Adam, 89, 123
Sober, Elliott, 96
social contract theory, 57, 65–67, 70, 74,
    77–78, 189
sociobiology, 95, 97
Socrates, 1–2, 48–49, 53, 60, 85, 104–5,
    150, 155, 170–71, 211
solipsism, moral, 18, 23–24, 60, 95
Sophocles, 102
Spinoza, Benedict de, 46, 123
state of nature, 18, 24, 39, 66–67, 70,
    78, 88, 204
Stephens, Leslie, 146
Stevenson, Charles L., 195–96, 229
Sumner, William G., 19, 24
supererogatory act, 9, 230
supervenient properties, 221

teleological ethics (consequentialism), 10, 37, 102–3, 143, 147, 228
theism/theists, 173, 177, 181–83, 185
theological virtues, 147
Through the Looking Glass, 204
tolerance, 6, 19–21
Turnbull, Colin, 15, 24

universalizability, 7, 125, 130–31, 134, 199

verification principle, 193–95, 206
vices, 11, 15, 57, 72, 90, 147, 152, 158, 161, 176, 190, 209, 213

Virtue of Selfishness, 90
virtue theory, 11, 147, 151–2, 210
virtue/virtues, 10–11, 15–16, 18, 21, 23, 57–58, 71–72, 81, 90–91, 108, 124, 127–28, 136, 147–64, 166, 168, 172, 175–76, 178, 190, 204, 210, 229, 231–32

Warnock, Geoffrey, 159–61, 204, 206
Werner, Richard, 217–18
Williams, Bernard, 115
Wilson, Edward O., 24, 26
Wolf, Susan, 150